IAN MURRAY was born in Edinburgh in 1976.
game in 1985 whilst at Dumbryden Primary S
Education Centre at the age of 16 to study Soci.. - _ ..
the University of Edinburgh. After graduating, he briefly worked in financial services before starting his own event management business, 100MPH Events Limited. He ran one of the largest events at the Edinburgh Festival and was an innovator in broadcasting on the internet. He also owned and ran a hotel and two bars in Edinburgh.

Alongside running his own businesses, he was elected to the City of Edinburgh Council in 2003 for the Alnwickhill ward and was re-elected in 2007 for the larger Liberton/Gilmerton Ward. As a Councillor, he specialised in economic development and planning.

In 2010, Ian was elected as the Member of Parliament for Edinburgh South. He was appointed Shadow Minister for Trade, Industry and Employment until the General Election in 2015 when he was returned to Parliament as the sole Labour MP from Scotland. He was promoted to Shadow Secretary of State for Scotland in 2015 and held the position until he resigned in 2016.

He was re-elected with the largest majority in Scotland at the snap General Election in 2017 and currently serves on the Foreign Affairs Select Committee.

In 2013, he was appointed independent Chair of the Foundation of Hearts and served on the Board of Heart of Midlothian Football Club 2014–15. He is a Trustee of the McCrae's Battalion Trust.

Ian is a lifelong Jambo and has always lived in Edinburgh. *This is Our Story* is his first book.

TO

Sandra and John

This is Our Story

How the Fans Kept their Hearts Beating

IAN MURRAY

Hnay

Luath Press Limited

EDINBURGH

www.luath.co.uk

First published 2019

ISBN: 978-1-912147-95-3
The paper used in this book is recyclable. It is made from low chlorine pulps produced in a low energy, low emission manner from renewable forests.

Printed and bound by Ashford Colour Press, Gosport

Typeset in 11 point Sabon by Lapiz

For every Hearts supporter who believed.

Dedicated to the memory of my dad, James Murray, who left the pitch far too soon.

To my brother, Alan Murray, who has shared all these footballing memories with me.

In memory of Robert Wilson, Elaine Bruce, Elaine Spence, John McBride, Jane Rankin, Ron MacNeill and Pilmar Smith.

Contents

Acknowledgements   9

Relevant Chronology   11

INTRODUCTION   It's the Hope that Kills You   17

CHAPTER 1   The Romanov Rollercoaster from
            Marmeladentörtchen to Salt and Sauce   21

CHAPTER 2   Hearts in Green and Yellow   35

CHAPTER 3   Hearts Nearly Stop Beating   47

CHAPTER 4   The Fans' Battle to Keep Hearts Alive   57

CHAPTER 5   Ball Kickers, Tyre Kickers and CICS   64

CHAPTER 6   To Chair or Not to Chair   79

CHAPTER 7   The Right People, the Right Time
            with Not Enough Time   89

CHAPTER 8   Founding the Foundation   100

CHAPTER 9   Budgein' the Figures   111

CHAPTER 10 A Pint for £2.50?   125

CHAPTER 11 The Tip into Administration   136

CHAPTER 12 Hearts and the Hobbit   149

CHAPTER 13 Bids and Bobs   163

CHAPTER 14 Three, Two, One... Preferred Bidder   179

CHAPTER 15 A Chorus of Drawdowns and Putdowns   193

CHAPTER 16 Scrooge Jackson Cancels Christmas   204

CHAPTER 17 Deal Done   220

CHAPTER 18 Relegations, Celebrations and Budgements   239

CHAPTER 19 And Now, the End is Near...   255

With special thanks to the Foundation of Hearts team and all who helped

Foundation of Hearts Board:

Henry Snedden, Calum Robertson, Jane Lewis, Bill Alves, Brian Cormack, Alex Mackie, Jamie Bryant, Garry Halliday (and his mum), Alasdair Bruce, Stuart Wallace, Louise Strutt, Donald Ford, Barry McGonagle, Donald Cummings, Dougie Masterton

Advisors to the Foundation of Hearts Board:

Lawrence Broadie, Andy Grant, Kevin Windram, Marcia Campbell, Iain McLeod and Richard Atkinson

Those who helped to make it happen:

Rt Hon Lord George Foulkes, Ken Stott, Willie Hunter, Colin Chisholm, Tam Cowan, Steve Kilgour, Barry Cole, Gary Mackay, Leslie Deans, Jambos Kickback, Scott Wilson, Kenny Whittman

The team at Heart of Midlothian Football Club during the period of administration:

David Southern, Paul Kiddie, Fiona Sinclair, Janine Brown, John Murray and the team

All the players, former players and managers who helped, especially, John Robertson, Dave McPherson, Jim Jefferies, Dylan McGowan, Gary Locke, Billy Brown, Allan Preston, Rudi Skácel, Paulo Sérgio, Jimmy Sandison, Gilles Rousset and Stéphane Adam

BDO and their team:

Bryan Jackson, Trevor Birch, Robert Barclay, Duncan Raggett and the team at BDO

Peter Duff and Keith Anderson at Morrisons LLP

The key players in Lithuania:

Asta Skaisgirytė-Liauškienė and her team at the Lithuanian Embassy
Deimantė Korsakaitė, Gintaras Adamonis and their team in Lithuania

Professional advisors:

Grigor Milne, Chris Walters and the team at Dundas & Wilson
John Reid, Kristopher Keane and the team at Deloitte
Graeme Henry and his team at DLA Piper

June Sinclair at JS Accounting Services
John Walker, Alan Glen, Kay Thomson and the team at Scott Moncrieff

Members of the press and media

Others who contributed to the book:

Archie Macpherson, Stewart Fraser, George Burley, Shaun Milne, Euan
McGrory, Martin Whitfield MP, Andrew Frame, Ken Fruish and
Mark Smith

Ann Budge, Eric Hogg, Craig Levein, Ann Park, Scot Gardiner, and all at
the club

Relevant Chronology

1874 Club founded

1875 Became members of the Scottish Football Association

1878 The famous maroon colours were adopted after a laundry accident bleached the white kit

1881 Moved to Tynecastle Park in Gorgie Road

1891 Won the Scottish Cup for the first time

1895 Division 1 champions

1896 Won the Scottish Cup for the second time

1897 Division 1 champions

1901 Won the Scottish Cup for the third time

1906 Won the Scottish Cup for the fourth time

1914 In August, started the season with eight straight victories

Sir George McCrae got permission to raise the 16th Royal Scots Battalion

1915 In September, Pte. James Speedie, 7th Cameron Highlanders killed in action

In October, Cpl. Thomas Gracie, 16th Royal Scots died in service

1916 On 1 July, Sergt. Duncan Currie, 16th Royal Scots killed in action; Pte. Ernest Ellis, 16th Royal Scots killed in action; Pte. Henry Wattie, 16th Royal Scots killed in action

In August, L-Cpl. James Boyd, 16th Royal Scots killed in action

1917 In April, Sergt. John Allan, 9th Royal Scots killed in action

1922 In April, the club's war memorial was unveiled at Haymarket before a solemn crowd of 35,000

1926 Gunner Robert Mercer and Hearts captain in 1914–15, 16th Royal Scots died of disease related to wartime gassing

1928 Sir George McCrae, 16th Royal Scots died

1933 Pte. Paddy Crossan, 16th Royal Scots died of tuberculosis

1955   Won the Scottish League Cup for the first time

1956   Won the Scottish Cup for the fifth time by defeating Celtic 3–1 at
        Hampden

1957   Division 1 champions

1959   Won the Scottish League Cup for the second time

1960   Division 1 champions and won the Scottish League Cup for the
        third time

1963   Won the Scottish League Cup for the fourth time

1980   Championship winners

1988   Reached the quarter-final of the UEFA Cup and defeated Bayern
        Munich 1–0 at home

1994   Chris Robinson and Lesley Deans purchased Hearts from
        Wallace Mercer

1995   Jim Jefferies became Hearts manager for the first time

1998   In February, Stewart Fraser appointed Finance Director and
        Company Secretary

        In May, won the Scottish Cup for the sixth time by defeating
        Rangers 2–1 at Celtic Park

2000   Jim Jefferies sacked as manager to be replaced by Craig Levein

2004   In January, Chris Robinson announced the sale of Tynecastle to
        clear club debts. This led to the proposal to move to Murrayfield,
        the home of Scottish Rugby

        In April, Lord George Foulkes became Chair of Hearts
        In September, Chris Robinson agreed to sell his shares to Vladimir
        Romanov
        In October, manager Craig Levein left Hearts to take over at
        Leicester City to be replaced by John Robertson

2005   In January, Romanov cancelled the sale of Tynecastle and
        guaranteed debt of over £20 million

        In February, Romanov gained 29.9 per cent of Hearts to get
        control
        In May, Phil Anderton replaced Chris Robinson as Chief Executive
        and David Southern joined the club as new Marketing and
        Communications Director
        In June, George Burley was appointed manager after sacking of
        John Robertson

In August, Hearts got off to their best start to a season since 1914
In October, George Burley was sacked after eight wins and two
draws in the first ten league matches, Lord George Foulkes resigned
as Chair and Phil Anderton was sacked. Vladimir Romanov's son,
Roman, took over from both Lord Foulkes and Anderton
Graham Rix appointed manager and Stewart Fraser resigned as
Board Director but remained Company Secretary and Head of
Finance
In November, Campbell Ogilvie appointed Operations Director

2006   In March, Graham Rix was sacked as manager to be replaced by
Valdas Ivanauskas

In May, qualified for the Champions League for the first time
Won the Scottish Cup for the seventh time by defeating Gretna on
penalties at Hampden

2007   In March, Valdas Ivanauskas was sacked and replaced by Anatoliy
Korobochka

In July, Hearts debt reached £37 million

2008   In January, Anatoliy Korobochka was sacked as manager and
replaced by Stephen Frail
In March, Campbell Ogilvie became Chief Executive
In July, Hearts announced a debt of equity to reduce debt by
£12 million and sacked manager Stephen Frail to be replaced by
Csaba László
In October, player wages were not paid on time
In November, players were not paid for the second time

2010   In January, Csaba László was sacked as manager to be replaced by
Jim Jefferies for his second spell in charge

In September, David Southern became Chief Executive after Cambell
Ogilvie left to become President of the Scottish Football Association
In September, Hearts reduced debt by a further £10 million by
selling shares, giving Romanov 98 per cent of the club. Following
this, the debt stood at £25 million
In October, Alex Mackie, Brian Cormack, Garry Halliday, Donald
Ford and Jamie Bryant formally constituted the Foundation of
Hearts (FOH)

2011   In April, Stewart Fraser left role as Company Secretary
In August, Jim Jefferies was sacked as manager to be replaced by
Paulo Sérgio

In October, player and staff wages were not paid again
In November, player and staff wages were not paid again

2012 In May, won the Scottish Cup for the eighth time by defeating arch
rivals Hibs 5-1 at Hampden in the 'salt and sauce' final
In June, Paulo Sérgio left as manager after new contract discussion
broke down to be replaced by John McGlynn
In October, Hearts launched a share issue to raise £2 million
In November, Hearts were issued with a winding up order by the
Court of Session in Edinburgh for repeated failures to pay tax
liabilities on time. Ian Murray became involved in helping Hearts
with the tax case
Hearts Board issued a statement saying the St Mirren match could
be the club's last
Foundation of Hearts offered £450,000 to pay off tax debts in
return for ownership of Hearts
St Mirren match was played after successful negotiation on tax
liabilities
In December, share issue raised over £1 million

2013 In February, John McGlynn was sacked as manager to be replaced
by Gary Locke
ūkio Bankas entered administration, with Hearts owing £15
million secured against the stadium
In March, Hearts lost League Cup Final to St Mirren 3–2 at
Hampden
In April, Ian Murray became Chair of FOH and was joined on the
FOH Board by supporter groups representatives, Henry Snedden,
Jane Lewis, Calum Robertson, Bills Alves and Dougie Masterton
In May, Hearts issued a statement saying they needed £500,000 to
survive the summer and put entire squad up for sale
In June, Hearts entered administration, Bryan Jackson and Trevor
Birch from BDO were appointed as administrators. Fans were
asked to buy 3,000 extra season tickets to prevent liquidation
In July, FOH-backed bid from BIDCO was submitted with proposal
to take club into fan ownership for £2.5 million
Hearts started the Premier League season with a 15-point deduction
In August, FOH-backed BIDCO bid was given preferred bidder
status
In November, Hearts parent company, UBIG, formally declared
insolvency and entered administration

2014 In April, Hearts were relegated despite a 4–2 victory at Partick Thistle

In May, the FOH-backed BIDCO deal was completed and Ann Budge took control of Hearts as the new Chair and Chief Executive. Eric Hogg was appointed Operations Director. Ann Park was installed as Head of Commercial

Ian Murray joined the new Hearts Board as FOH representative

Craig Levein appointed as new Director of Football

Gary Locke and Billy Brown left Hearts after not being offered new contracts, due to Ann Budge changing the management structure of the club

BIDCO deal with FOH agreed to see fan ownership in five years

Supporter groups representatives resigned from FOH with Alastair Bruce joining the FOH Board

Hibs were relegated to the Championship after a play-off defeat to Hamilton

In June, Hearts officially exited administration

In July, David Southern announced he was to leave Hearts

In October, Donald Cummings from Dundas & Wilson joined the FOH Board and Marcia Campbell became a special advisor

In December, FOH held its first AGM and members elected Barry McGonagle to the FOH Board

2015 In March, Hearts won the Championship by 21 points and with seven games remaining

In May, Ian Murray resigned as Chair of FOH and representative on the Hearts Board to be replaced by Brian Cormack

In September, Donald Cummings appointed to Hearts Board as second FOH representative

In December, the FOH AGM was held and Louise Strutt became a Director of FOH through a vote of members

2016 In May, Hearts finished third in the inaugural season back in the Premier League and qualified for the Europa League

FOH approved £3 million contribution towards the funding of the new main stand and delayed repayment of BIDCO for two years

In August, Hearts lodged a planning application to build a new main stand

In December, Robbie Neilson left Hearts to become manager at Milton Keynes Dons to be replaced by Ian Cathro

2017   In February, Brian Cormack stepped down as Chair of FOH
        and Hearts Board representative to be replaced by Stuart Wallace
        In May, Hearts finished the football season fifth in the
        Premier League
        In June, John Robertson left Hearts Ambassador role to take up
        the managerial position at Inverness Caledonian Thistle. He was
        replaced by Gary Locke
        In August, Ian Cathro was dismissed as manager to be replaced by
        Director of Football, Craig Levein for his second spell in charge
        In November, FOH held their AGM

2018   In May, FOH completed the final instalment of the £3 million
        towards the new main stand
        Hearts finished the Premier League season in a disappointing
        sixth place
        In December, Hearts officially opened their new 7,000 capacity
        main stand and FOH held their fourth AGM

2019   In May, Hearts finished in a disappointing sixth place in the
        Premier League but reached the Scottish Cup Final losing 2–1 to
        Celtic
        In July, Ann Budge won the prestigious Edinburgh Award for
        business success, community work, and services to sport in the city

2020?   In June, FOH will become the majority shareholder in Heart of
        Midlothian Football Club and take it into full fan ownership with
        a 79.9 per cent shareholding after contributing over £10 million to
        Hearts finances

('Premier League' is reference to the top league of Scottish Football. This has
been called the Premiership and First Division. Reference to 'Championship'
means the second-tier league in Scotland.)

It's the Hope that Kills You

This is my story, this is my song.
Follow the Hearts and, you can't go wrong.
For some say that Rangers and Celtic are grand.
But the boys in maroon are the best in the land.

AT 4.55PM ON Saturday 25 May 2019, more than 22,000 Hearts supporters funnelled out of Scotland's national football stadium, having watched a spirited display in the Scottish Cup Final. As the fans filled the air with the famous Hector Nicol Hearts song, there was pride that their favourites had brought the curtain down on the 2018/19 campaign with a performance that had lifted the spirits after an up-and-down season. We didn't bring the legendary old trophy back to Edinburgh, having lost to Celtic by two goals to one, but it was certainly a case of 'what might have been'. The historic precedent of supporting Hearts was that it is always the hope that kills you. This was upheld that day.

The very fact that Heart of Midlothian FC was even able to play in a cup final was the real victory. Hearts' last final in 2012 ushered in the most uncertain and rocky period in the 145-year history of the club.

As the fans, who had sung themselves hoarse, were meandering and weaving away from Hampden Park looking forward to their summer holidays, they should have been the proudest fans in the world. Not only did they save their club but they were now on the brink of owning it. The history of Hearts safeguarded for everyone to enjoy and the club secured for future generations of 'Jambos' to return to Hampden Park for showcase matches.

In just six years, the fans have gone from the nightmare of having to comprehend the club that they love being confined to the history books of Scottish football, to seeing their favourites come within a whisker of winning the cup and returning to the pinnacle of the game.

It doesn't really matter which football team you support, we can all share the joy and pain of fellow fans. That's what makes football the most magnificent of sports. It brings people and communities together like no other. Lifelong loyalties are forged and tested. The old saying that you can choose your friends but not your family is no longer true, as you can even choose your family these days. One thing is true: when you become a supporter of a football club, it is for life. It's an association that will always be with you 'til death do you both part. Nick Hornby wrote in his enthralling footballing book, *Fever Pitch*, 'Few of us have chosen our clubs, they have simply been presented to us'. That was certainly the case for my elder brother, Alan, and me. We were presented with Heart of Midlothian Football Club by the wider Murray family. That was it. We were born into this world and therefore we would be Hearts supporters for life.

I had travelled to the Cup Final with Alan. We had gone to every final and semi-final together since 1986. Despite the apprehension of the game, we had to keep reminding ourselves that this was only the 15th Scottish Cup Final that Hearts had participated in since the club was founded in 1874. We have only won seven. These were the moments that all Hearts fans should savour. After all, history shows us that we may never see another one.

This cup final in particular had a more poignant resonance than any of the others. It came almost five years to the day since Heart of Midlothian Football Club exited administration after the most turbulent period in its history.

It may not have been most poignant or memorable for my brother though. I think that may have been the Scottish Cup Final of 1998 and for non-footballing reasons. Hearts hadn't won the Scottish Cup for 42 years when we defeated Falkirk in the semi-final in 1998. We would play the all-conquering Rangers in the final. After the semi-final, he called his partner, Nicola, as we celebrated the victory at the Dell Inn in Edinburgh. He decided that, given the long wait for a Scottish Cup victory, he could confidently promise that he would ask Nicola to marry him should we go on to win the final.

I wouldn't want to speculate but I think the offer was made through the prism of an overindulgence in post-semi-final euphoric alcohol consumption and his attempt to get permission for a few more hours in the pub. Anyway, to those not of a Hearts persuasion, we won the final by two goals to one and lifted the trophy for the first time since 1956. Alan followed through on his promise made whilst tired and emotional and married Nicola in 2000. So, whilst I have said that sometimes you can choose your family, in this case, it was Hearts that chose Alan's family. I told this story during my best man speech at their wedding. I departed from the usual protocol and said that winning the Scottish Cup in 1998 was the best day of our lives. I winked at him as he gave a thumbs up in front of his new wife. I don't think he was even kidding. That is what Hearts means to us Murrays.

And that's what football means to all Hearts supporters. When the club needed them most, they rallied to the cause. The fact that we were able to make another Scottish Cup Final at all was down to them. The coming together of more than 8,000 ordinary supporters donating their hard-earned money to saving the club would be at the forefront of my mind as we headed to Hampden. These are the fans, like me, who were 'presented' with Hearts as their club. These are the fans that have all celebrated the highs and cried at the lows. In fact, many will have also cried at the highs. I know I have. This Cup Final was for them.

Back in 2005, Hearts supporter Craig Watson wrote a book called *The Battle for Hearts and Minds*. It examined the period from the early 1980s up to the proposal by owner, Chris Robinson, to sell Tynecastle and move to the home of Scottish rugby. The final chapter of that book is how Lithuanian oligarch Vladimir Romanov bought Hearts to prevent the sale of our historic Tynecastle Park ground. The final two sentences of the book say:

> Those who guard Heart of Midlothian's destiny today should take heed of the club's past perils, recent and distant. There must never again be any need to save our Hearts.

Within seven short years after this was written, Hearts was again in the eye of a financial storm that provoked a need to 'save our Hearts' for the second time in less than a decade. It was a crisis that engulfed the club to the extent that Hearts may have played their last ever game. Those who bought Hearts in 2005 to 'safeguard the destiny' of the club were on the verge of eclipsing the 'past perils' resulting in Hearts disappearing forever – becoming the Third Lanark of the 21st century.

What I think some owners forget is that Heart of Midlothian, or any football club for that matter, should be bigger than one individual. I'm afraid recent history shows that for much of the last few decades that has not been the case. A succession of owners has failed to handle that most important of points.

The supporters rallied back in 2005 to prevent their spiritual home from being sold and they would have to rally again as never before. It was for that group of fans to ensure that, finally, Heart of Midlothian would move away from a fickle ownership model to be owned by them – the club's best customers, its loyal support. That way there was a chance that the sentiments expressed in Craig Watson's book would come true.

11 June 2019 would be five years to the day since the Court of Session approved the legal documents that resulted in FOUNDATION OF HEARTS (FOH) tweeting:

> The club is officially out of administration. We said in March [2014] to put the champagne in the fridge. Today you have permission to pop the cork.

Although the journey from Hampden that Saturday is a good place to start this story of how the fans saved their Hearts, the end of that journey will come shortly after the Scottish Cup Final in 2020. Hearts may or may not appear in the final for a second year in a row but what will happen will be much more significant – the supporters of Heart of Midlothian Football Club will become the majority shareholder owning 79.9 per cent. They will own the past and can shape the future. They will have saved it for future generations and ploughed in over £10 million. That has the chance of allowing the club to fulfil its true potential, not only as the heart and soul of Edinburgh, but the heart and soul of Scottish football. This book is about that fight, how it was done, and how the supporters became the owners of Hearts.

The only constant in any football club are its supporters. It is only supporters who are genuinely interested in its well-being. Heart of Midlothian Football Club should therefore belong to the people who care for it the most. This won't be a story that will be unfamiliar to supporters of many football clubs, but this is the story of my club. The fight for the very existence of Heart of Midlothian Football Club was at stake. The stories in this book are my recollections. Some may disagree with the detail but this is how I saw and recorded it. It is a marvellous journey from the threat of the last ever Hearts game to a fan-owned club.

This is my story, this is our song…

CHAPTER I

The Romanov Rollercoaster from Marmeladentörtchen to Salt and Sauce

THE FINANCIAL PROBLEMS at Hearts were not a new phenomenon. The early 1980s saw the club crippled with debt. It was only by the intervention of previous owner and Chairman, Wallace Mercer, with his close ally, Pilmar Smith, that saved the club from dire circumstances. However, this was, in the history of the club, a mere temporary reprieve.

Although Hearts was back from the brink in the mid-1980s with regular title challenges, Cup Finals, and the flirtation with the very best in European football, the financial situation was no different to most other clubs.

For a club like Hearts, there is always the need to try and compete with the big two of Celtic and Rangers. Their financial prowess and spending abilities are many multiples of the next nearest. The decision for any football club owner is whether you live within your means or take the gamble to try and break the duopoly. Some have succeeded in the form of the 'New Firm' of Dundee United and Aberdeen in the earlier part of the 1980s. No club has managed a title-winning side outside the big two since.

Hearts comfortably occupy third place in the all-time Premier League standings behind the top two of Celtic and Rangers respectively. It is hardly surprising that, just now and again, there is a glimmer of hope in taking the league crown, progressing to the lucrative stages of European competition, and building an infrastructure that sustains this for a few seasons. I have been watching Hearts since the mid-1980s. At that point in Hearts history, anything was possible. We even flirted with the Premier League title. Regular European football saw some of the best clubs in Europe grace the Tynecastle turf. Looking back, who would have thought that Hearts would defeat the mighty Bayern Munich in the first leg of a European cup quarter final? The return leg in Munich was heartbreaking for the 'Jam Tarts'. We should have won it comfortably. The semi-final would have brought Diego

Maradona's Napoli to Edinburgh. The match in Munich has been replayed by Hearts fans for the last 30 years.

My favourite story is recalled by a friend and former colleague, Andrew Frame, who was in Munich with future assistant referee, James Bee. As a souvenir, they picked up a German fanzine that contained a summary of Hearts history translated into German. It had a section on nicknames. Bayern Munich have several but we know them best as 'Bayern'. The literal translation of 'Jam Tarts' is 'Marmeladentörtchen', meaning a tart of jam. Bayern fans would come up to Andrew and James in the street, point to their Hearts scarf and proclaim 'Marmeladentörtchen' as a friendly acknowledgement.

Football has moved on considerably since those days. The chances of Hearts competing at that level are, if we were being honest, all but gone. The consistent problem is the one of finance. This book is not about the history of Heart of Midlothian Football Club, but I think it is right start by examining how the club got into the financial mess. A mess that questioned its very existence.

When former co-owner and Chief Executive of Hearts, Chris Robinson, and major shareholder, Lesley Deans, sold their majority shareholding in the club to Vladimir Romanov in 2005, the club was teetering on the brink. It had an eye-watering debt reported to be close to £20m and had proposed to sell their spiritual home of Tynecastle Park to Cala Homes. That sale would pay off crippling debt but force them to move to the home of Scottish Rugby, the 67,500-capacity Murrayfield Stadium. At the same time, Scottish football was probably going through the worst financial crisis in generations. It is little wonder given the way football was supported by the financial institutions they banked with.

Stewart Fraser, Hearts Finance Director, and Chris Robinson would go to the Bank of Scotland headquarters on the Mound in Edinburgh on an annual basis to see if they could extend the club's overdraft. After winning the Scottish Cup in 1998, the Hearts Board decided to invest in re-signing players who had featured in the famous Cup run, along with new players, both at higher wages than previously. This was in the belief that it would be paid for with the income from increased attendances brought about by our historic success. Hearts wanted to keep the winning team together but also to invest. Unfortunately, crowds remained pretty much the same as previously. The Hearts Board then spent the next few years trying to bring the wage bill down to get the turnover ratio back to industry norms. In the meantime, this necessitated requests to Bank of Scotland each year to increase the overdraft by £1 million. That was unsustainable. The real problem began when Halifax bought over Bank of Scotland. Ten of the 12 Scottish Premier League clubs were customers of the Bank of Scotland. All were put into their over exposure and high-risk centre.

That resulted in a very stark message from the bank to Chris Robinson. He was told he had to do 'something creative' to get Hearts' overdraft down. A stadium move was the only real option for raising the kind of sums required. That was where the idea to share a stadium with Hibs at Straiton came from. There was a subsequent meeting of the Federation of Hearts Supporters clubs in the Gorgie stand to discuss the Straiton option. The Federation was against it. Hibs initially supported looking at the idea as they were in a similar financial situation but they abandoned it when their fans went against this in a big way. That left Hearts on their own. They really couldn't make the finances of it work without a partner.

Many ask where the Murrayfield option came from. Allegedly, someone in the crowd at the Federation meeting shouted, 'Have you ever thought of going to Murrayfield?' and a bulb went off in Chris' head. That was when the club started to look at it. Chris took many people across to Murrayfield and everyone came to the same conclusion that it wouldn't work. The problem was options were running out and so was the patience of the bank. £20.5 million was being offered by Cala Homes. It made financial sense if nothing else, if only to sort the club's finances.

This was not what the supporters wanted and it sparked a furious reaction. Many fan-led organisations like Save Our Hearts (a pressure group formed by the Federation of Hearts Supporters clubs and the Hearts Trust that was disbanded shortly after Romanov took the reins) sprung up to try and stop Robinson from selling the ground. The 'not fit for purpose' document produced by the club to show why the ground had to be sold was roundly criticised. Ironically, the document would play a not inconsiderable part in the saving of Hearts a decade later.

One of the only other avenues was to find a suitable buyer who would have deep enough pockets to take on the massive debt and invest in the future. There were not many people coming forward, let alone being a serious proposition.

The only two that had even bothered to turn up to Tynecastle was a guy that called himself 'Johnny' from Nigeria. He had a rather nice lunch with Finance Director Stewart Fraser and Chairman, Lord Foulkes. After lunch

Johnny went into the club shop for a look around. He availed himself of a large amount of Hearts merchandise. He had bags of strips, scarfs, mugs and hats. Everything that was maroon and white made its way into the hands of Johnny. Of course, he never paid a penny for any of this. Stewart Fraser pursued him for some months for payment but he was never seen or heard of again.

Then there was a consortium of Thai businesspeople. They were taken around the stadium by Stewart but all they really wanted to do was take pictures of the grand old lady and subsequently disappeared. I suspect these potential buyers were never serious contenders but the Board of the club had to leave no stone unturned in trying to find a way out of the financial mess that Hearts was in.

Two other potential purchasers, who would become regular names when it came to the ownership of Hearts, were Pat 'the plumber' Munro, who walked into the reception at Tynecastle one afternoon to say he wanted to see Chris Robinson to buy the club. He got palmed off on Hearts employee Kenny Whitman.

The other was Bob Jamieson. He will feature later in this story. At this time, he arrived at Tynecastle and tried to hand a cheque to Chris Robinson. It transpired, as I have been told, that after a little bit of due diligence, he was discovered to be a shoe salesman that others alleged was found to be living in a caravan just outside Edinburgh. You can see that there were very few potential buyers with any financial clout.

The only person was Vladimir Romanov. My good friend, and Chairman of the club at the time, Rt. Hon Lord George Foulkes described Romanov as being 'the only show in town to buy Hearts and save Tynecastle'. Romanov had been to see other Scottish clubs – Dunfermline, Dundee and Dundee Utd – looking for a lame duck. There was no club lamer than Hearts at that time. It did save Tynecastle.

He did have the advantage of involvement in football. He already owned FBK Kaunas in his home country of Lithuania (who would later be seen as a sort of Hearts' unofficial feeder club) and he had a stake in MTZ-RIPO Minsk from Belarus. There was a credible school of thought that Romanov was looking to launch his bank, ūkio Bankas, into the UK financial system. This required a rare banking licence that was not easy, or cheap, to obtain but having a successful business in Edinburgh, as one of the largest financial services sectors in Europe, would go a long way to establishing the credibility he required. His association with Hearts would help convince the financial authorities that ūkio could operate here. Hearts could prove to be a useful conduit for that purpose.

Many supporters will have a Marmite attitude to Vladimir Romanov. I think it would be unfair to label him as some sort of pariah. It is worth remembering that, despite his obvious eccentricities, he did deliver some of the most memorable moments in the history of the club. Who can forget the blistering start to the 2005/6 season under new manager, former Ipswich, Derby, Southampton, Crystal Palace and Scotland boss, George Burley?

It was new Hearts Chief Executive Phil Anderton who approached Burley to see if he would be interested in speaking about joining as manager. Burley was attracted by the challenge of Hearts under new ownership and with some money to spend to develop his own squad. Phil recommended to the Board that they appoint him and he was offered the job a few days later. Burley told me:

> I quite fancied the challenge in Scotland and Edinburgh was a real draw. Hearts was an attractive proposition. I was aware that the team had a lot of positives with four or five great players and good characters. I was particularly enticed by the talents and potential of the spine of the team in Andy Webster, Paul Hartley, Robbie Neilson, Steven Pressley, and Craig Gordon. I would be able to invest in the team and build on that superb spine.
>
> We had a nucleus but needed players, but Romanov had to give the go ahead. There were never going to be any fees involved but we had to pay big wages. We were paying very big wages.
>
> Hearts always had a good youth set up with really good people behind it and that was the driver of getting good young players through. It is important to keep and nurture that for the future of football and I think in a few years' time Hearts will really benefit from being ahead of the game on this.

Burley's Hearts won the first eight games, including the one against Rangers at Tynecastle that resulted in the fans singing, 'We are unbeatable'. The run also including a 4-0 humiliation of Hibs. It was this match that Burley recalls as the one that gave him his best memory. He recalled:

> I have many, many happy memories from my time at Hearts. It was all too short but superb memories. I really enjoyed it. My best was against Hibs. You can't beat the feeling of winning a local derby match, especially at home. The atmosphere at the club was already superb when we hammered Hibs four nil. My old mate Tony Mowbray was in charge of Hibs and I still remind him of that result to this day. He hates it. It still hurts.

It was the best start Hearts had enjoyed since the 1914/5 season; not only did they sit on top of the Premier League, they were 11 points ahead of champions Rangers. Many have said that Romanov was obsessed by wrestling the Championship title from the Old Firm duopoly and regularly competing in the Champions League. He certainly invested in the playing side to give that a shot.

Hearts fans were witnessing the start of something very special indeed. They were flocking back to Tynecastle like never before to watch players of a quality never witnessed before. The squad was peppered with Champions League and European Championship winners. There were players who had played at the very highest levels for club and country. There were players that would become historic cult figures, talked about in the pubs around Tynecastle for generations to come. The Mackay, Conn, Bauld and Wardhaugh of the 21st century.

Many supporters will often sit back and marinade themselves in their memories of Hearts but, for me, there were two pivotal moments that will always shape the Romanov period. Back on a dark Wednesday night at Tynecastle Park, Hearts played Aberdeen where a win would give them enough points to render the last day of the Scottish footballing season (when Hearts was due at Ibrox to play Rangers) irrelevant. Three points against Aberdeen at home would secure second place in the Premier League. That would mean Champions League football for the first time in the history of the club. Hearts would become the first non-Old Firm team to qualify.

What a night that was. A tense affair. As if there was ever any other type of affair when it came to critical games watching Hearts. It turned when, after 52 minutes, the referee, Stuart Dougal, pointed to the penalty spot. Aberdeen defender Russell Anderson had handled in the box. As the floodlights lit up the famous old ground, 17,327 Hearts supporters, clad from head to toe in the famous maroon, stood in almost complete silence as cult hero and player of the season, Paul Hartley, placed the ball on the penalty spot. For what seemed like an age, he struck the ball into the back of the net for a 1–0 win.

As the final whistle sounded, the famous Champions League anthem, 'Zadok the Priest' by George Frideric Handel, reverberated around a jubilant but stunned Tynecastle Park. Vladimir Romanov took to standing on the barrier in front of the Directors Box as 'Vladimir Romanov, Vladimir Romanov' rang out from the stands to the tune of 'La donna è mobile' from Verdi's opera, *Rigoletto*. Hearts had made it to the Champions League qualifying rounds and we were going to enjoy that. There were a few happy tears shed that night. As an aside, the hundreds of Hearts supporters sitting reading newspapers at the start of the meaningless game with Rangers at Ibrox the following weekend was a fun sight. Everyone deserved that after a memorable season.

Many will have written about the following summer's excursions into the Champions League but it is fair to say that a small part of the five-year plan to win the title and play regularly in the Champions League didn't seem like such an unachievable dream after all.

In the end, it was a disappointing qualifying campaign. Hearts didn't quite make it to the group stages after a 5-1 aggregate loss to AEK Athens but we could all say we were there. I don't think the irony of playing Champions League home matches at Murrayfield was lost either. The maroon Romanov juggernaut was well and truly hurtling down the tracks and everyone was enjoying the ride.

Then there was arguably the most famous victory in the history of Hearts. The 2012 Scottish Cup Final win over Hibs. We had won the trophy in 2006 when we defeated Gretna on penalties but this was the first Scottish Cup Final between the two Edinburgh clubs for as long as anyone alive would have experienced.

Maybe this wasn't the pinnacle that Romanov wanted but it was for the fans. I remember the semi-final against Celtic at Hampden. I couldn't make the game so Alan and I went to Diggers Bar to watch it on TV. The nervousness that envelops watching most Hearts matches on TV manifests itself in drinking too much alcohol. Each pass, throw in or incident is greeted with another slurp of Diggers' finest. To add a little more anxiousness, our bitter rivals Hibs had beaten Aberdeen 2-1 the afternoon before. They were awaiting the winners of our tie in the final. Gulp.

The script was playing out as expected. Hearts hero Rudi Skácel opened the scoring early in the second half and, if previous history was a guide, Celtic would equalise and go on to win the match. When Celtic did equalise, a deflated Diggers crowd was silent except for the odd 'I knew it' emanating from an exasperated fan. But the usual script was about to be ripped up. The improvisers had got hold of this match and they were going to do what Hearts fans had rarely witnessed – they were going to award a penalty to Hearts in the dying minutes. What joy. What pain. What nerves.

What was about to happen was extraordinary. History was about to take a great leap forward. I always remember my mate, former election agent and dyed-in-the-wool Jambo, Mike Howard, posing a question one night: 'What is the difference between a great night out and an ordinary night out?'. After a great deal of toing and froing with guess after guess, I gave up. 'Stories to tell,' he said. And my goodness, if we were to apply this to our love of Hearts, we were just about to turn an ordinary football match into a great memory. We would recall this moment for years to come.

Striker Craig Beattie, signed after being released from Swansea in early 2012, decided that the history books of Heart of Midlothian Football Club deserved to have his name etched on this chapter. He stepped up and scored the penalty. 2–1 to Hearts with minutes to go. Diggers erupted. Gallons of alcohol of all flavours and styles flew through the air accompanied by an enormous roar. Every TV in sight was adorned by the image of Craig Beattie running behind the goal in front of the delirious Hearts supporters. He was stripped to the waist, twirling his number four shirt above his head. It would become the must-do thing for all celebrating Jambos in the coming weeks (I haven't done that – well, at least not in public). He only made five appearances for Hearts but what an impact. All football fans dream of scoring an important winning goal and doing a 'Klinsman' or 'Shearer' or other dramatic celebration. Hearts fans now had the 'Beattie'. We are all thankful for that.

The final whistle blew at Hampden that afternoon after a few lengthy minutes of onslaught on the Hearts goal from Celtic. But as the arms of Hearts fans at Hampden and in Diggers were raised in celebration, there was a realisation of what was about to come. I remember turning to my brother after our final whistle embrace and saying, 'What the fuck have we just done?' The enormity of a Scottish Cup Final against Hibs, who had not won the Scottish Cup in 110 years, was sinking in. The first Edinburgh Derby Scottish Cup Final in over 100 years. The Romanov Rollercoaster was to continue. All the financial problems were to be put to one side for a single match in May 2012 at the national stadium in Glasgow.

As an avid fan, I had quite enjoyed the run up to the 1998 Scottish Cup Final when Hearts defeated Rangers 2-1 to win their first Scottish Cup since 1956. Back then, the expectations were lower as we lost to Rangers two years previously in the League Cup Final and three years prior in the Scottish Cup Final. It is always difficult to defeat either of the Old Firm in a final so when it came it was slightly unexpected. The best day of my life. Was that about to be eclipsed in 2012?

The run-up to the 'salt and sauce' final was a little more fraught. I didn't really sleep properly for over three weeks. Long nights lying in bed playing over and over in my head all the potential scenarios, wondering what the outcome would be. One of the key members of my parliamentary office team, John Griffiths, is also an ardent fan. He looked more and more tired as the weeks wore on when I walked into my office on Minto Street every Friday for my weekly advice session. We could barely discuss what we thought could or would happen. We sort of had an unspoken understanding that if we didn't discuss it, the nervousness would disappear. When we did mention the unmentionable, it was to try and reassure each other. The omens were all pointing to Hibs breaking their 110-year Scottish Cup hoodoo against us. It just couldn't happen. These conversations were like a mutual support group. They certainly didn't help.

I'm sure fans of all clubs go through this in the run up to huge games but this, for me, was completely different. My experience was one of nervousness and fear. Others had altogether more acute problems. Calum Robertson, who would go on to become a key Director in the FOH, had a heart attack in the week leading up to the final. That is how much it affected him. However, respected comedian and football broadcaster, Tam Cowan, says it was nothing to do with the anticipation of the game and more to do with the fact that Calum was a 'fat bastard'. Tam has never let Calum forget this. The travesty for Calum was that the doctors forbid him to watch any of the final. He was not in a fit state to do that to his heart.

Hearts fans will have repeatedly spoken of the run-up to the game and the day itself at every possible opportunity. It would be remiss not to give my short story as part of this book. The game was significant and the financial consequences utterly critical for the survival of the club.

The day itself started as any other away match did. I would make the short journey to Sighthill Bowling Club where the Longstone Hearts Supporters club buses were leaving from. Getting hold of a spare bus to take us to Glasgow was not easy given the number of fans from Edinburgh heading to our national stadium. That was made more evident to me when, after a quick pint (it was 10.00am), my brother, our fellow voyagers for decades and I left the bowling club. We were presented with a bright red double decker, emblazoned with the words 'Golden Eagle'. It was hired from a company in North Lanarkshire. It was primarily used as a school bus and had a speed limiter of 40mph. It was less of a golden eagle and more of a dead parrot. This was not going to be a quick journey to Glasgow.

The bus crawled along the M8. I'm sure if we had walked it would have seemed quicker. Every other maroon- or green-clad vehicle on the motorway that morning sped past us. You could imagine the mocking that was going on inside their vehicles. Not only was its maximum speed 40mph but it took what felt like three days to get anywhere near that top speed.

Anyway, the lengthy trip allowed us time to reflect on away days of the past. We made comparison with the 1998 Scottish Cup Final, the final at Hampden when Rangers beat us 5-1 and some of the other sun-soaked semi-finals days out we had enjoyed as fans.

And what better place for a few pre-match pints in Glasgow at lunch-time than a nightclub? I know. The experiences of that day will never be matched. Hundreds of Jambos cramped into an establishment that would normally not see such an attendance until at least 2.00am on a Sunday (and, for that matter, a crowd of a much lower average age). It may have been a rather unorthodox start to a Cup Final day but it was great. The nightclub had arranged large screens where previous goals against Hibs were being replayed. The drinks were flowing, the songs were being sung, old acquaintances and new were being established and a good time was being had by all.

When I was looking around the company that Alan and I were in, it made me reminisce about what Hearts meant to me and to him. We were still the same group of friends that had grown up together, bound by our love of all things maroon – Gogs, Smitty, Gav, Shaun, Laughton, George, Alan and me. The only difference was that we were all older. We had gone through the highs and the many lows together. Here we all were, in a night-club at lunchtime, enjoying each other's company. Mums, dads, aunties, uncles, sons, daughters, nieces, nephews, grandparents all enjoying the day. All of this started when my own dad, Jim, lifted me over the turnstile at the Wheatfield Street entrance to Tynecastle back in 1985. I wonder how many supporters start their footballing journey with that kind of story.

I thought about my dad a lot that day. He died back in January 1986 at the age of 39. He was just a few years older than I was on the day of the Cup Final. He also passed away halfway through one of the most successful seasons in Hearts' recent history. Yes, in 1986, they did fail to win the Premier League title with seven minutes to go on the last day of the season and, yes, they did lose the Cup Final to Aberdeen the following weekend, but he would have cherished every minute of the journey. He would also have been lapping up the day we were having. A Jambo through and through and, like many other sons who have lost a father, if I had one wish – just one – I would have wanted to spend the 2012 Cup Final with him. What a day that would have been. He made me maroon. He was as maroon as any Hearts fan and I thank him for that lifelong passion that I was lucky enough to inherit.

Anyway, on to the match. We left the nightclub rather bleary eyed at 2.30pm. We weren't bleary from the few pints we had had (or cans as it was) but from surfacing into a rather fine sunny Glasgow day. We had spent the best part of two hours like moles in a very dark nightclub.

We walked the 15 minutes or so to the ground. I was struck by the almost silent optimism of the Hearts supporters. There were many enthusiastic songs on the streets but that was tempered by a palpable apprehension. You could almost see it. The other quite humorous observation was the way that almost everyone, including myself, checked the pocket that contained our match tickets every few steps. There was no way we wanted to miss this game.

Into the ground we went. What an atmosphere and what an occasion for Edinburgh, both football clubs and the Scottish Cup. It was absolutely electric. We took up our seats in the traditional Hearts end behind the goal to enjoy the 'salt and sauce' Scottish Cup Final between our beloved Hearts and our bitter rivals, Hibs.

I hadn't felt this way at a football game since the 1998 final against Rangers at Celtic Park. I was 21 in 1998 and with the same group of friends. Hearts hadn't won the Scottish Cup since 1956 and it all came down to 90 minutes of football. I don't need to explain to any Hearts fan that we were 2–1 up with ten minutes remaining. I left my seat and went to the concourse under the stand. I, along with thousands of others, couldn't bear it. I have always proudly claimed that I have never ever smoked. That isn't entirely true because I spent a few precious minutes on the concourse puffing away on a cigarette handed to me already lit by a complete stranger. I bumped into my brother and he had a puff too. It seemed that the entire population of the west of Edinburgh was on the concourse smoking, avoiding the nervousness of what was happening on the pitch. We were all just hoping not to hear a muffled roar from the Rangers fans to signal they had equalised. That muffled roar never came and the final whistle went to bring home the famous old trophy for the first time in all our lifetimes. It was magical. I have never considered smoking since (I probably didn't even inhale) but I came close to it in the run up to the Cup Final with Hibs. (I didn't, though, if my mum is reading this.)

Back to 2012. The teams at Hampden came out to a rapturous reception. I just tried to take it all in. Looking back, it was a blur. A combination of a not inconsiderable amount of cheap lager (I think it's called tired and emotional having barely slept for near on a month) and the enormity of what we were about to witness must have had a lasting effect on my memory of the pre-match pleasantries. The whistle blew for the start of the game and the nervousness, intense chats, sleepless nights and playing all the connotations of the game in my head disappeared.

And then it happened. The hero of the hour Darren Barr poked the ball into the Hibs goal at the far end of the ground. Mayhem in the Hearts support. Only 15 minutes gone. The tension of the game evaporated into a frenzy of clenched fists, jumping up and down with my brother and going wild with delight. The Hearts end absolutely erupted. I have never seen scenes like it (apart from perhaps at the 1998 Cup Final or when Hearts took the lead against the mighty Liverpool at Anfield).

Another goal from cult hero Rudi Skácel before half-time looked to have us on easy street. Wait, this can't be right – Hearts never do things the easy way. Where are the heart palpitations? Where are the moments of biting my fingernails to the quick? Where are anguished faces and hands over the eyes? Well, they came. Just before half-time, Hibs were thrown a lifeline with a goal by their captain, James McPake. It was 2-1 at half-time. There was still a long way back into the game for Hibs but it ruined my half-time. Could we begin to dream the unbelievable?

The second half started with Hearts on the front foot. They were now shooting into the Hearts end which was always a much more comfortable position for me. For some reason I have a superstition that when the team are shooting into their own fans, it makes it somehow easier for them. What do I know about football after all?

With just 47 minutes on the clock, Suso Santana burst into the penalty box from the left and went down after a tug on the shirt from Hibs defender Kujabi. 'PENALTY,' we all screamed in unison. The referee, Craig Thomson, didn't even hesitate and pointed to the spot. To our sheer delight, the referee also brandished a second yellow card for Kujabi and sent him for an early bath. Was this actually happening? 2-1 up with just 47 minutes played. A penalty for us and Hibs down to ten men. Surely if we dispatched the spot kick, there would be no way back for the men in green.

Almost complete silence descended on the stadium as Danny Grainger placed the ball on the spot. The concentration in his eyes could be seen by all. He stepped up and stroked the ball home. Total and utter delirium from everyone wearing maroon. 25,000 Hearts fans could start to dream. We could see the Cup coming home. We could touch the possibility. It was utterly joyous.

It was at this point that Calum Robertson dismissed his doctor's advice and succumbed to watching the rest of the game. He had chaired the Hearts Youth Development Committee for many years. What a job he and his committee had done for the club. All the players knew he was ill and been unable to go to the game. It was wonderful that he got a call from the team bus on way back from Hampden and spoke with captain, Marius Žaliūkas and hero of the day Rudi Skácel. A lovely gesture that just emphasised the Hearts family.

And, of course, at 3-1 we weren't finished yet. Despite singing ourselves hoarse, we got to celebrate what has now become an iconic headed goal from our Australian youngster, Ryan McGowan. The scoring was rounded off by none other than the exquisite left boot of Rudi Skácel. The final whistle blew and we celebrated as if our lives depended on it. A 5-1 victory against our rivals in the Scottish Cup Final. The score line would go down in history (and provide the Foundation of Hearts with one of its more popular donation rates of £51). The score 5-1 would never be the same again. My only disappointment – with 20 minutes still to play – was that we should have turned the screw and made it ten.

Our Lithuanian club captain, Marius Žaliūkas, went up the famous Hampden steps to collect the trophy. As he held it above his head, a moment that all of us will never forget was delivered. It was only eclipsed by Rudi Skácel holding aloft the trophy whilst standing on the barrier. He was wearing a curly maroon and white wig. The scenes were simply incredible.

For me, the highlight of the post-match celebrations was the Hearts song. Most of us will have sung it loud and proud hundreds of times at matches. Many of us will have sung and whistled it in the shower or the car. Maybe we have given it a few verses at parties and even weddings. This was special. That day was the best ever for me. 25,000 utterly overjoyed Hearts fans singing it in unison. The YouTube videos of that three and a half minutes are a must-watch for all Hearts supporters.

I have described my Cup Final day as I saw it. Many fans will have their own stories to regale for years to come, stories that our children, grandchildren and great grandchildren will never get fed up hearing. The story of our time watching Hearts that takes on the same stature and significance as the story of the 1956 Cup Final from our own parents, grandparent or great grandparents. The memories of a stunning day and an unforgettable reminder of why we love Heart of Midlothian and football in general.

Now this book isn't about my favourite games but I wanted to touch on just two specific instances of where Vladimir Romanov took us on a rollercoaster as supporters. I could have, of course, talked about the 4–0 hammering of Hibs in the Scottish Cup semi-final in 2006 and the subsequent cup victory against Gretna, or various forays into Europe. I could have mentioned my best goal celebration ever at Anfield in the Europa League but I wanted to show how the 2012 Scottish Cup triumph was not only one of our greatest moments but pivotal in the survival of the club financially.

The money generated from this Cup run and the League Cup Final later that same year gave Hearts the financial reprieve that allowed it to limp on to the end of the 2012/13 season, without which the club would almost certainly have died.

But it all went wrong for Hearts long before the hammering of Hibs at Hampden in 2012...

CHAPTER 2

Hearts in Green and Yellow

LITTLE DID ANY Hearts supporter know that when we left Hampden Park on that glorious day in May 2012, the club would be a matter of months away from potentially playing its last ever game. We had won the biggest game in our history. The memories would never fade but would we ever see the likes again? Was our club about to die? Were these memories about to become just that?

Hearts was owned by ūkio Bankas, a Lithuanian bank that was a subsidiary of the Lithuanian UBIG Group – companies owned by Romanov. The club was reported to be in over £28 million of debt. It wouldn't have taken an accountant to work out that the way the club was spending, and the size of the debt, was not being serviced by the turnover of the club. This position may have been sustainable had it not been for other factors but it was not just the global financial crash of 2008 that caused the problem. The warning signs had been there from 2005.

The Finance Director at that time, Stewart Fraser, had a constant battle. He insisted on a clause in the published annual accounts in 2005/06 that highlighted the precarious financial position that Hearts was in and the fact that it was unsustainable.

In November 2008, Campbell Ogilvie as Chief Executive, David Southern as Marketing Director and Stewart insisted on the HMFC Board convening with the club's lawyers on the basis that the Board would be liable if they ignored the perilous financial position of the business. At this meeting, the prospect of administration was discussed in some detail as was the nature of events. The club was being run on a hand to mouth basis with no real plan or strategy as to when finance would be required from the owners. The result of this meeting with the lawyers was a short-term injection of cash from Lithuania. This stabilised Hearts for a short period but the situation couldn't go on.

There was also an email that Stewart sent to the Board in March 2008 that said:

Unless we sort this situation out now, the closure of the company is now certain, the only uncertainty is when...

It may have been four years later that Hearts fans were anticipating watching their last ever game, but Stewart was correct.

There is a copy of a letter that Romanov wrote when he first took over Hearts. The letter stated that the wage costs would stay the same and he would pay any of the additional costs beyond that base. Every year, for the annual accounts and auditors, Stewart had to get a letter to say that the owners would stand behind the overdraft and spending. It was a Public Limited Company (PLC) so they had legal reporting responsibilities. Romanov didn't like this. He hated that it cost a lot of money to maintain, so he decided to take Hearts private.

Romanov would service the club by sending money from Lithuania. That was fine and boosted the club's finances. However, two years down the road, these turned into loans at the insistence of parent bank ūkio Bankas. Romanov's right-hand man at Tynecastle, Sergejus Fedotovas, handed Stewart a very large package of loan agreements. These came completely out of the blue. All the money that Romanov had put into the club to support the day-to-day spending on players' salaries etc would be loans. It wouldn't have surprised anyone if the owners of holding company UBIG, of which Romanov was just a part and had no overall majority control, had insisted that these payments were turned to loans to protect their financial position.

For two years, Campbell, David and Stewart continued to warn on the direction the club was heading, including in formal letters to the Board and the parent company, UBIG. They also travelled on a number of occasions to Lithuania to speak directly with Romanov to appeal to him that the company be financed on a more secure footing and that wild spending be reduced or stopped. The 2008 economic shock merely magnified these issues.

Late one Friday afternoon in 2008, prior to a home match the following day, Campbell, Stewart, David, John Boag, the facilities manager, and Pedro Lopez, who was helping Sergejus, spoke about how they couldn't get the match played. It looked likely they would have to forfeit the points. The police, security and safety personnel hadn't been paid and would not turn out unless their accounts were settled. They had literally two hours to get in touch with all the suppliers, who were a very patient and understanding bunch, to negotiate their way to ensuring the game would be played. In this instance they were successful, but it was not an isolated problem. It would become a running issue for the years ahead.

Some of the spending was wild. There would be instances on transfer deadline day that a dozen players would be brought in with no thought as to the financial implications. They would be on huge salaries with extras that were clearly unsustainable. Contracts would contain compounded win bonus clauses that increased with every consecutive win.

One of the most outrageous contracted bonuses was given to Finnish player, Juho Mäkelä. Sergejus signed him. He hadn't played very well in his trial and was poor in his first few games so didn't really play again. His contract contained a clause that gave him £5,000 a goal as a 'golden goal'. It never cost the club in the initial stages as he never scored. Hearts played a cup tie at Alloa in September 2005 and Mäkelä scored a hat trick, bagging £15,000 as a goal bonus. Pedro Lopez, brought over from Lithuania by Romanov to help Sergejus, kept saying to Stewart, 'That's another £5,000, Stewart.' The owners never listened to these kinds of issues and it cost the club a lot of unnecessary resources. Finally, they managed to pay off Mäkelä. It became clear after he left Hearts that Mäkelä never asked for the golden goal clause. It was Sergejus that insisted it went in. Sergejus didn't really understand football. He was a basketball man. He didn't get the consequences of such a generous clause. Not bad for a few goals at Alloa though.

The Lithuanian owners were also well known for their love of wheeling and dealing. A particular example was with the Scottish Media Group (SMG). SMG owned a large minority stake in the club. When they bought out their share, they put an attractive offer on the table. Just as they were about to sign the formal contracts, the Lithuanians would remove the contract and place a much-reduced offer. SMG was so far into the contractual obligations at that point that they just signed. It was perhaps a different cultural way of conducting business, but it was unorthodox.

I was told of one occasion on the last day of a January transfer window when Romanov came into the office at 11.00pm and demanded to know who the best player in Scottish football was at that time. The assembled staff said Barry Robson at Dundee United. He demanded that the club fax Dundee United and see if the player could be signed. Cost was not a consideration. Hearts didn't sign him in that transfer window but it goes to show the kind of resources the club was spending and what the owners were willing to do to get what they wanted.

There is no doubt that without the considerable financial support of Romanov the club could not survive. But with that financial umbilical cord comes dictatorial management. We all know of rumours of the famous fax machine where accusations would be made that Romanov was picking the team. These were never proved or disproved and the managers at that time denied that these actions ever took place.

He did, however, give each player a score out of ten after every match to assess whether a player had done enough to merit being picked the following week. There were players he liked and disliked. It was known that he never had a great deal of time for fans favourite, Julien Brellier. He never marked him with anything more than a five despite performances that were recognised by the supporters and rewarded by praise from the manager. That led to him insisting that an on-loan Brazilian player called Samuel Camazzola should play in midfield in place of Julien Brellier. This was obviously against the wishes of the manager and, given he didn't play, it gave the manager a rare victory against the Romanov regime. That may have been Burley's only and last victory over Romanov. It may even have been the major contributor to Burley leaving the club. Burley said:

> I would recommend players but couldn't get them approved. My first team scout, Simon Hunt had loads of contacts that allowed him to recommend a number of outstanding prospects for Hearts. There was a friendly game against Steve McClaren's Middlesbrough and I was keen to get some of these prospects in to have a further look at them. I had already managed to sign Julien Brellier and wanted to add Roman Bednar, Michal Pospisil, Takis Fyssas and a certain Rudi Skácel.
>
> I was confident that if I could get them on the pitch I could persuade Romanov to sign them. The players I got over, including Rudi did very well. Their agent, who could speak Russian persuaded Romanov to bring them in. The problem though wasn't me just trying to get players passed the Romanov test. I used to say 'no, no, no', to all Romanovs suggestions but he did sometimes get his way. On one or two occasions someone would come over for a trial and I would say no and then the player would arrive on a three-year contract. Most of them were pretty hopeless. I just refused to play them.

I haven't been able to get a handle on the influence these player scores and records had on the team, nor if it influenced the manager or who would be the manager, but it showed a level of control and obsession that was ever present in the day-to-day operation of the club.

It wasn't as if employees of Hearts didn't try to bring some sense to the spending decisions. Campbell, David and Stewart used to do joint emails to

Romanov to try and get some responsibility to sort out the company finances. They were powerless in practice though. Stewart couldn't even sign a cheque for one pound. Sergejus was so against using standing orders or direct debits that he asked Stewart to cancel them all. He wanted full control. This was a paranoia that nobody had witnessed at Hearts or in business before.

Often Campbell and David would say to Stewart, 'We think it is time for another one of your letters.' Those letters to the owners were from Stewart, as company secretary, reminding them of their responsibilities as directors of the business and their legal obligations to keep the company solvent.

I was told that they went to see specialist administrator, Blair Nimmo, with Sergejus to talk through what would happen in the case of administration. Sergejus liked the idea of being able to negotiate and forego debt. He asked, with no irony or hesitation, 'Can we appoint Stewart Fraser as our administrator?' He was bluntly told 'No' and that the current owners would lose all their power and relinquish control of the company. That was the end of that discussion. It does show that administration was never far from the minds of the owners and the day-to-day reality for the club. There were some incredible decisions made. Some publicly known and others not so.

It's well documented about the sacking of Burley. It was met with sheer dismay from supporters and also the majority of the footballing world. He had won eight out of ten league matches and taken us to the top of the Premier League. We were being seriously considered as title challengers. Burley himself knew that:

> I genuinely thought we had a really great chance in the league title that year but behind the scenes was difficult. The mentality of foreign owners was just a different culture. It wasn't deliberate for Romanov, but he got more and more bizarre. Foreign owners don't help managers and it makes the job more and more difficult. It becomes more of the norm and that is damaging. They see control as more important than success.
>
> I was not surprised by the results as I knew we had a great team, but I was slightly surprised by the consistency of a fairly new team. The form was excellent, and the fans responded as Hearts fans always did. I remember the match away to Dundee United at Tannadice and the Hearts fans filled two thirds of the stadium. It gave everyone at the club a boost and the players loved it. The stadiums were filled with Hearts fans wherever we went. I knew the team needed time, but they did really well when people gelled.
>
> What would have happened is anyone's guess, but I would have liked to have thought that we could have gone on to win the title. I had two years

in Europe as the manager of Ipswich and took Derby and Southampton to the play-offs so my record showed that we could have achieved Europe as a minimum that season.

There has been lots of column inches devoted to the reasons for Burley's exit from Hearts, including an uneasy relationship with the owner, but none of them can be justified in footballing terms. Was it that Romanov just didn't get on with the manager or were there much deeper problems that became untenable? Burley himself is very straightforward about what happened:

It was becoming more and more difficult to manage the team. It had been brewing for a long time. I'm maybe an old-fashioned manager but I was brought up on a diet of Sir Bobby Robson and others. They had total control as that was the way they delivered success for their teams. As an example, Sir Bobby Robson used to choose the grass seed for the ground staff and that was the way he wanted to do things. That was the way he knew how to deliver success. I needed total control of the football department or I couldn't do the job properly and get that success that we all wanted. That was when I knew I had to go.

This was the first instance where Hearts fans truly started to see the unpredictable nature of Romanov. Did he want to own Hearts to overturn the dominance of the Old Firm and take on the Champions League or was this just a plaything for a very rich owner? We may never know but it started a long list of decisions that would have fans dismayed and, on some occasions, very angry. The sacking of Burley came a day after Romanov had announced he was taking full control of the club by taking it back into private ownership. Burley knew this would not end well for Hearts supporters after he left:

I felt sorry for the superb fans at Hearts. They had ploughed their money and all their passions into the club and it was almost completely ruined. When you have an owner that wants to win games and trophies it makes it much easier to create success. The fans will stay right behind the team and it was the fans being right behind the team at Hearts that saved the club.

The sacking of Burley also had the consequence of resulting in the sacking of the Chief Executive, Phil Anderton. Phil had tried to create a different match day experience for Hearts fans by introducing pre-match fireworks (he was called firework Phil after all), adorning the stadium with huge mosaics of famous players, and instilling a siege mentality at our home stadium. All of this was attracting fans back to Hearts and helping the team to an invincible position.

My understanding was that on the day Burley was sacked, Phil Anderton was told by Romanov to say it was because of an alleged contract breach by Burley. Phil rightly refused to portray the sacking in such a way. He was dismissed as a result. It was clear Romanov was looking for an excuse as Burley had too much control.

Lord Foulkes as Chair, Stewart as Finance Director and Company Secretary, and Phil himself voted against the sacking but the Lithuanians had majority control on the Board. It was approved. Romanov took no part personally, as he had no voting power, but at the point of the decision to sack Anderton, Romanov knelt down beside him and said in broken English, 'You now no Director, you are now barely a manager' and left.

That left the club without its undefeated manager and innovative Chief Executive. It was left to the club Chairman, Lord Foulkes, to deliver the devastating and numbing news of Burley's departure to the fans. Lord Foulkes has always regretted not resigning from the Board there and then. He felt a sense of responsibility to ensure the situation didn't spiral out of control to the detriment of the club he loved. He famously said, 'I am not happy making this statement…'

The news that Lord Foulkes was considering his position was intimated to Romanov. This sparked a charm offensive that seemed out of character for the owner. He desperately wanted to meet his Chairman but Lord Foulkes refused to travel from his home in Ayr back to Edinburgh for what would be an inevitable showdown. To the utter shock and surprise of Lord Foulkes, Romanov arrived at his home in Ayr with a bunch of flowers and box of chocolates for his wife, Liz. They were described as the local petrol station's very best. The meeting was cordial but the discomfort he felt at not resigning was clear to Romanov.

It is difficult to fathom what the Romanov strategy had become. After that showdown, Lord Foulkes would no longer play a key role in the club. Lord Foulkes had made his mind up to resign and would do so at the next Board meeting. However, news came through to him that the club would have a hastily arranged emergency Board meeting that Monday evening without Lord Foulkes either being invited or, as would be the normally practice, calling the meeting. When Lord Foulkes arrived at the Board meeting that Monday, Romanov was shocked to see him. He tendered his resignation and left his role of Chair of the club. He was replaced by Romanov's son, Roman Romanov.

This commenced a period of what was described as 'paranoia' from Romanov that manifested itself in him having a 'spy' in every department and office of the club. He would place a Lithuanian or friend at Tynecastle in roles ranging from finance to ground staff. This paranoia was most evident on the managerial department. The decisions on who would become Hearts manager perplexed most supporters and were seen as Romanov trying to dominate footballing decision. The dismissal of Burley would have been dampened if Romanov had brought in another high-profile boss. There was lots of talk of Claudio Ranieri, Sir Bobby Robson and other top European names, but after Phil Anderton's dismissal, the chances of getting a big-name replacement for Burley was almost impossible. To everyone's utter astonishment, Romanov appointed former Portsmouth manager, Graham Rix. In 1999, Rix had been sentenced to 12 months in prison for having unlawful sexual intercourse with a 15-year-old girl. The strange irony was that Romanov still insisted that Burley was sacked on moral grounds. It didn't help when Roman Romanov dismissed the fans' anger with his now infamous saying, 'A man who has been beaten by life is worth two who are unbeaten.'

If you were to ask anyone what they think would be the worst managerial appointment following the euphoria of Burley, they would have never contemplated Graham Rix. Romanov had led the fans to expect a household name, not a controversial figure whose own ambitions were to apply for the vacant manager's position at Crawley Town. The one thing that appointment achieved was to temper some of the shock of Burley leaving. It was far worse.

It also resulted in the resignation from the Board of Finance Director, Stewart Fraser, as he had no knowledge of the decision and simply didn't want to be associated with the announcement that the 'Board of Heart of Midlothian Football Club has appointed Graham Rix'. Stewart stayed on as Company Secretary but felt he could no longer sit on the Board.

Rix didn't last long. What followed was a revolving door of managers that were known to Romanov in Lithuania. They were supported by Directors of Football that also had close associations with the owner. One thing is clear from the statistics of that period, the managerial appointments didn't get anywhere near delivering the results for the team that was commensurate with the money being spent on players. By the end of the season that had started so promisingly for Hearts, they were managed by Lithuanian Valdas Ivanauskas and had no fewer than nine Lithuanian players in the first team.

None of the subsequent nine managerial appointments by Romanov achieved anything even near a 50 per cent win rate. The club became a home for poor Lithuanian managers whose only qualification was a connection with Romanov – Eduard Malofeyev, Eugenijus Riabovas, Anatoliy Korobochka. A second spell from Valdas Ivanauskas was punctuated by several spells of John McGlynn as caretaker and short reigns by Stephen Frail, and afterwards by Csaba László. A second spell as manager for the legend that is Jim Jefferies steadied the ship but only just before cult hero Paulo Sérgio won the 2012 Scottish Cup. What started as a project to create invincibility at Tynecastle ended up a damp squib.

As if the sacking of Burley, the loss of the renaissance team of Phil Anderton and Lord Foulkes, the paranoia and the managerial decisions were not enough, there were some other astonishing decisions that are hard to believe. I wonder if there has ever been another instance in world football where the owner of a club has put a player through a lie detector test in order to determine if they were of sound enough character to play for the club. I don't know if this is an issue that should have been taken up with the Players' Union, but it is certainly unorthodox. There is also the instance when the marketing department managed to put a stop to Romanov introducing a tartan home kit. The usual process for designing and implementing a new kit for the forthcoming season was taking place. Without any notice or intention whatsoever, Romanov appeared with what has been described to me as 'not quite a detailed design' for what he envisaged the kit looking like for the following season. He obviously wasn't too concerned about the marketability of the product to the supporters as it was described to me as a:

> kitsch, partly tartan design that I'm not even sure we would be able to get permission from the footballing authorities to wear.

Romanov demonstrated the design by taking a picture of Hearts Cup winning, goal scoring hero, Stéphane Adam, who was featuring in the match day programme. He overlaid the famous white strip from the 1998 Cup Final with the tartan wrapper from a Walkers shortbread packet. He had carefully cut the packet into the shape of the shorts. It was 6.45pm on the Friday before a match day and everyone was eager to get home. The doctored photo of Stéphane Adam adorned the desk of Hearts commercial manager, Ally Russell. Somehow, they managed to persuade Romanov that it would not be the best look for a new strip design. David commented that 'tartan was for tourists' and hastily left the building.

As if the tartan kit wasn't enough, the most astonishing consideration was Romanov proposing to change the club colours from the famous maroon and white to that of the colours of the Lithuanian club he owned.

Kaunas FC played in green and yellow – the colours of our Edinburgh rivals, Hibs FC, and indeed almost exactly like the Celtic FC away kit at that time. The very thought of associating anything with the colour green at Hearts would bad enough but to make a serious proposal to the marketing team that the club colours should change to green and yellow was absurd. The new kit of green, yellow and perhaps even a little tartan to 'bring the two countries of Lithuania and Scotland together' was simply a non-starter.

It took all the diplomacy of a top Foreign and Commonwealth Office official to persuade Romanov that this would not be one of his better ideas and could irreparably damage his relationship with the supporters. Commercial manager Ally Russell did actually meet with some of the fan groups and asked for their views on some of the designs. I hear they gave their honest assessment! It wasn't positive.

Thankfully, for the sake of the club, the proposal was dropped. It was pointed out that the financial consequences would be an unmitigated disaster. The projections on replica shirt sales started at zero and didn't really move beyond that ambitious figure. Can you imagine for one minute a new owner coming in and changing the colours of the club to that of your rivals?

These stories are not told to do anything other than highlight the continued rollercoaster ride that Romanov brought to Hearts. It was a rollercoaster not just for the fans but also for all those who worked at the club. These decisions also contributed to the perilous financial situation.

Romanov was a stickler for negotiating player sales despite the need for cash to keep the club solvent. There was the well-documented offer that had come from Burnley for Andrew Driver. He was undoubtedly a prized asset at the time under the management of Jim Jefferies. He had returned to the club for a second spell as manager to try and steady the ship. Jim had negotiated a deal worth £1.5 million in cash rising to over £2 million with add-ons. Romanov insisted that Jim went back and asked for another £250,000. Jim did and Burnley agreed. This went on until the deal had reached £4 million with £2.5 million in cash up front. At this point, Romanov wanted Jim to go back and get another £250,000. As I understand it, Jim refused. He had already returned on four previous occasions despite a deal having been agreed. In the end, I don't know if Burnley withdrew their offer or Hearts pulled out, but Driver remained a Hearts player. It was described by those involved as a game. For £250,000 extra, Romanov was willing to forego £4 million.

Player sales were always needed to stave off the non-payment of wages, settle bills to HMRC or ensure matches could be fulfilled. Despite them, it only ever temporarily removed the financial problems. Yes, there were sporadic injections of cash from Lithuania but there was also the timely sale of prized playing assets. One example that allowed the Executive Board to breathe a huge sigh of relief was the sale of Christophe Berra to Wolverhampton Wanderers on the last day of the next transfer window in 2009. Almost £2 million dropped into the club's bank account. It was immediately used to pay wages and the tax authorities. This ultimately gave the club more time. There was also the £9 million sale of Craig Gordon to Sunderland for what was a world record transfer fee for a goalkeeper in 2007. That was huge money.

But the late payment of wages and tax bills was an all too familiar feature during the reign of Romanov. Most of the late payment of wages was well documented but it occurred on no fewer than 13 times between June 2010 and March 2013. This was not all of the players every time but at least some were paid late. The Players' Union was involved on a number of occasions. It is worth also remembering that the non-payment of the wages of playing staff was against the rules of the Scottish Football Association and would have severe repercussions should they continue not to be paid.

The non-payment of November 2011 players' salaries resulted in Romanov claiming that he was going to put the club up for sale. The playing squad's October salaries were late and the November salaries were paid so late that they arrived just one day prior to when the December payments were to land in the players' bank accounts. The December salaries failed to arrive and that was when the Players' Union got involved. A complaint was lodged with the Scottish Premier League (SPL) by the Union at the same time that many fringe players at the club were advised to leave and seek employment elsewhere.

On 4 January 2012 the SPL ordered the club to pay all outstanding wages within a week and to settle the January payroll on time, which was by the 16 January. How was the club to do so without any financial support? Well, with the sale of Icelandic midfielder, Eggert Jónsson to Wolverhampton Wanderers. The fee was reported to be around the £400,000 mark and that allowed Hearts to settle the December wages and make the commitment to pay the January salaries as well. There was some dispute about whether Hearts actually made the SPL deadline but what was clear was that the situation had become untenable. The footballing authorities said they would not allow this to happen again.

It wasn't just the playing staff. The non-playing staff were paid late nine times over a similar period. One staff member in particular was paid seven weeks late. It was testament to the dedication that staff had to the club that they kept working. Their dedication should never be forgotten as they strived to ensure matches took place and the club ran on a day-to-day basis.

Then there were debts to HMRC. Tax debts were paid late on numerous occasions and many payment plans were put in place until HMRC lost patience. It was this loss of flexibility with the tax authorities that finally broke the pretence that Hearts could continue as a going concern.

The dye was setting on Hearts future...

CHAPTER 3

Hearts Nearly Stop Beating

THERE WAS LITTLE doubt that the club had been limping along financially for almost four years. Their hand-to-mouth existence, alongside the increasingly erratic decisions of the owner, had to break at some point. That breaking point came when HMRC finally ran out of patience. Would HMFC v HMRC be the most difficult match in Hearts history?

It was at this point in November 2012 that I got involved in trying to help the club. I received a call from David Southern to see if there was any way I could assist in the ongoing issues with HMRC. Hearts was due around £450,000 in non-payment of taxes on wages. The club had been served with initial proceedings towards a winding up order that would ultimately have led to the business being liquidated. It seemed like a relatively small amount of money, but I hadn't appreciated the gravity of the situation. There had been both a history of non-payment alongside and the club breaking previously agreed payment arrangements. This particular winding up order was in addition to HMRC claiming unpaid tax liabilities in the region of £1.75 million. These related to loan agreements for a number of players who joined Hearts from Romanov's Kaunas FC since 2005.

The £1.75 million legacy debt had only come to public attention when Hearts issued a share prospectus to raise funds. The document stated:

> HMRC claimed unpaid tax liabilities of circa £1.75 million (excluding interest and penalties) in relation to the arrangements between the company (Hearts) and Kaunas FC in relation to certain players who were loaned to the company by Kaunas FC.

I committed to do everything I could to try and assist them in setting up a payment plan for the £450,000. I was a Shadow Business Minister in Parliament so had a few people I could call upon. It was important to get to the bottom of what was going on and that could really only be done quickly through the Government.

The Exchequer Secretary to the Treasury at that time was Rt Hon David Gauke MP. I knew him a little bit from sparring across the parliamentary chamber and doing secondary legislation committees with him. I also knew he was a very approachable and sensible Government Minister. I rang him to see what could be done and to seek advice on the best way forward. What had become clear was that time was of the essence. The winding up petition would be heard in the Court of Session in a matter of days, so we had no time to lose.

David Gauke gave me the number of the footballing sector specialist at HMRC. He would be able to walk me through the process and provide me with chapter and verse as to the plight of the club. There is absolutely no doubt in my mind that the only way to resolve this situation was a cheque with HMRC's name on it. I wasn't sure they would be able to get that. I made contact with Mr Des Dolan, who was hugely helpful and incredibly experienced. As I understand it, he had been the lead of the football sector for a substantial time so spoke from a position of historic knowledge.

I was a little perplexed as to why HMRC were pursuing Hearts so vociferously for such a small amount of debt. They had been assured it would be paid 'in a matter of weeks'. I wanted to impress on HMRC that the political and public fall-out from such a winding up petition would utterly dwarf the monies due and that the club just needed some time to get their house in order. I couldn't understand why HMRC would put at risk the millions of pounds of future revenue that Hearts would pay to the Treasury for the sake of a short-term fix. I have since learned that, regardless of the sector, company or individual, HMRC rarely, if at all, takes into account the fact that they will earn much more in the years ahead by keeping businesses alive. That may have changed now but it was my experience at that time. HMRC took a hard line with no exceptions.

I'm sure everyone in the position I was in at that time would have made the same demands of HMRC and would have tried to seek some common ground that would resolve the situation. I was shocked at what Mr Dolan told me. He went through the problem in detail and what the process would be in terms of the winding up petition. He then responded to my challenge that the money would be paid very soon. He explained that he had been in his current role for over 12 years and the files of three clubs had never left his desk. Those were Coventry City, Portsmouth and Hearts.

The winding up order was by no means the first to be issued by HMRC. The club announced in February 2012 that they had paid an outstanding tax bill after being given eight days to pay or face being served with a similar winding up notice – likewise, in 2009, 2010 and 2011. Mr Dolan empathised with the situation the club had found itself in but could not justify another reprieve given the long history of debt and non-payment. It's a very difficult thing to argue against.

The great thing about Mr Dolan was that he was a 'football' guy. He understood the passion of supporters and the dedication of all those who made their clubs as good as they could be. He understood the heartbreak of seeing clubs being served with winding up orders, but he also knew that the only way to get some clubs to pay and comply with their tax responsibilities was through the Courts.

Everyone was pulling out all the stops to help. I know the former Chancellor of the Exchequer, Rt Hon Alastair Darling, was also involved in making similar representations to HMRC as a fan and the MP for Tynecastle.

I received a letter back from HMRC on 16 November from the Director of Debt Management and Banking that simply said:

Thank you for your detailed correspondence to our Chief Executive about Heart of Midlothian Football Club.

I understand that Des Dolan has spoken to you regarding your concerns and you are now aware of the current position regarding HMRC and this football club.

It appeared to me that HMRC would not really move on their position and the latest winding up order was the last straw for them. The long and short of all the discussion was that the winding up order would go ahead but the order would not be actioned for a few weeks. That would give the club time to fulfil the promise that the monies would be paid. But how would they do that?

It brought into sharp focus the perilous state of affairs at Hearts. The club, at that point, was reported to be in debt to the tune of over £24 million and there was no way of either bringing in a profit to help reduce that debt or getting an injection of cash. The wage bill to turnover ratio had gone from 29 per cent when Romanov took over to 131 per cent. Given the rule of thumb on wages to turnover ratios is around 50 per cent, you can see how unsustainable the situation was. The context was even more pronounced when you consider the complicated ownership structure of the club and that the funding streams from both ūkio Bankas and UBIG had dried up.

The club had only reduced the debt to £24 million by significant debt forgiveness from the owners in both 2010 and 2011 totalling £16.6 million. So, at the point of serious financial difficulties, the debt would have been over £40 million had the parent company not written off a considerable amount.

The club had effectively already been put up for sale by Romanov when he launched, in October 2012, a share issue aimed at selling 11 per cent of his 98 per cent shareholding. He hoped to raise the best part of £2 million in working capital to keep the Hearts afloat. There was no doubt that Romanov couldn't keep the club going himself. He wanted to leave in a dignified manner from his ownership and had hinted previously that he was an admirer of the ownership models in Germany and Spain. Was this the start of his exit strategy?

Their need to find new funding had become even more pressing after the club failed again to pay the wages of the players in September and October 2012. As a result, Hearts was hit with a transfer embargo by the Scottish Premier League until the end of 2012.

As all of this financial turmoil was playing out, there had been ongoing work to improve the operational efficiency of the club and reduce operating expenses. However, the onerous wage bill and associated tax burden continued to weigh heavily. The share issue was open to all supporters and the open market. It started on 26 October 2012 and was to end on 13 December.

The 'Share in our Future' prospectus contained a long list of risk factors. The first of those risks was most telling,

> The Company's balance sheet is negative, and the Company would be insolvent (on the basis of being unable to pay its debts as they fall due) without the ongoing support of UBIG or alternative funding. While the Company has short-term comfort from UBIG that it will not call up its debt, there is no guarantee that UBIG will not do so in the future...

This was key, especially given that all the funds that had been given to the club by the owners to support player recruitment, wages and running costs were converted to loans. Interestingly, the prospectus also said something that would have a greater resonance in the months ahead: 'You're already part of it. Now why not own a piece of it?'

The stakes were high, and it was getting desperate. A covering letter I received, signed by anonymous Hearts Director, Vitalijus Vasiliauskas, painted an altogether more positive but dishonest picture. It talked of the need to raise funds to continue the 'club's off-field intention to develop a stadium befitting of one of the top teams in the country' and that this was an opportunity for 'groups to invest in this vision'. The letter concluded that the enclosed share prospectus:

> also demonstrates the opportunity for supporters to take an increased inter-est in the club and we are hopeful that it will capture the interest of the many thousands of people who are closely aligned to the club.

This prospectus was a cry for help. Everyone knew it was nothing more than a charitable donation to keep Hearts afloat. If the share issue was offering such sunny uplands, why was it followed by a devastating bombshell?

Just two weeks after launching, the severity of Hearts' financial position was brought into sharp focus. On the morning of 6 November 2012, the club was teetering on the brink once again. This time there was no safety net offered by the owners. That morning, David Southern took a call from one of the club directors in Lithuania. He made it clear that the club was now on its own. The club had just been served with the HMRC winding up order and was struggling to pay player wages. This would have been the third month in a row. The owners left David in no doubt that it would impossible for them to be able to fund the club, even in the short term. The club had to raise the funds necessary to keep operating. There was no notice, no step change. It was instant.

David was very well aware of how difficult the club's financial position was. He and his team had succeeded for almost 18 months in operating without support from Lithuania. Prior to that, David had been relatively successful in securing funds from Lithuania to underwrite overheads. He thought that by showing a track record of reduced reliance on the owners he may be given some support. This was different. There was simply no money left.

David had visited Lithuania on a number of occasions with both Camp-bell and Sergejus to request funding. He was subsequently monitoring the parent company's own business fortunes. He was in no doubt that the club's very future was in severe jeopardy. If Hearts could not buy enough time for the club to be sold or offloaded, liquidation of Heart of Midlothian Football Club was a certainty.

In David's mind, the owners would not have hesitated to sell Tynecastle as part of a land deal to realise funds to provide short term liquidity. That liquidity would not have been for Hearts. Don't forget that ūkio Bankas and

UBIG were trying to keep themselves alive. It wasn't a case of the padlocks being put on the gates of Tynecastle. There was a very strong view that there would not be any gates to padlock.

From that instant, David moved the skeleton staffing at the club to full crisis management. The share issue had been launched and was now becoming a lifeline for the club. This was no longer about a dignified and managed exit of Romanov from Hearts. This share issue was now more of a do or die situation.

The club statement that day did not sugar coat the problems. David needed to let the staff, sponsors and supporters know as they'd be crucial in supporting efforts to save the club. Surprisingly, Sergejus and the other Directors agreed to issue a statement. This was unusual for David as his suggestions to communicate through the media were normally either rebuffed or the process for sign-off was so cumbersome that the moment passed. This was the occasion that David understood the severity of the situation.

Many have told me that one of the characteristics of the owner and Board – arguably to a fault – had been a 'never-say-die' attitude. That included showing no weakness no matter how precarious the position. They would be admitting weakness this time.

There was a number of forthright conversations with Lithuania. The conclusion was that any club statement had to leave no one in any doubt that this could be the end of Heart of Midlothian Football Club. If insufficient funds were raised to pay the current bills, including to HMRC, and to provide some working capital, it was the end.

David and his team went about writing the statement for Lithuanian sign-off. He wanted to ensure that there was no misinterpretation as to the severity of the situation. Hearts would die if this didn't work. David has since told me that he wrote it with honesty at heart. David, to all who know him, is as honest as the day is long. His unassuming but steely character had served him well in his time at the Hearts. The 'bunker' mentality that he and his team had was one of the reasons that Hearts kept going through some extraordinary times.

David sent the draft statement to Lithuania in the knowledge that it would be returned with so much red pen on it that it would render it meaningless. To his utter shock and surprise, the message came back that the statement could be issued with no alterations.

The full statement said:

Today the Board of Heart of Midlothian PLC is writing to you with the express wish that every supporter provides emergency backing for the club.

This is not so much a request as a necessity.

To use the words yesterday of John Robertson, one of the greatest players in this club's history, this is a 'Call to Arms'.

There is no greater need than now for supporters to invest in the club in whichever way you can, without delay. How can you do this?

1. Invest in the Share Issue! Take time to look at the Share Offer brochure and give some thought to what you might be able to afford to commit to the Offer. There are risks, we know, and these are laid out clearly so be very sure this is right for you before committing but please at least consider it.

2. Buy a ticket for you and a friend for the St Mirren game next weekend (Saturday 17 November KO 3.00pm)!

3. Buy a ticket for you and a friend for the Celtic game on 28 November. It's always a cracking atmosphere under the floodlights at Tynecastle and we will welcome the champions for what we expect to be a cracking game. Let's fill the stadium and help the club continue to operate.

4. Buy a ticket for you and a friend for the Aberdeen game on 8 December.

Without the support of fans there is, as we issue this note, a real risk that Heart of Midlothian Football Club could possibly play its last game next Saturday, 17 November against St Mirren.

This isn't a bluff, this isn't scaremongering, this is reality.

Discussions on whose name is above the door, talk about how the money has been spent and debate on whether the investment in silverware has been appropriate is all natural but quite simply worthless at this moment in time.

The only valid debate now is how can you help the club. Is the club worth less than £110?

This club has been supported for the last seven years by generous funding from the majority shareholding business ūkio banko investicinė grupė (UBIG) and we continue to seek the support of UBIG at this stage. However, no business is immune to the financial realities of the current global economy and for this reason the club's reliance on its supporters is greater than at any point in the last seven years.

Our partners, our opponents, media, football bodies, many others – all are watching and judging how we will respond to the challenge. If we cannot demonstrate that we are united, and we represent a force then there will be no due respect to the club from anyone around.

Without your help now, we could be entering the final days of the club's existence. There are limited options for the Board of Directors to take to avoid the catastrophic consequences that a funding shortfall would mean for the club.

In a footballing sense alone Hearts would have suffered an immediate 17-point penalty unless they could make it to the end of the season. This would just be the start of a painful process that will affect every one of us and could lead to far more damaging actions that threaten the very existence of the club.

The power is still in the hands of every Hearts supporter and for that reason we want to be as honest and transparent with you in the hope that you, too, believe that this club is worth saving.

Now please make every effort you can to take any or all of the four steps outlined above and help this great sporting institution survive.

The statement was unambiguous and was met by a combination of shock and numbness from supporters. However, the challenge had been set and the supporters had to rally to save their favourites. The clarity around the debate about ownership, criticism of previous decisions, and the direction of the club was for another day. The focus was solely on survival. David hit 'send' and the response was immediate.

It was during this period that David and Sergejus met with representatives of the supporters. The G10 fans' group was, firstly, asked to back the share offer and, secondly, invited to make a bid for a 51 per cent shareholding in Hearts. They wholeheartedly backed the share offer, although they suspected it was a sham. If they hadn't, they knew what would happen to the club. They also agreed to meet with Supporters Direct Scotland (SDS) to explore how they might put together a bid for fan ownership.

One of the concerns at the time was whether the money that was raised by the fans would stay in the club. They didn't want their efforts rewarded by raising funds to prop up the other parts of the crumbling Romanov empire. That prompted the club to reassure fans that all their money would stay at Tynecastle.

Would this help with HMRC? A club spokesperson said:

We have guaranteed future revenues from forthcoming games and related broadcast income as well as additional guaranteed transfer income which will more than cover the outstanding amount stated in this petition.

We would therefore be hopeful that HMRC will accept that winding up the club would be totally unnecessary.

'Unnecessary' it may have been but for the purposes of saving Hearts, it proved to be totally necessary.

As the club teetered on the brink the fans rallied round. Despite the trial and tribulations behind the scenes, football was still being played. Hearts travelled to Inverness on 10 November and a last-minute penalty by club captain, Marius Žaliūkas brought a point back home. But was this to be the last point Hearts would ever win?

HMRC pursued the winding up order and, as a result, the £450,000 had to be paid by end of day on Friday 16 November. Luckily, an agreement a few days before allowed the debt to be settled by Monday 3 December provided that all other tax payable for November and December 2012 was paid on time. The St Mirren match was on.

The only task now was to raise the funds to pay HMRC and ensure that the St Mirren home match was not going to be the last time anyone watched their team play in maroon at Tynecastle Park.

Huge numbers turned up and packed the ground. 16,443 was about 4,500 more than the fixture would normally have attracted. As an aside, one of the assistant referees for the game was avid Hearts supporter, and now occasional host at Tynecastle, James Bee. A poor game saw Hearts win the match 1-0 with a deflected goal from a Danny Granger shot. But it wasn't really about the game – it was about the occasion and it was about the fans. The match programme was dedicated to the supporters and many key figures in the club praised their support.

The manager, John McGlynn opened his contribution with:

> The fact that I am able to address you today ahead of kick-off against St Mirren is to a large extent due to the magnificent efforts of the fans in the last week or so.

Club Captain, Marius Žaliūkas echoed the remarks of his manager:

> Their loyalty, dedication and willingness to go the extra mile to assist the club in any way they can has been outstanding and has underlined to every one of the players what a great football club Heart of Midlothian is and how proud we are to represent it.

Scottish Cup Final goal hero, Danny Grainger, was the player profile for the match day programme and added:

Thanks to the incredible efforts of the supporters, allied to the players' deferral of their November wages, the club managed to agree a payment extension with HMRC. With the financial problems we have created a special bond between players and fans... Seeing it in black and white this could have been the club's last game...

But the most interesting contribution came from Sergejus, who also thanked the fans fundraising efforts but added:

Delighted as we are by the fans' contribution to the cause, it is important to stress that there remains a long way to go before we emerge from this situation... So, don't delay. Play your part today.

So, the baton for the continued survival of Heart of Midlothian Football Club lay in the hands of the supporters – the very customers who had ploughed their hard-earned cash into the club for years, decades and generations.

Although the focus had to be on short-term survival, there was much discussion about how the club could fulfil all their fixtures to get to the end of the season and what would happen with ownership. That is where the FOH and other supporter groups would come in.

But would the Hearts stop beating?

CHAPTER 4

The Fans' Battle to Keep Hearts Alive

THERE WAS NO doubt that everyone with an interest in Hearts was battling to keep their football club alive. Huge praise was poured on the Hearts support and not one word of it was out of place. For the few staff that remained at the club, to see the fan base mobilise in such a way boosted everyone in continuing their efforts to keep the club's head above the waterline. The players also helped by deferring wages and assisting with fundraising efforts.

It was announced before kick-off at the St Mirren match that Hearts supporters had raised £500,000 since the launch of the share issue. This was incredible. The staff and players came out on to the pitch before the game to applaud those efforts. I remember having a lump in my throat. It was a very emotional moment on a poignant day for the club. The staff offering their thanks was especially touching. You have to remember that the club had been hollowed out over the previous four years. David and his small team of staff had become the last line of defence within the club and they were determined not to let the ship sink on their watch. Failure was not an option for them.

David has always praised them. Every time anyone talks about that period at Hearts, he reflects on the fact that the core team that remained were the true heroes. And he is correct. Many worked without the security of a salary when they had mortgages and rent to pay and families to support. I would fathom that it was this fighting spirit that brushed off on the fans. Everyone was truly all as one with the same goal. We would collectively not let this go.

And none deserves greater credit than staff like Elaine Spence. Elaine worked hard in the ticket office but sadly died in early 2015, at the age of just 40. Elaine was well liked at the club as a loving mum to daughters Amy and Kristen. Elaine had been bravely battling illness for the three years prior to her passing. A hugely popular member of the Tynecastle team that she joined in 2006, Elaine was one of the nicest and toughest during some of the clubs most challenging times. Hearts said at her passing:

> She will be long remembered for the way she inspired everyone in her handling of adversity.

And that adversity was not just her battle with illness but the way she battled in her job. As David said, these were 'the true heroes'.

David did, however, highlight the contribution a playing legend made in the immediate battle, one of the unsung heroes of the fight to keep Hearts in existence – John Robertson. Robbo was a legend on the pitch having been Hearts' all-time top goal scorer but his value off the pitch was every bit as high. He may have scored 271 goals for Hearts and netted 27 times against Hibs but all of that would pale into insignificance with what he was about to do. This was his most important legacy and I don't mean being at my 40th birthday party and actually buying a drink! To help sell the share issue, David spoke to Robbo for over an hour, answering all his detailed questions and trying to appease some of the real hesitancies that anyone would have being asked before taking on such a role. Robbo always felt he had been treated badly by the owners when he managed Hearts, so he wanted to be certain. David asked him to become an ambassador for the share issue – a share issue that launched as an avenue for the supporters to take a stake in the club but ended up being the life support machine.

All Hearts supporters and everyone associated with the club had massive admiration for Robbo. From a business viewpoint, he was able to see beyond the emotional aspect of the increasing disquiet regarding the ownership of the club. That was crucial at that time. As it turned out he was instrumental in the efforts to save the club by helping people focus on what actually mattered.

He agreed to take on the position as ambassador in October 2012. It gave David confidence that when the two of them toured the country and visited supporter groups across the UK, he believed in what he was saying. He was as powerful an advocate for the fundraising efforts as anyone could be. He was Mr Hearts and what Robbo said would be heard.

David zig-zagged the country with Robbo. They went from Inverness to Manchester selling the virtues of the share offer and laying out with honesty the perilous situation the club was in. Their UK wide tour made its first stop in Inverness on a Friday evening before Hearts played there the following day. Over 100 people turned up to hear a very sobering assessment.

David knew the best strategy was to be honest. There was no point in downplaying the dire situation. The fans needed to know the true position. Robbo gave a tear-jerking passionate speech about how much Hearts means to us all and how we all have to rally in the hour of need. I heard he told the fans at a meeting, 'As long as I'm alive this club will not die.' So, if you are a Hearts fan, the next time you see the 'Hammer of Hibs' don't just thank him for goals, thank him for putting his reputation on the line to preserve Hearts.

The stories about what supporters did to raise money to buy shares could fill a book in itself. Their efforts were extraordinary. There were stories of young fans turning up to Tynecastle and emptying their piggy banks out on to the counter, pensioners handing in their last £10 note, families fundraising together, and ordinary supporters digging deep by buying anything and everything maroon. The fan chatroom, Jambos Kickback, ran a huge fundraising campaign and bought tens of thousands of shares. Every fans group rallied. Hearts Youth Development Committee turned all its focus to fundraising to keep the academy alive. The Federation of Hearts Supporters organised fundraising rallies and events. It was an overwhelming effort by everyone who cared about Hearts.

By 4 December, the share issue had raised in excess of £600,000. This settled the HMRC tax bill and the latest winding up order. Hearts had survived to fight another day.

The following day, the club announced that they had come to an agreement with HMRC that they would pay £1.5 million over three years to settle the legacy tax issue. Progress was being made, albeit on a hand-to-mouth basis.

By coincidence, the share issue became the start of discussions about how to deliver supporter ownership and spawned the creation of the supporter groups coming together more formally. This would prove crucial in the months ahead. The club had engaged former Hearts Communications Manager Lawrence Broadie to meet with SDS to determine if there was any potential in commencing tentative talks with supporter groups about how best to transfer to supporter ownership.

David, SDS and Lawrence met to try and come up with what became known as the 'Maroon Solution' or 'My Hearts'. The proposal would be presented as an initial seed idea to the supporter groups and the owners with the purpose of determining if there was any traction in taking it forward.

Many years before, the club had set up the 'GIO' so there was a ready-made vehicle to make initial consultations. The GIO was an attempt to bring together all the fans organisations associated with Hearts under one umbrella. They discussed matters affecting fans such as ticketing, kit designs, and hospitality options. They were also charged with the task of helping to develop a supporters' charter. It had been a reasonably successful initiative. The GIO consisted of two members of each of the four existing supporter organisations: Heart of Midlothian Shareholders Association (HMSA), Federation of Hearts Supporters clubs (FHSC), Supporters Trust (ST) and the Fans Forum (that was dissolved) and replaced by the Hearts Youth Development Committee (HYDC). There were also two members of the clubs' senior management.

Under the tutelage of SDS, the groups were looking at ways of formulating a plan that would allow the current owners a dignified exit from the club. The plan would concentrate on prevent the club from going bust and provide a platform to raise necessary funds. Paul Goodwin from SDS led a presentation at a meeting in November 2012 about their preferred model of buying a 51 per cent majority share. I don't know what happened at this presentation meeting but the GIO were very unhappy at Paul Goodwin chairing the meeting and whilst they were comfortable with the involvement of SDS, they wanted to have them in an advisory capacity only. They certainly didn't want SDS driving the process with preconceived conclusions. This resulted in Lawrence becoming the independent Chair for most of the meetings with Henry Snedden, Vice Chair of the FHSC stepping in as acting Chair when Lawrence was unavailable.

Interestingly, Henry was very much a natural choice as acting Chair. He was a former diplomat and had spent much of his UK Civil Service career chairing complicated partnership meetings involving differing views and agendas. Those skills would be required in spades.

At no point in any of these discussions did either the club owners or the fan groups attempt to quantify what percentage Romanov would be willing to sell, nor was there ever a value put on the club, although Romanov did bandy around £51 million at points. Romanov regularly used the phrase 'wanting to sell to real fans' but wanted recompense that he felt his efforts and spending deserved.

Other organisations were gradually invited to the meetings, like FOH, who had been around for over 18 months prior, but nobody had really heard of them nor had they attempted to make themselves known to other supporter organisations. I have been told on a number of occasions that FOH weren't comfortable in this GIO structure as it was set up as a meeting of equals led by the club. The FOH at that time thought, as I understand it, that they should have a far more prominent role in the discussions about future ownership. That was why they existed. This would be a point of contention for a long time into the future.

It was at the time of the share issue that the GIO was called together to attend the SDS fan ownership presentation. Romanov was always attracted to the idea and, in a perfect world, would sell his stake in Hearts to the supporters over a period of time. It was clear, at this meeting though, that Romanov had been 'grossly insulted' by an earlier approach made by FOH to then Lithuanian owners.

Against the advice of many advisers to FOH, including, as I have been told, Ann Budge, they made an offer to Sergejus to take control of the club in return for settling the £450,000 debt to HMRC. All debts would be carried by the current owners, including the £24 million due to ūkio Bankas. This was dismissed as derisory by Sergejus and Romanov. They described it as 'demonstrating a staggering misjudgement of the value of the club' and 'a worrying lack of understanding of the situation'. It did a significant amount of damage to the reputation of FOH with the current Board and other members of the GIO. It just wasn't realistic or credible nor was it clear where the money would come from or how the club would be financed as a going concern. The relationship between Sergejus and FOH never really recovered after that despite the owners genuinely wanting to find an exit from Hearts.

There was also the setting up of the 1874 Fighting Fund (1874FF). This was spearheaded by former Hearts aces Gary Mackay and his teammate Scott Crabbe in conjunction with the Save Our Hearts campaign group. Fans were being encouraged to donate whatever monies they could. It would work in tandem with Hearts' own efforts to remain in business.

The 1874FF organised events that would fundraise to help the club: dinners, quiz nights, functions, fun days and any activity where they could raise money. They were originally part of the GIO group but didn't have any members to represent, nor were they set up to try and seek ownership of the club. They merely wanted to raise as much money as they could through their connections in the footballing world. They also became a central point for individuals to make donations and encouraged other organisations connected with the club to donate to them. They raised an extraordinary amount for the benefit of Hearts. Regular substantial cheques were arriving from the Merchiston and Orwell Hearts Supporters clubs. The individual donations ran into the tens of thousands of pounds.

One of the initial donations came from former Tottenham Hotspur manager, Harry Redknapp. He was Spurs manager when they played at Tynecastle in the Europa League qualifying stages the previous year. He became a bit of a cult hero at Hearts. He was followed by a host of former club legends, with the likes of Paul Hartley, Steven Pressley, Gilles Rousset, Stéphane Adam, Tosh McKinlay and George Cowie committing to get involved. Jimmy Sandison gave an extraordinary amount of help to support the fund.

The 1874FF used their funds very well indeed. They spent a great deal on making sure the stadium was maintained and repaired. These were costs that the club couldn't afford at the time. They also paid for an overnight stay in Dingwall for the first team the night before a match against Ross County.

Jambos Kickback also got involved. A regular contributor under the name Gregorski was selling prints of Tynecastle and artwork that raised an astonishing £6,000. A dinner at a local bowling club contributed over £5,000. It was a critical contribution over an 18-month period.

Fundraising was relentless. I think it is worth giving a special mention to *Off the Ball* presenter and BBC Sport pundit, Tam Cowan. Despite his love for Motherwell he went above and beyond to support the Hearts fans' activities. He would often be the after-dinner speaker at a variety of events and not only would he donate his fee, but he would give more. He drew large audiences to hear his irreverent humour and football anecdotes. Tam not taking fees and providing so much revenue with his presence will always be appreciated. He holds a very special place with Hearts supporters and it is well deserved. When the real footballing community had to come together, it was led by people like Tam.

There were others who looked to help ease the situation (although it could be seen as capitalising depending on the outlook). Rangers owed Hearts £800,000 in fees from the transfers of Lee Wallace and David Templeton. Although Rangers had gone into administration, the SFA rules were that all football debts had to be paid off before the Charles Greed-led consortium were allowed a new SFA membership. The deal with Rangers was that they were to pay Hearts £300,000 in January 2013 and an additional £500,000 at the end of July 2013. They offered £500,000 to settle the deal in November 2012. That would help pay the HMRC debt that was due. Romanov rejected this offer outright.

It is worth acknowledging that other clubs that also helped. Inverness Caledonian Thistle, Partick Thistle, Ross County and Motherwell donated all, or part, of the gate receipts generated by the visiting Hearts supporters in the season 2013/14. This totalled more than £15,000. These combined efforts bought the club the required breathing space to get it to the end of the season. In the end, 4,200 supporters took up the share issue. They contributed the best part of £1.1 million and were instrumental in ensuring the club survived. They also rallied round in huge numbers by packing Tynecastle for games and participated in large-scale fundraising activities.

It also indirectly provided the fan groups and, latterly, FOH, with valuable time to reinforce their own position as a viable organisation with a common strategy and clear goal to takeover Hearts. In parallel, the fan groups decided to work together as part of the existing legal framework of FOH. The agreement was conditional on the appointment of an independent Chair and a fresh strategy. There was a fear from the supporter groups that the previous attitude and approach by FOH to fan ownership was too static and wouldn't go down well with ordinary fans. After all, it was the fans that would be required to fund the proposals.

The one constant was that the fans would not let their club die without a fight. They had battled on many previous occasions to save their club and they would do so until all hope was lost. The momentum from inside the club and from the supporters was extraordinary.

But was it all too little, too late?

CHAPTER 5

Ball Kickers, Tyre Kickers and CICS

BEFORE HEARTS TIPPED into administration at the end of the 2013 season, a lot of work had been done between the last game calamity against St Mirren in November 2012 and that point. The focus up to the end of 2012 ensured the share issue was a success and all other revenue streams could be maximised. There were many activities going on outside the share issue and club initiatives. I was working along with others on ways to try and find a buyer and give the club a more sustainable existence.

I took a much more active interest in Hearts following my involvement in the HMRC crisis. Lord Foulkes and I decided that we could not allow the club to continue to stumble from one crisis to another. Something had to be done.

One of the things we decided to do was help the club with the share offer and the sale of match tickets. I had a long chat with Hearts supporter and Scottish Government Finance Secretary at that time, John Swinney MSP. Despite us being political adversaries, we were as one when it came to assisting Hearts. We decided that we would try and get our respective political supporters to come together for a joint press conference and encourage fans to participate. It didn't quite come off, but we did manage to get former First Minister, Alex Salmond, Alastair Darling MP, prominent former Scottish Conservative leader, David McLetchie MSP, and local Liberal Democrat MSP, Mike Pringle, to show their support. It was a major coup to get everyone to work together. The common cause was more important than anything else. It is amazing how football can pierce even the most hostile political rivalries. It was all hands to the pump and we did what we could.

Two things also happened in the post-HMRC crisis. Firstly, I had built up a great deal of trust with both David and Sergejus. They had invited me on a couple of occasions to watch Hearts from the boardroom as a thank you. That's where I met Romanov and his team. He was very pleasant and genuinely grateful for the effort being put in to helping. The second was that I became a bit of a honey pot for others who were concerned at Hearts plight and wanted to either try to help or potentially purchase the club. There was a growing realisation that the inevitable was just a matter of time and I felt that much of the work to find a new owner would have to start in earnest.

I didn't know at the time that the G10 and others were meeting regularly and that SDS were involved in looking to pursue the My Hearts supporter ownership option. What I did know was that my beloved Hearts was in trouble and I was in a position to try and do something about it.

My former university friend and fellow founding member of the original University of Edinburgh Hearts Supporters club, Mark Bathgate, was supplying me with regular updates on the position of both ūkio Bankas and UBIG. It was very clear that their liquidity problems were so severe that they were being described by financial analysts as 'dead ducks'. That was pretty evident given what was happening at Hearts but it did highlight the severity of the situation. Mark was an international financial analyst and he was able to see what was happening on the ground in Lithuania and how it could potentially topple Hearts. There was one email in mid-November 2012 in which Mark described the debt that Hearts was due to ūkio Bankas as being 63 per cent of the entire value of the bank. Their share price was plummeting like a stone and that would inevitably lead to their administration. That brought with it the urgency required to ensure Hearts was not swept away by financial and other circumstances out of our control.

Lord Foulkes and I tried our best to convene groups of meetings of everyone we knew to have an interest and influence on what could be done. We had many a lengthy meeting in the Council offices of former Lord Provost and ardent Jambo, Councillor Eric Milligan. He would make sure that former co-owner Leslie Deans, David Henderson, the former Chief Executive of Scottish Equitable/Aegon, former Hearts Board Director, Brian Duffin, and others were in attendance to provide insight and potential investment. The two biggest problems we had were not having a definitive timeline or when Hearts would fold, but also if there was really a genuine interest in Romanov relinquishing control – and at what price. These meetings, though, were very helpful in disseminating information to the correct influencers and keeping the issue at the top of the agenda.

One such meeting took place on 28 December 2012 in Councillor Milligan's room. A rather plentiful supply of particularly nice wine was generously provided by Eric to wash down the festive mince pies. The serious talk of Hearts' plight was all that was discussed but after that was disposed of, we retired to the legendary Milligan hospitality. We did as all good Hearts fans do – we recalled our best stories of our time watching Edinburgh's finest football club. It was a fine evening of wonderful Hearts memories that merely emphasised what the club meant to us all.

Subsequently, Lord Foulkes and I decided to empty our contact books and try to see if we could find a buyer. This was by no means going to be an easy task. A complicating factor was the circling of vultures over Tynecastle. As an example, Italian Angelo Massone, who hadn't had the best of reputations when he owned Livingston Football Club, was sniffing around. He had been rumoured to be preparing a £4.5 million takeover that was dismissed by Romanov. Yes, he may have been a potential solution but I, and pretty much everyone else, was not convinced he either had the resources available or would be a fit and proper new owner of Hearts. He was certainly a serious 'tyre kicker' but there was never really any offer on the table, nor could we identify if there was any visible money. We did think that it would be difficult to justify going from one dictatorial owner to another but perhaps it was the only option.

There was some press speculation that Edinburgh businessman, Mr Pat Munro, who failed to buy Hearts in 2005, 2007 and 2008, had been keeping a keen eye on events and wanted to team up with the Massone bid. It was perhaps not seen as a credible approach given that Romanov dismissed even the speculation by publicly commenting through his spokesperson, Charlie Mann, 'Vladimir would be more interested to hear from Marilyn Monroe than Pat Munro.' That avenue was certainly dead.

There may have been a long line of potential new owners waiting in the wings for administration –or even liquidation –in order to pick up the club at a pittance, but we did not know who they were and couldn't afford to wait to find out if any actually existed. From a purely business perspective, Hearts may have been a more attractive proposition if it was in administration as that would allow it to shake off its crippling debts for any new owner.

In late 2012, Lord Foulkes made contact with an investment professional from Berkeley House Investments, Mr Barry Cole. Berkeley specialised in matching wealthy individuals and corporations to potential investment opportunities. Barry was involved with a number of client investors who were trying to acquire a lower English Football League club. He had been involved in various other potential deals with clubs outside the Premier League. He had built up a number of attractive connections with individuals and companies who had an interest in owning football clubs.

It was all very promising. Barry told us that his current client had access to around £300 million of investment and was very attracted to the English Championship. It was obvious that there were vast riches available to an owner who can take an English Championship club into the English Premier League. We had to convince Barry that his client would be more than delighted with the purchase of Hearts in the Scottish Premier League and it would cost them a tiny fraction of an English Championship club. Barry was a lovely guy. That made him a very easy person to work with. He was passionate about football and hugely knowledgeable about his industry. He was a real find.

After some introductions from Lord Foulkes, I managed to have a long conversation with Barry about the situation and opportunity at Hearts. He was keen to understand what benefits an investment into a club like Hearts would have for prospective buyers. Two of the strongest arguments are always the history of the club and the potential. People with little or no knowledge of Hearts are fascinated by the story of McCrae's Battalion and what they did for the World War I effort. Hearts fans pride themselves on the contribution their club made when the country required them to step up. Barry was touched and impressed by the story but also the business opportunity.

The second argument is the potential. If you are looking to buy your way into football and be an owner, it is huge risk. There is the old saying: 'How do you turn a billionaire into a millionaire? Buy a football club.' Investment is a risky and expensive business. But perhaps a club like Hearts is very good value for money. It would be very expensive to buy an English Championship club and it would also be disproportionately expensive to buy either of the Old Firm in Scotland. That leaves Hearts as a very good option. For a fraction of the price, you get a club with potential in a very competitive league that will regularly win trophies. Hearts also has the advantage of being from Edinburgh. The city itself is a huge draw for players with its quality of life. However, it is the potential of regularly playing in the Europa League or even Champions League that was the most powerful argument. There is very little chance of many of the English Premier League teams playing in Europe let alone a Championship team. If your horizon was towards European competition, then Hearts was a very good buy indeed. Scottish football gives a wider access to European competition that English football doesn't. Barry, despite being a committed Watford fan, understood this and commenced the development of a proposal for his client list.

The proposal document that Lord Foulkes and I finessed had, as its conclusion, a paragraph that summed up the club beautifully:

> Heart of Midlothian FC is club steeped in history, supported with distinction by a faithful band of supporters. The club has been focused on building upon these roots and increasing the professionalism and attention within the club to ensure it grows and remains a force in Scottish and European football for another 140 years.
>
> The opportunity to become the new owner, and steward, of Hearts is an exceptional one offering not only the opportunity for real financial upside but also to garner the history and goodwill within the community and broader football spheres to deliver broader personal and business interests, where mutually compatible.

It went down well and, in late January 2013, we met in Parliament with one of Barry's clients in Parliament, Charles Lissack. We went through the potential opportunity with him. Charles had been a long-standing director of Watford FC. An experienced property investor with a keen interest in football and a good knowledge of players.

It was difficult not to get too excited. The person sitting in front of us had both the ability and the client base to save Hearts and perhaps even allow the club to achieve its full potential. We had a really good discussion about football in general, investment and Hearts. Charles explained that he would be looking to bring in some equally seasoned people with the expertise to take Hearts to the next level. He, in one respect, would have been a shrewd choice as the new owner as he understood the football and commercial side of the club. We'd even discussed the idea from Charles that he would be keen to approach some accomplished English championship managers who had a proven pedigree, such as a Neil Warnock type to get the best out of the players. It was a wide ranging and constructive meeting. Perhaps we went a little too much into the detail but the fact that we did was a hugely positive outcome for us.

Charles left the meeting with Barry and said he would seriously consider what we had said and come back as soon as he could. An email from Barry that very same afternoon explained that Charles had warmed to both Lord Foulkes and me, was very comfortable with our involvement and trusted what we had to say. He saw the potential was there and that the club was a great asset. Barry concluded by saying that Charles wanted to digest everything and speak to his associates. He was very positive and upbeat during their post meeting debrief. He was keen to visit Tynecastle and see a match but we never quite managed to deliver this. A good start, we thought, and even at this early stage any potential investment from the consortia led by Charles could have a sizable element of supporter ownership.

Barry made many approaches to potential suitors. He met with an individual who was representing a Middle Eastern group with a Royal Family connection from that region. Their representative was very guarded as to their exact identity and indeed Barry questioned if there was a geopolitical or strategic reason they would consider buying a Scottish club. It was rumoured that they were in the advanced stages of buying an English Championship club and the 'family' wished to buy two more. They were very interested in the story and potential of Hearts but wanted a little time to determine if it would work for them. I don't think money was going to be an issue. Ultimately, they indicated to me that Hearts possibly lacked the kudos of a club like Newcastle or Chelsea that had vast potential. Barry deduced the buyer was really looking for a trophy club and I don't think they meant the Scottish Premier League trophy! I wonder if they went on to purchase another club.

There was also a lengthy and constructive conversation with a former Chelsea player who was involved in a bid for Rangers. He had been working on a bid for Everton on behalf of clients. He wanted to remain anonymous but said he'd been following Hearts as a potential target for some time and had a long connection with Barry. He was going to discuss the Hearts opportunity with his clients and press the case that this was a good opportunity. There were lots of irons in the fire at this stage.

The issue with finding a buyer was not really the amount of money required as it was relatively modest in footballing and investment terms. In fact, it was almost too little. The real question was always whether there was the potential to build Hearts into a big club in terms of support and finance. Most people Barry, Lord Foulkes and I engaged with spoke warmly of the club but felt they were the third largest fish in a relatively small pond. Barry was asked by one hardnosed buyer how much money could the club make if they won the SPL and qualified for the Champions League. I recall providing him with the figures at the time and he said he could buy an English Championship team, get them into the Premier League and get so much more by many multiples of millions of pounds. The example they gave at the time was that they could purchase a Barnsley or Burnley and invest to get them into the English Premier League where there was a guaranteed minimum of £70 million.

That is the challenge for Scottish football in general. Barry was great though. He would always say to prospective buyers that you don't buy a club like Hearts, or most football clubs for that matter, because you want to make money. You do it because it's your club and not because you're going to make millions. As I said previously, if your investment strategy is to become rich then don't buy a football club.

Barry spoke to many mainly England-based buyers who felt that, whilst the team was doing well, everything would be fine but if the team was on a bad run the English owner would get the flack. Those people were obviously a little naïve as to how football operates as it is clear that any owner of any football club is loved as long as they are investing and making what the fans think are the right decisions. If you don't as an owner, you'll get criticised whoever you are – English, Middle Eastern, Lithuanian or not.

Ultimately, whilst these discussions were productive, they never really went beyond an initial interest.

During this entire process I was keeping in close contact with David and the club to ensure he was fully abreast of what was going on and to get all the facts and figures that may be requested by potential purchasers. David put together an informal prospectus that we could share on a non-disclosure basis with potential funders.

There was a coincidental link in our relationship with Barry. When the prospectus was formulated, Lord Foulkes sent it to a contact he had at PKF, the international global network of accountancy firms. That contact was an Alan Jenkins who would later be involved with Hearts administration through BDO. Lord Foulkes was keen for a prominent international financing expert that had experience in the football industry to look over the prospectus and see if there was anyone they knew that may be able assist in trying to find a purchaser. Alan subsequently sent the information to the very person who would fit those qualifications. He turned to someone who had previously been appointed the administrator of Portsmouth and been on the Board at Chelsea, Trevor Birch.

There was a pressing need for us to get some good professional advice both on the structure of a consortium, on making a bid, due diligence, legal obstacles and negotiations. On 12 February 2013, we met with Alan and Trevor in the Pugin Room at Parliament to discuss the situation at Hearts and examine some of the options that may be available. Little did we know at the time that in a matter of months Trevor would be leading the administration of Hearts. Given what we all know now, we were very lucky to have BDO, with Bryan Jackson and Trevor at the helm, taking on the Hearts administration. We couldn't have had a more experienced and knowledgeable team.

The meeting with Trevor and Alan really allowed us to sharpen our focus on what would interest investors and how best to sell Hearts as a proposition. Alan, in particular, had a contact on the ground in Lithuania who was able to confirm that a temporary administrator was about to be appointed by the Central Bank of Lithuania to look into the status of ūkio Bankas. The temporary administrator would report within the week on the status of the bank, and decide on further punitive actions (restructuring, administration, bankruptcy, etc). It appeared that the demise of the companies that effectively owned 79.9 per cent of Hearts was imminent.

Lord Foulkes was very aware of the existence of FOH but hadn't really engaged with them for a while. He committed to meeting his long-term friend, Iain McLeod, who was involved in the Save Our Hearts campaign back in 2004. The purpose was to try and reinvigorate FOH and see what progress they had made after the previous bid to purchase Hearts had fallen through. This was pretty much the first I had heard about FOH, but it seemed like a well organised and well-meaning project.

Shortly after the investment meeting with Barry and Charles, we met Paul Goodwin from SDS to see what support they may be able to provide to Hearts' plight. We knew they had already been speaking to the club and some of the supporter groups about the potential options on the journey to supporter ownership. I always thought SDS would play a pivotal role in the months ahead but the one thing that did irk me was that they seemed rather stuck in their ways with the approach to take. I acknowledge that this was partly the way they were constituted, but, it didn't seem nimble enough to adapt to either the rapidly changing circumstances at Hearts or, indeed, the diverse nature of football clubs across Scotland. Nevertheless, their input was invaluable and the work they were doing would prove to make a significant contribution.

What we didn't appreciate was that SDS was quite a long way further forward in their thoughts than we were led to believe to the extent that SDS representatives were meeting formally with Hearts Directors, including Sergejus. A meeting had been arranged after a game against Kilmarnock at Tynecastle in February 2013. The Lithuanian owners would be in attendance to hear SDS propose a joint ownership of the stadium with Romanov. The current owners would gradually reduce their shareholding over a period of ten years with supporters gaining full ownership at that time. They envisaged a 'Maroon Solution' with a large supporters' rally and meeting at the Usher Hall in Edinburgh where all associated with Hearts, past and present, would endorse the plan and urge fans to subscribe. This would form the basis of discussion between the club and the GIO group over the coming weeks. The challenge for Lord Foulkes and I at this point was to try and keep some sort of handle on all the things that were going on. That wasn't easy.

The other component of Hearts' plight was undoubtedly political. We were essentially dealing with a business that had fallen into financial difficulty but football clubs have a very special place in the lives of so many and the communities in which they operate. Given what had happened to Rangers, with their liquidation a few years previously, it may have been the final nail in the coffin of Scottish football if Hearts had also disappeared. Everyone was all too aware of the high-profile nature of Hearts and the position they had found themselves in with Lithuanian ownership. It was important that we were able to impress upon the Lithuanian authorities that, despite it being a small fraction of the liabilities of ūkio Bankas and UBIG, the political and societal consequences could be much more significant.

The only way to ensure that the significance of Heart of Midlothian Football Club was known to the Lithuanian Government and financial authorities was to engage with the Lithuanian Ambassador. We had to make sure she was fully versed on the consequences of Hearts going out of business. It just so happened that Lithuania were about to take on the Presidency of the Council of the European Union for the six months from July to December 2013. That was a great lever to pull as it was the first time that they had held this prestigious position and they wanted to showcase the country as a modern economy where it was easy for other European nations to do business.

We met with the Lithuanian Ambassador, Asta Skaisgirytė-Liauškienė, in late February 2013. She was a hugely impressive Ambassador. She was well briefed, came across as genuinely interested, and listened intently to what we had to say. It is often difficult to judge a senior diplomat but both Lord Foulkes and I got the impression that she was serious with her offer of help and fully understood the potential and serious political damage that could occur as a result of Hearts' plight.

The main conclusion from the meeting was the Ambassador would pass us the contacts for the ūkio Bankas administrator. That would allow us to open up a direct line of dialogue with the administrator, Mr Adomas

Ąžuolas Audickas. He would become an important interlocutor and key to the survival of Hearts. We would be contacting him as soon as possible to ascertain his thoughts on the position of Hearts within the wider context of ūkio. He would also make the decision about who to appoint as administrator of Hearts. The important point from this is that any administrator of ūkio Bankas, who held the security over Hearts stadium against their debt, would represent the people who were creditors of the bank. Those creditors would come first and, in order to protect their interests, Mr Audickas would attempt to get maximum value for all of the assets. Those assets included Hearts.

We brainstormed many more potential avenues. One such idea was to ask the ūkio Bankas administrator if he could use his position to dismiss the current Directors of Hearts and install their own Directors. It was a potential long shot but worth a try. There would be considerable issues around legal liability, professional indemnity and fiduciary responsibilities as Directors, but it was a potential avenue to wrestle control away from the Romanov regime. At the very least, it would shine a light on the exact position and how long, realistically, was left before Hearts fell into administration.

We were all encouraged by the number of leads we were generating. It was always going to be difficult, and require a lot of luck, to find a buyer that would be able to conclude a quick deal. There was always the naked business perspective that many potential new owners wouldn't care about Hearts' plight and would rather wait until the club was in administration or liquidation. This would give them the opportunity to purchase at a much-reduced cost without the hangover of a large debt or the problems with negotiating with the current owner. No one thought that Romanov would be easy to deal with.

Barry fully understood the challenges but always thought that the supporters taking a sizeable stake may be able to open up other self-financing avenues. Lord Foulkes and I had explained that the GIO and FOH, with the help of SDS, had been looking to take a percentage of ownership in the club for some time. That interested Barry a lot. He had been involved in devising a plan to make funds available to buy Watford on behalf of the Watford Supporters Trust. He had delved quite deeply into the practical facets of raising the money: who would be responsible for the day-to-day running of the club and ultimately paying the money back to the individuals or institutions who would provide the initial capital. He had done all the work on the plethora of hurdles that would need to be overcome.

The largest hurdle was always going to be the need to raise sufficient sums to buy out the current owner and provide working capital to run the club for a period. Don't forget that the purchase of any football club is only a small part of the outlay. The very fact that Hearts had been haemorrhaging money for years meant that it would need investment and significant working capital until it was at a break-even position. Hypothetically, if the purchase and working capital figure was £20 million, how would the club repay that money at the end of the loan? What would happen if the supporters' organisation running Hearts required additional money for a major stadium repair or a particularly bad football season – where would it come from? Would the supporters Board be prepared to stump up 15 per cent or so (£3 million) that would be required to raise the initial loan? In the event of default, that 15 per cent would be taken as part of the security as well as the other assets of the club. Would the members be clear that their decisions whilst running the club could jeopardise that 15 per cent and the very existence of Hearts?

Barry was really challenging. He raised the notion that even if the initial capital could be raised it would be a long and difficult road to sustainability. He also advised on something that would become a point of major debate and discussion for FOH in the future. This was that if you have a business run by an individual or a family, they set out their strategy, provide funds to implement their plans and work full-time to ensure success. With a group of perhaps eight or ten individual supporters operating as a Board, there would need to be the same coherent plan and shared vision as with the family-run business, which – in any business, and more so football with its passions and emotions – is sometimes hard to achieve. Would the manager be sacked every time Hearts lost an important match – to Hibs, God forbid?

I remember a meeting with Barry when we went through all this and tried to get a handle on how the financing would work. This financial structure was a possibility but would put all the onus on the supporters to save the club. Barry made the commitment that he would like to try to do this type of capital funding idea as it could become a model for lots of other clubs. He did say, though – and this would become very evident for me personally in the coming months – that for the FOH members it would cease to be fun supporting their club. Football would become a business for those fans and would need to be made to work. How true a statement that would become.

I continued to pursue all options both commercially and politically, working alongside many others and the club. Keeping dialogue open with as many people as possible was not easy. We were not in a position to determine if individuals had the required resources or whether they were serious. We heard constant talk of a Norwegian consortium but had no idea who or where they were.

Keeping all options on the table led us to a meeting with the Rangers Chief Executive at that time, Charles Green. We were aware he was in London and thought it would be beneficial to get information on the process that Rangers went through and if there were any lessons that Hearts could learn. We didn't know at that time that Charles would cease to be in post at Rangers in a matter of months. He genuinely wanted to help. He saw the Hearts situation as detrimental to Rangers and Scottish football as a whole as it could start a domino effect of Scottish clubs going to the wall.

The main question we asked was how any consortium or fan groups can raise enough capital to buy Hearts. He offered three potential solutions. The first was to see if he knew any high net worth individual who could help. He would ask his commercial Director, who worked in the City of London, to look into it and he was willing to set up a meeting.

Secondly, he suggested a friendly match with Rangers could be organised both as a fundraising exercise and also as an olive branch. It would work as a fundraiser for Hearts but would also do a bit of a favour to Rangers fans – they were unlikely to get many matches against SPL sides over the next few years given their demotion to the third tier of the league system. It could raise a substantial sum to give the clubs much-needed cash.

The third suggestion, and I must say it was off the top of his head, was to take advantage of Rangers being unable to buy any players until January 2014 due to a transfer embargo. His idea was that if a consortium looking to buy Hearts needed cash in order to make a bid, then Rangers could buy options on Hearts players. Those options would come into effect after the transfer embargo was lifted. Rangers would give a loan to the prospective bidding consortium, which they would then pay off with a player or players of Rangers' choosing. In essence, it allowed the consortium access to some of the value of the club in order to make the purchase. Rangers would benefit by being able to take the player at a lower price. We didn't know, and Charles also wasn't sure, if this would be allowed under the football rules and regulations but he was willing to at least look into it.

What Charles also did was give his experience of dealing with administrators. Whilst he acknowledged Hearts was in a different position, he was able to move quickly with the administrators of Rangers because he gave them a non-refundable deposit. That gave his consortium an exclusive option for a couple of months. This involved some risk for the consortium but at the same time made it clear to the administrator who the serious player was. It also stopped them being distracted by other potential bids, many of which never materialised. Given the Hearts situation was riven with other potential bids that turned out to be spurious, this was not a bad idea to consider. It would certainly have saved a considerable amount of angst and time with the many 'tyre kickers' that emerged to 'buy' Hearts. It was certainly worth having the meeting and the ideas were useful. We were not in a place to not consider them. Lord Foulkes and I were to put this into our 'no stone unturned' file that we would come back to if required.

In March 2013, Hearts got to the final of the League Cup against St Mirren. The irony being that despite all the off-field problems that were engulfing Hearts, there was the potential to have both the Scottish and League cups at Tynecastle. As Sergejus was going to be in Edinburgh for a short period to attend the final, I thought it was important to reach out to him directly.

Sergejus wasn't a total stranger as we spent some time together back in 2005 when we both attended the annual commemoration at the McCrae's Battalion cairn in Contalmaison in the Somme. I was there as a representative of the City of Edinburgh Council and he of the club. I was impressed by him when we met. He was engaging, kind and had the very best interests for Hearts. Sergejus was also aware of my involvement in the discussions with the Treasury and HMRC senior officials with regards to the tax issues the previous year.

I explained to Sergejus that I, and others, had been working with people who were looking seriously at purchasing Hearts, but they wanted to stay anonymous until clarity could be given on what any potential sale process would be, who actually owned the club and the state of the financial situation. They were also keen to know who they would be dealing with in any meaningful discussions. The fundamental question was an indication of price. This was key to determine if anyone would want to move to the next stage.

Sergejus knew that neither FOH nor SDS were in a position to purchase the club at that moment. However, there may have been a mechanism for pulling all the parties together to do a deal that would be acceptable and quick. He responded almost immediately, which made me think that a

discussion about potential buyers was something he would be very interested in having. His reply also invited my brother and I to the League Cup
Final against St Mirren at Hampden as a thank you for our efforts.

I met with Sergejus late that Friday afternoon in the old administration
block at Tynecastle. It was a constructive meeting where he outlined the
aspiration of Romanov to sell the club 'for the right price and in the right
circumstances'. David and Finance Manager, Fiona Sinclair, attended the
meeting and it was agreed that they would prepare detailed information
about the current financial health of the club alongside turnover projections
and costs for me to pass to potential purchasers.

Coincidentally, that very same day, a press release was issued on behalf
of the GIO and SDS that outlined the process of setting up a formal organisation that could take a fan ownership model forward. The GIO had been
invited by Hearts to investigate them forming a Community Interest Company (CIC). This vehicle would be used to purchase the shares of Hearts on
behalf of the fans. As was explained to me at the time, the CIC would raise
money to make an offer to the current owners of the club. This way forward
was the preferred model used by SDS at other clubs like Clyde and Stenhousemuir. The attractiveness of a CIC was that assets owned by the company like the stadium are 'asset locked', meaning they must be used for the
benefit of the community and can't be sold or transferred. The CIC had to be
run as a socially responsible company with a significant community interest.

The press release stated that a consultation would be launched to seek
approval of supporters and develop a fundraising programme. The CIC's
objective was to secure at least a 51 per cent majority control in Hearts. In
doing so, they would have the ability to appoint directors to a new Hearts
Board under new ownership. Full and open democratic elections to the
Board of the CIC would be held amongst its shareholders. To get the initiative moving, a 'working group' would be set up comprising of GIO members,
specialist advisors and club representatives. This 'working group' would
resign upon conclusion of any deal with the owners. The GIO would also
appoint an independent Chair to take this proposal forward.

This process had been agreed with the club and their official response in
the press release was telling. They said:

What Supporters Direct Scotland has tonight offered GIO is an opportunity
to organise themselves with a realistic prospect of making a bid that could
open the door to them taking control of the club.

The club are empowering them to do so, and whilst there is no guarantee that this process will ultimately work, by supporting them fully to do so,
we want to give fans every chance to have a significant part to play in the
future of this famous club.

As you can see, there were so many irons in the fire at this point. All we
needed was to try and get something over the line to save the club from
imminent disaster. Big questions were still at the forefront of our minds.
Would Romanov sell? At what price? Did we have time? Could the fans be
the catalyst for a sale? What was the implications of ūkio Bankas appointing administrators? Would we stumble across a white knight? How much
money would we need? Were we wasting our time with tyre kickers who
really had no interest in buying the club? And could we, at the very least,
see the club through to the end of the season to prevent punitive points
deductions and certain liquidation? The key point was to prevent administration at all costs to find time to identify the right buyer. That was not
going to be easy.

To make matters worse, that Sunday, Hearts lost to St Mirren in the
final of the Scottish League Cup by three goals to two. St Mirren continued
to be Hearts' bogey team: the memories of their capitulation to the hands
of Celtic on the last day of the 1986 season that cost Hearts the Premier
League title, the club we would have faced in our final game and now the
loss of the League Cup final. We all hoped for a better story against them in
future years.

At this stage, I just wanted to have any Hearts story to tell at all...

CHAPTER 6

To Chair or Not to Chair

ONE OF THE consequences of being a member of the UK Parliament and working 400 miles away from home is that nights tend to be taken up with catching up on work. Wednesday 17 April 2013 was no different. I had to stay back to the end of the day's parliamentary sitting as the former MP for Ochil and South Perthshire, Hon Gordon Banks, had an adjournment debate on the closure of the Alloa Crown Post Office. As the Shadow Minister responsible for postal services, I was on the front bench for the debate on behalf of the Official Opposition. Some MPs have all the fun! After the debate, I was sitting in my House of Commons office ploughing through masses of emails whilst, on the TV in the background, West Ham and Manchester United were drawing 2-2.

A notification popped up on my phone to say I had a Twitter message from a Lawrence Broadie. The message said that he had got my details from Lord Foulkes and could he give me a call to discuss a Hearts related proposition. I was only too delighted to speak with Lawrence. I had never met him previously and he had never met me, but any credible approach that may lead to a solution for Hearts was worth pursuing. Lawrence impatiently said he would have to speak with me the following day at the very latest.

Lawrence and I spoke at length early the following morning. He explained that he had prepared a presentation that he delivered to the expanded G10 at a meeting at Tynecastle (the expanded G10 included the FOH and Save Our Hearts representatives). He explained that it didn't go down well at all. They were really concerned that the Lithuanians were asking fans to put their hands in their pockets again to the tune of £20 per month to buy the club over a long period of time, with no guarantee that they would keep their promises or keep the club alive as a going concern. One of the biggest obstacles that Lawrence had identified was the disparate nature of the supporter groups. It wasn't a criticism but rather the reality of a patchwork of groups that existed and operated for different purposes. They all shared the common purpose of doing their very best for Hearts and that was a good starting point.

The GIO agreed to convene a series of meetings to find a way forward. At one such meeting, the members met in the Bobby Walker suite at Tynecastle with Paul Goodwin from SDS to discuss the submission of a proposal to the Lithuanian owners that would facilitate a move towards supporter ownership. This was the culmination of talks between SDS and Hearts. The group were to examine fan ownership models in more detail and try to agree a possible way forward. Progress was painfully slow and cumbersome. There were ongoing tensions between SDS and FOH on who should lead this group. The Chair and founding Director of FOH at that time, Alex Mackie, thought that FOH should take up the Chair. Paul Goodwin thought that he would be more appropriate as he did not have an existing association with Hearts. Lawrence, who was chairing at that time, said there was lots of bickering about these issues and what the group should be called, how it should be constituted and what the strategy would be for trying to take forward the ownership ideas that had been presented.

There was no consensus in the group that either Paul or Alex should become Chair. The consequence was that Lawrence would continue, albeit on a temporary basis. It was something that he didn't want to do, and it never really worked, despite him being seen as a neutral in the eyes of the fan groups. He did have a long association as an employee of the club with David Southern as his boss for most of his time there. That was surely seen by the group as an asset. It wasn't. There was always suspicion of anyone who was perceived to have had a previous relationship with the 'Lithuanian regime'.

Lawrence described a follow-up meeting as 'the most torturous two hours' of his life and one of the most awkward meetings he has ever had. There was a constant pitch battle with FOH. They felt that they were the only people professional enough to take anything forward. That didn't go down too well with the other groups who had all contributed huge amounts to the club over decades. Some didn't handle the challenge very well either. SDS were being hugely helpful in facilitating the meetings and providing valuable experience but it was clear that Paul was not the most diplomatic of contributors. That didn't assist the already fractious dynamics of the group. I guess the club wanted Paul to lead the group as he had developed a relationship with the owners and had not angered them as FOH had done previously.

The key challenge for Lawrence was a need for everyone to address how they saw themselves – how they fit into the picture with what was the SDS' preferred model of a Supporters Trust on one side and FOH on the other, both wanting to buy the club their way and with their strategy. Then there was the shareholders association in the middle alongside the representatives of the supporter groups who just wanted to save the club.

The frustration from everyone resulted in the G10 getting nowhere fast. Lawrence, at a meeting at the end of March 2013, proposed that the group look elsewhere for an independent Chair. They had to come together and find a way to do that. It needed to be someone of sufficient status and experience, who could unite the fans and drive forward the ownership agenda quickly and efficiently. The supporter groups had agreed on one thing at least and their homework for the next meeting was to suggest names that could take on the role of the independent Chair. Lawrence was going on holiday, so it would give them breathing space to look at potential candidates before they next met.

It was desirable if that person was a passionate Hearts supporter, had no previous links with any of the groups, had an understanding of the current plight of the club, could present to the media and wider supporters and have credibility with all stakeholders. As a minimum, the candidate had to be a person that didn't offend. They didn't have to be loved by every member of the group but they could not be offensive to any of them. Everyone knew that time wasn't really on their side, but no one had any real idea on how much or how little time was left.

This conversation with Lawrence was a real eye opener for me. It was true that we didn't know what was ahead. What we did know, though, was that the club was in deep trouble and something had to be done.

It would be unfair and wrong to suggest that the G10 hadn't made any progress. They had made some decisions that would help shape the way forward. They had agreed that only one unilateral solution supported by all groups should go forward. That would create an unstoppable strength of fan power. They couldn't afford for there to be any splinter groups or anything other than one voice. To deliver on that objective, they knew that there would have to be a laser-like focus on marketing, communications and PR. They also recognised that the group was too large and unwieldy. It was now involving nearly 20 individuals. They would have to form a smaller 'steering group' made up of all those currently engaged so far, including the 1874 Fighting Fund who had joined at the meetings in late March. That would be achieved by each group putting forward only one representative rather than the current two in order to move, debate and decide on issues quicker. Or would it?

There was a strong recognition that if the Lithuanians were unwilling to provide a price, the group would have to use the expertise available to them and, based on land, assets and brand value analysis, establish a notional price for the club. That price could be used as a negotiating point for the discussions with Romanov and his representatives. And, of course, they had reluctantly agreed to appoint an independent Chair.

I initially thought Lawrence was asking for my help to find someone to fill the role, so I was taken aback when he put the proposition to me. He wanted to recommend to the meeting that I become the independent Chair of the G10. There was to be a meeting later that same evening where Lawrence would present to the group my candidature and seek their approval.

Lawrence was a canny operator. His long-term relationship with David was invaluable at this time. They trusted each other implicitly and that helped to oil the wheels. Lawrence had already had a conversation with David about the independent Chair idea. Lawrence was totally drained by the whole process and knew he had taken it as far as he could. He could have taken it on but was convinced that unless there was an independent arbiter who could come in, with no baggage and with a fresh impetus, that it would not be able to get on the right path to saving the club. The problem Lawrence had was that he had set the group the homework to come up with suggested names but didn't, at that point, have one to suggest himself.

Lawrence suggested to David, after a number of conversations with others, that he would approach me. He knew I had been quietly involved in the HMRC tax issue and hadn't offended the Lithuanians. I had no previous connections with any of the groups (apart from travelling on the Longstone Hearts Supporters club buses for many years) and the club. I was a fresh name that the supporters would perhaps know from my profile in politics but nothing more than that. I was seen as new and energetic and not about the past, and had political and business experience. The big thing for Lawrence was that I would have a thick skin, be able to do media and, critically, would be a credible suggestion to the group. Lawrence knew that, as an objective decision, the group would struggle to find any way to disagree with me when comparing my candidature to the original set criteria. David agreed with Lawrence that it was a great idea. Lawrence had his name and would seek to get it through the next meeting.

I didn't immediately say yes to Lawrence. I had a number of concerns about both my involvement and the situation that he had detailed to me. Although I would be doing this in my spare time, I would have to dedicate most of my already limited spare time to the role. It was not going to be an easy sell to my constituents, nor to my personal life. I was a Shadow Business Minister at the time, had a slender 316 majority and was completely consumed by serving my constituents. There was also the small matter of offending the green and white portion of my electorate. These were all matters I would have to deal with and consider.

What concerned me more than anything else was the current situation with the G10. Could this be a hiding to nothing and would they come together? I was really grateful to Lawrence for being so forthright and honest about the situation. He could have downplayed the recent history of the group to encourage me to take it on but he didn't. That's all credit to him. After all, he was starting his own business and couldn't commit the time to be chair, although in the coming months his experience and dedication would be invaluable to the saving of the club. He was one of the many unsung heroes.

If I was to have listened to my heart at that time, then this was a no brainer for me. I knew how much trouble my beloved Hearts was in. The work that I, Lord Foulkes and many others had done over the previous few months had demonstrated that finding a white knight buyer was not going to be easy or indeed even possible. The only realistic option, and one where we could control the outcome, was supporter-led. There was a tangible prospect that supporters could not only save their Hearts but also own their club. That was a purpose worth fighting for.

My head was telling me that this was a huge risk. What if this process failed? What if the club went into administration, was subsequently liquidated and disappeared? What if we made mistakes that hastened the club's demise? We were, after all, just amateur volunteers trying to do our best. How would this affect my political career? Did we really want to be at the helm when the history books were written about the death of Hearts FC? What would the effect be on my private life? Did I want to invite the potential for fans' protests and anger towards me and others? It had happened before. These were all serious questions and the only way to answer them was to make this project a success. The only problem was that success had such a small percentage attached to it. For me, could I let my heart rule my head?

Regardless of which football team you support, we all share the same passion for our club. I love Hearts. They have provided me with a lifetime of entertainment, joy and hurt, almost in equal measure. I would always joke with people that don't support a club that they have something missing from their lives. What do they actually do at 3.00pm on a Saturday afternoon? Are their lives diminished by not having that racing heart and anxiousness as you log on to look for the result of the game? When I was growing up, my brother and I would watch away matches on Ceefax. It was painfully slow. Every 30 seconds to a minute, the screen would refresh, causing your heart to jump in anticipation of seeing if Hearts or the opposition had scored. You would know that the game finished on a Saturday at 4.45pm or midweek at around 9.15pm but Ceefax was so slow that you would still be transfixed on the screen for at least 15 minutes after the final whistle had blown and until the 'FT' icon was displayed.

It's not like that now of course. Social media is as instant as you can get and, of course, accessing Sky Sports or BBC Sport is as easy as the click of a mobile phone button. However, my heart still races as I hit refresh on the screen to see the latest or final scores, staring intently at the Hearts goal column hoping it ticks upwards.

We are all the same in that regard as supporters. We cheer at the goals, swear at conceding goals, rise in our seats like meerkats as the team marauds forward or gets a corner. I just couldn't imagine what life would be like without having Heart of Midlothian Football Club as part of it.

These were all thoughts that ran through my mind as I considered whether or not I could accept the proposal from Lawrence. What clinched it for me though was this: it is not often that you get opportunity to play a part in saving your football club. Hearts did mean so much to me. It was a key component of the Murray family. It had been for generations. There were three conditions of being a member of the Murray family. You had to be a passionate supporter of everything Scottish from the national football and rugby teams to the Scottish Olympic champion curlers and world darts champion, Jocky Wilson. If it was Scottish, you supported it without condition. The second was to boo at the television every time Margaret Thatcher or our local MP, Malcolm Rifkind, appeared (these are probably my first political memories). The third, and probably most important, was to support Hearts. Now, I don't know if I would have been adopted out of the family if I broke any of these cardinal rules but that was the basis of a wonderful, fun and loving upbringing of dark blue, red and maroon.

And then there was my dad. I've mentioned him already but he was a huge factor in me making the decision to take on the independent Chair. What would he have said to me, I wonder? I guess he would have invoked a similar phrase to Lord Kitchener in that famous World War 1 poster by

Alfred Leete. I'm sure he would have said, 'Your club needs you'. And what would I have done had Hearts gone bust and disappeared? Yes, there were huge risks and not many upsides, but the fact of the matter was that I could help, should help and had to help. To walk by on the other side and see the club die would have filled me with regrets for as long as my own life. My dad and late uncle as brothers were as avid Hearts supporters as my brother and I are. I had to do it for them if nothing else. I decided to do it.

I phoned Lawrence back and told him that I was in and he could propose my name at the meeting that evening. I know Lawrence was confident of getting me approved but it was by no means certain.

At the meeting at Tynecastle that evening the G10 was asked by Lawrence to present their homework on who it could approach to be the independent Chair. A number of possible candidates were put forward but these were all discounted by others on the basis of not meeting the criteria or having a previous association with another party or being deemed not to be independent. Lawrence was always of the view that it would be easy to knock down the suggestions of the groups, not for any other reason that their experiences of Hearts were formed in the circles they operated in. That would naturally guide them towards potential candidates that they knew or had worked with previously. It was a perfectly natural approach to the exam question to reach out to people you already knew and trusted. Despite this, each member was asked for their thoughts and rationale. What became clear was they were bringing names that could be discounted or have a biased connection, as Lawrence rightly deduced. Henry Snedden proposed former non-executive advisor at Johnston Carmichael Chartered Accountants and Maven Capital Partners UK LLP, Jack Ogston. Despite him having a glittering and successful corporate career, nobody really knew of him, so it didn't get much traction.

Other suggestions included former Hearts ace cum football agent and businessperson, John Colquhoun, and a former partner at KPMG and Chair of Spartans FC, Craig Graham. There we also suggestions of ex-HMOST, Martin Laidlaw, and Chief Financial Officer of the EDI development group, Eric Adair. The last suggestion was David Watson. David was Chair of the Ayr United Football Academy, a former senior management consultant and chartered accountant with expertise in organisational restructuring. He was a Hearts Shareholder too. These were all fantastic candidates that would have done a superb job. However, they all suffered from the same disadvantage: they were suggested by certain individuals in the group that meant others would not accept them.

Lawrence didn't reveal my name immediately. He kept it private until the process of each member proposing names and testing them was exhausted. This was not a quick process. The meeting was the last where two representatives of each group were present and everyone wanted their opinion aired. Lawrence then asked the group if he could be permitted to put a name forward. It was met with a bit of surprise but only the FOH reps objected. The rest of the group were very happy to hear an alternative given they were all pretty much resigned to the fact that they couldn't get agreement for their own suggestions.

Lawrence knew he didn't have any voting rights or actually much skin in the game at this stage but at the end of a very fraught meeting he put forward my name. I have been told that FOH didn't like the idea as they still held to the position that they should take this forward. After another long and fractious debate, the FOH reluctantly agreed to a consensus and, as a result, my candidature was agreed unanimously.

Lawrence had taken a gamble. He knew that this was in the best interest of Hearts to get an independent Chair that could try to bring everyone together. His strategy and approach were right despite it meaning he lost the respect and credibility of some in the group, especially the FOH representatives. It's all, of course, water under the bridge now but, for me, it was the start of an incredible journey.

Lawrence bowed out of the group formally at the end of this meeting. His involvement was not to disappear. In fact, it was probably about to intensify beyond his comprehension.

I had agreed with Lawrence that if my appointment was approved that we would call an early gathering at Tynecastle for me to meet with everyone and get a full briefing on where they were, what the plans were, and how we could take it forward, both from the G10 and the club.

I got a direct message on Twitter from him very late that evening that simply said:

Hi Ian, the group unanimously approved the motion to invite you to chair. Hope you can accept! We can talk specifics tomorrow if that's OK?

I immediately replied saying that I would absolutely accept.

I hadn't had much time to formulate my own thoughts. This had all happened so quickly. I was confused by all the groups and patchwork coalitions of various organisations. I knew who they all were but I didn't have a handle on who was who or how they all fitted together. I knew of FOH by then and the GIO but had no idea of the characters involved. Would it be FOH, FOH and the GIO, or something new? My only thought at that stage was whether we needed to start afresh. Given what had been described to me by Lawrence and others, I was firmly of the view that perhaps a fresh approach was required in order to get everyone to wipe their slates clean and leave their historical baggage at the door.

That Saturday, after another long conversation with Lawrence (long conversations with Lawrence and others would become a firm feature), I agreed that I would send an email to the group to introduce myself and express a few initial thoughts. The email pretty much summed up the position of Hearts at that time and what needed to be done. There may also be a small white lie in the second paragraph! The email read:

> I just thought I would drop you a quick note to, firstly, thank you for considering me as the independent Chair of the group and, secondly, to introduce myself to you all informally.
>
> It took me about a nanosecond to accept the invitation for a number of reasons. Firstly, on a very positive note, getting the club onto a stable footing would signal a very bright and exciting future for an organisation that we all cherish and love.
>
> Secondly, we should all want to ensure that future generations can support the club. The thought of there not being a Hearts fills me with dread.
>
> Thirdly, the timing is here and now. The ball is firmly in our court and if we can produce the results that we all want to see, we can do this. The window of opportunity is not large, and the scale of the task is enormous – but it can be done.
>
> I recalled last night a question that was once asked of me by a journalist. He asked why I was so passionate about Hearts. My reply was that that I had jumped too many jigs of joy, kissed too many strangers and shed too many tears not to have a deep passion for the club. The opportunity to try and forge a future from a very uncertain few years is something we should all grasp as tightly as possible.
>
> Lastly, if I could ask a small favour. This will not be an easy task for me. Politics is a tough game and it is even tougher when you have a small majority and a high-profile Shadow Ministerial position. I want to do this for Hearts, but I can only do this why it does not compromise me or my position both personally and professionally. I would hope that our relationship can be one of mutual trust and that the pages of the newspapers are the very last thing on people's minds.

Make no mistake, there is no white knight out there, there is no other game in town at the moment and that's why it's important for us all to make rapid progress as a single unit for the sake of our club.

The inaugural meeting with me as Chair was arranged to take place in the Directors Suite at Tynecastle a couple of weeks later. David and Fiona would open the meeting with the current state of play at the club before handing over to me. I have to say, after all my initial anxiety and caution as to whether I should accept the role as independent chair, I was as excited as a young child on Christmas Eve, or maybe as excited as a Hearts fan heading in to the away end at Easter Road to see another famous victory over our greatest rivals!

I had no doubt that I had made the correct decision...

CHAPTER 7

The Right People, the Right Time with Not Enough Time

BY THE FIRST meeting that I would chair of the G10, it looked as though the fan ownership vehicle was going to be the only way to see Hearts into new ownership and out of the hands of the Romanov regime. There were still a number of irons in the fire but I am not sure the fire was lit. There were also a number of tyre kickers, many of whom would become a real problem in the months ahead.

Barry Cole and his team were still seeking opportunities and he was also putting together a proposal that would give a substantial upfront investment to the supporter groups, with the investment repaid over a period of time. That approach would sit alongside the potential for other white knight owners.

That left the responsibility for finding a solution to the small number of Hearts fans who had volunteered from their respective organisations to form this new group. At a previous meeting it was agreed that the number of representatives per organisation would be reduced to one each. This would form the steering group.

The meeting of the steering group was set for Friday 26 April 2013 in the Directors Suite at Tynecastle Park. There had been some discussion and decisions made before this meeting that I was made aware of in conversations with Lawrence and David. The group had decided that they were uncomfortable with the continuation of Paul Goodwin representing SDS. It wasn't personal, it was just a style clash with some of the group. I understand Paul left SDS shortly afterwards due to the Scottish Government reducing their financial support. If SDS were to continue to be involved, then they needed someone else to give advice and present the case. It was disappointing not to have Paul's experience and knowledge but we were extremely lucky to get the support of Richard Atkinson from SDS in his place. He became a key contact for the group, not just from his SDS experience but he played a pivotal role in setting up the 10,000 Hours project with his colleague, a Glasgow-based solicitor, Chris Stewart. 10,000 Hours was started to provide a vehicle and project for the supporters of St Mirren Football club to purchase a majority stake. Richard was Commercial Director at St Mirren so had a wealth of football experience and impressive business credentials through his own family firm, the Maxi Group.

The 10,000 Hours project involved setting up a CIC for the purpose of taking the majority shareholding of St Mirren into community ownership. That ownership would have a number of elements but be primarily the individual supporters of the club. They endeavoured to raise £2 million for this purpose. The key element of this CIC model was that the football club would be constitutionally, through its company classification, a community asset. That would allow 10,000 Hours to access specialist funding, including soft loans, grants, patient capital and social investment, for the purchase of community assets. In this case, the community asset would be a 52 per cent interest in St Mirren, controlled by 10,000 Hours. The club would then operate as a community hub in order to benefit the club and wider local community. The initial capital required to purchase the shareholding would come from a variety of sources, including the potential for a fan membership scheme.

The 10,000 Hours initiative was the blueprint for FOH. It was ultimately unsuccessful at St Mirren by a whisker. It fell just short of raising the necessary £2 million funds to meet the offer price required to take control of the club. St Mirren's loss was Hearts' gain as we benefitted from the vast experience of Richard. One of the key lessons was how to set up, develop and operate a supporter-based direct debit contribution system that could raise regular amounts.

My name as independent Chair was to be kept out of the public domain until just a couple of days before my first meeting. Lawrence thought that, in order to leave breathing space, the G10 would not name the Chair as it would get good media coverage that could help promote the agreed road map. Lawrence was clear throughout the process that being able to give the media an interesting and positive message would allow the detail of what we were trying to achieve, much of it very dry, to penetrate better into the minds of the supporters. There was almost a malaise and numbness in the Scottish sporting media following the demise of Rangers. That meant we needed to have in our minds at all times that this had to be a positive story that would contain colour and interest for the public.

It was also a very good way of controlling the amount of information that ended up in the public domain. We wanted to be the masters of our own destiny, so we would require a strict messaging policy with a clear media grid about what was said, by whom and when. This was never going to be an easy task when dealing with such an emotive and important issue of saving a football club. We would have to control the thirst for information from supporters. Absolute discretion was essential to protect the confidentiality of the group and trust between the members. It was very important to be a step ahead of what was put into the public domain. It was critical to ensure there was no room for sticking points or disagreements to be aired publicly. We all knew this was not going to be an easy process and there would be large bumps in the road on the journey but we had to have a public veneer that everything was smooth, working well and heading for a successful outcome.

To that end, the G10 issued a short statement prior to my first meeting that simply said;

The six key Hearts supporter groups have agreed that a unilateral solution is required towards supporter ownership and governance.

With that in mind, the group have agreed to appoint an independent Chair. Discussions will take place in the coming days and it is hoped that the position will be filled shortly.

The only problem with this strategy was that we required professional assistance to make it happen. Lawrence had been instrumental in getting the group to focus on the agenda and had persuaded me that I should take on the role of Chair. However, on issuing this statement to the media, he decided to tell us all that he was stepping back at the point of me being formally confirmed. Lawrence had dedicated a large and increasing amount of time to this project and felt that this was a good time to pass the baton. He was intensely proud of what he achieved as an employee at Hearts. He always said how much he loved his time there but thought this was the moment for him to retake his place as an ordinary supporter in the Wheatfield Stand and continue his work with Hearts-related charity, Big Hearts Community Trust.

He wasn't going to get away with that. I wasn't going to allow that to happen. Lawrence had got me into this and we would be doing it together or not at all. We needed the strong relationships he had built up at the club and in the sporting media to help us through this. He is a consummate professional, very good to work with and, critically, damn good at what he does. I needed someone of Lawrence's experience to come in and help with the messaging and marketing. David agreed so we set about making sure he would be tied in.

Lawrence was steeped in the short history of the project. His institutional memory was needed. On one occasion, just after the League Cup Final with St Mirren, Lawrence was invited to Alex Mackie's office in central Edinburgh with former Partner of Deloitte and FOH advisor, Robert Wilson, to essentially be 'interviewed' for the role with FOH. The interconnections were now becoming tangled, so it was right for Lawrence to stay involved and be a key element of the future success.

I remember the first meeting very well, not just because this was to be a seminal moment for me. It was exciting as an avid fan to be heading to the Directors Suite at my beloved Tynecastle for such an important occasion. I remember walking up to the entrance in the main stand and being taken up the stairs by David. I recall entering the Suite thinking that Hearts had provided me and many others with so many wonderful moments over the years. The stairwell was adorned with images of previous Cup Final wins and our playing heroes of those occasions. It was a rather surreal experience.

Lawrence wouldn't be attending the meeting as he had set out that he was going to take a step back. A key outcome for me would be to ensure I got agreement from the group that we ask him to stay. They all knew there was nobody else with his experience that could help us guide the messaging.

The meeting started with introductions. There was a little confusion as I had been briefed on the machinations of the group but also been told that there would only be one representative of each organisation. The group was to be made up of people I had heard of but never met or had any previous interactions with. The steering group was:

Independent chair: Ian Murray MP
Federation of Hearts Supporters clubs: Henry Snedden, Vice Chair
Foundation of Hearts: Garry Halliday, Director
Heart of Midlothian: Fiona Sinclair, Head of Finance (club group advisor)
Hearts Youth Development Committee: Calum Robertson, Chair
Save Our Hearts: Dougie Masterton, Representative
Hearts Shareholders Association: Bill Alves, Chair
Supporters Direct Scotland: Richard Atkinson (advisor to the group)
Hearts Supporters' Trust: Jane Lewis, Secretary

Although the FOH was represented on the steering group by nominated Director Garry Halliday, Alex, who was the founding and current Chair of the FOH, was a large part of the discussion due to his previous views on the way forward.

What was key from David's presentation was that it was utterly critical that, if the club was to go into administration, it had to do so after the end of the football season. It was inconceivable not to fulfil our fixtures. That would have created a position for the club that may not have been recoverable. It would have damned Hearts. Not only were there significant contractual issues but there was also sporting integrity that had become a much stronger policy from the footballing authorities after the demise of Rangers. Simply, though, it was about cash. Hearts had to play games in order to sell tickets and get the staged payments due from supporters who had purchased season tickets with their credit cards. The deal with the credit card companies was that they paid out a proportion of season ticket money with every home match played. By forfeiting fixtures, the credit card company would be liable to their customers for a refund and that would be paid from the funds due to the club. The financial, footballing and integrity issues of not finishing the season were not worth contemplating. Administration was pending. It was a matter of when, not if.

David carefully set out the position of the Lithuanian owners and reiterated their desire to find new ownership through the supporters. The club indicated that a bid should come in no later than 30 June and prior to this if possible. We agreed that we should work towards that date. A key decision had been made at our first meeting. It was a sobering but, as was David's style, a hugely honest assessment. Would we make it to the end of the season? Well, who knows, but the skeleton staff at the club and the players were doing all they could and it was great credit to them that they were.

Every member of the group asked David questions and gave their thoughts on where their organisation sat in the process. I remember thinking throughout the meeting that the best strategy for me was not to say too much and listen to the presentations, hear what others had to say, and get to know the characters and what motivated them. It was easy to know that they were all dyed-in-the-wool Jambos but I had to work fast to determine how I could utilise their skills. We were a bunch of well-meaning volunteers and had to remember that throughout this process. I had been given a download on each member by Lawrence but didn't want that to influence my own initial thoughts. The responsibility was extreme but the rewards would be immeasurable.

There were sharp tensions in the room. I don't know if everyone was on their best behaviour because I had come into the group from the outside but I could tell all was not well. It appeared that FOH felt a degree of irritation that the supporter ownership model that they had long championed was now the ownership of everyone and not just theirs. Alex would spend a lot of time at subsequent meetings describing the genesis of FOH, who was involved, why they existed and the importance of them remaining the dominant partner in the group. That, not unsurprisingly, didn't sit well with the others. They had come into this process in good faith, with no preconceived ideas as to how it would be constituted but with a deep suspicion of Alex. He had, in previous meetings, completely dominated discussion and decisions. There was a recurring difficulty in getting people to forget the recent past and move on.

What held them all together, though, was the sense of crisis engulfing the club. The fact that they had Hearts running through them all like a stick of rock helped. The club belonged to all of us supporters and we were merely short-term custodians for future generations. 'All I am here for is to help save the club' would be a phrase I would hear very regularly from all members of the group.

It was blatantly obvious why the decision had been made to get an independent Chair. As the meeting wore on, and it did wear on for many hours, one key outcome had to be to achieve unity between all the groups and find agreement for the vehicle to take it forward. I didn't have any predetermined notion as to what the vehicle would be. It was clear that most of the steering group recognised that FOH did have a significant advantage. They had been set up from the outset with the sole purpose of acquiring a stake in the club, so they already had a basic legal framework in place and an objective that differed from the other groups. The other organisations were set up for very different aims and objectives and had been around since the '70s and '80s, so it made sense to look at using the FOH framework as the starting point. The downside was that FOH had already made an unwelcome move to purchase the club and burned their boats with Romanov. We needed to tread carefully, show we had a fresh approach, and to present any future bid as credible.

Lawrence used the word 'torturous' to describe some of the previous meetings and if there was a stronger word, I would have used it. The discussions tended to meander around issues, regularly referring back to previous debates. I was always taken back to the history of FOH and why they were set up. We had to get some decisions made and move on from this but it was difficult.

What we did agree though was nothing short of a miracle and was really driven by Richard. There were only really two options as setting up something new would take too long. The preferred model for SDS would be using the Hearts Supporters Trust. This was ruled out easily as it was a very small organisation that wasn't equipped to take on such a momentous role. The only other viable option was FOH. It had the flexibility to achieve the 'seven principles of cooperative ownership' including fulfilling a 'one member, one vote' process of voting that was a red line requirement for SDS. It had an existing framework to build on. There was also the not inconsiderable element of FOH that they had 2,400 supporters pledged to give them a regular donation should they formalise the process. To that end, every member of the group would be issued with a paper proposing that FOH be used to try and purchase the club, current documents pertaining to FOH governance structures and articles of association that would be reviewed.

In what looking back now seemed completely unbelievable, we got early agreement that confirmed the steering group would formally trim down attendees to create working groups on key aspects of the bid and we would formally merge the steering group into the FOH organisation. We also agreed that all of the supporter organisations on the steering group would be invited to become full Directors of FOH and join their Board. I would become the Chair of FOH and Alex would step aside to allow that to happen. Garry, as the FOH representative, confirmed that this would be agreed with Alex after the meeting and would come into effect at our next meeting when the legal and procedural formalities would be concluded. I didn't know if this could be delivered by Garry but I had to trust that he could make it happen. I recall Richard saying that it might be a case of 'irresistible force meeting immovable object'. That still left the problematic and thorny issue of self-appointed Directors of FOH and what would happen in the future. We had to have a democratic process to elect Directors if we managed to acquire the majority shareholding in Hearts. It was agreed, after a considerable amount of blood, sweat and virtual tears that, at the outset, every Director of FOH would lodge a letter of resignation with me that would come into effect as soon as the aims and objectives had been achieved. There would be no reason to prevent the Directors from putting themselves up for re-election if they so wished, but they would do that from the same position as any other supporter who wished to be elected to serve the FOH Board. This was not universally welcomed by all of the group but it did allow us to move forward.

Garry, as the existing FOH Director present at the meeting, made a strong case that he didn't think it was necessary for the founding Directors to relinquish control of FOH. I had a certain degree of sympathy for that position. They had taken the initiative to set it up and get key figures interested but we had to engineer a situation that wiped the FOH slate clean. Compromise had to be on both sides and, if the supporter groups were going to agree to FOH becoming the means by which to deliver supporter ownership, then the founders of FOH had to realise that this would not be theirs anymore.

Despite FOH becoming the vehicle and taking on all five supporter groups as equal Directors, the constant reference to 'founding Directors' and the supporter groups Directors would become a firm feature of tension and annoyance throughout this entire process. To this day, I only ever received the resignation letters from the supporter groups and not from the founding Directors of FOH. In hindsight, it didn't really matter but it was an unnecessary regular distraction that didn't help to nurture unity.

We had made a huge amount of progress with clear action points on the way forward. Richard ranked the meeting ten out of ten and would have awarded me a bonus point to make it 11 out of ten if it had finished on time. I had enjoyed meeting those involved. It was inspiring to lead a group of ordinary Hearts supporters who simply just cared. Their motivations were nothing other than to ensure the survival of Hearts. It would be a turbulent and stressful period over the next 18 months with lots of self-doubt, anxiety and pressure but we all had one thing in common and it was the only thing that mattered. Heart of Midlothian Football Club was not going to die on our watch.

I remember speaking to Lawrence after the meeting. I recall saying to him, 'What the fucking hell have you just done to me?' Not only was I now in the firing line if Hearts didn't survive, I had also just risked my entire political career. In fact, would I have been able to live in Edinburgh again if this all went wrong?

Although I couldn't have been more grateful to him for the pre-meeting briefing on the dynamics of the group, the key issues of contention and the potential way forward, I was aggravated by how dysfunctional the group was. The distrust and suspicion FOH had for the supporter groups and vice versa was palpable. There was also a rather uncomfortable dynamic with Richard. He was challenging in his questioning and robust with his advice. That was a good thing in my view. Not everyone shared my positivity. We compared notes on the meeting and agreed that we had achieved a great deal. That was when I broke it to him that my first major decision was that he was not being allowed to walk away. He would be a key advisor to the FOH Board. The GIO would remain but no longer be about supporter ownership. It would still exist for the original purposes of club and supporter liaison.

The FOH was our focus now. Lawrence has since said to me that he thought about it for a few days but actually he was delighted to be asked to stay on and threw his heart and soul into the FOH project. This was not a universally popular decision as some in the group knew that Lawrence worked for Hearts during the turbulent period when owner Chris Robinson had suggested selling Tynecastle Park and moving to Murrayfield. It was seemingly an issue at the Dundee match the day after my initial meeting. Some supporters mentioned that they were uncomfortable with Lawrence tweeting out the agreed statement from the meeting. I didn't think those criticisms were fair or relevant, but it did highlight the long memories of some and added to the challenge of how to overcome them. It was at this point that Lawrence told me about his three-hour phone call with Alex on the day of the League Cup Final with St Mirren in March. These character dynamics would become all too familiar to me.

The next couple of days would be crucial. I wanted to hit the ground running and not let the initial impetus be lost. Fortuitously, Parliament was about to prorogue to allow for the next session. That involved a Queen's Speech, so I would be able to be in Edinburgh for an extended period. I also wanted to strike while the iron was hot on what had been agreed. I knew these meetings had not been overly productive in the past so by me playing a little ignorant of the obvious and visible problems in the group, I could maybe get more formal structures in place. That would involve setting up specific working groups on governance, marketing, operations, finance and relations with the club. Henry Snedden also helpfully suggested we set up a core bid team. Jane would utilise her contacts to see if we could access the databases of other supporter groups across the country. Hearts has a large international footprint with supporters in every corner of the globe. Jane would attempt to try and tap into that significant resource. We had given ourselves little over two months to get a credible and sustainable bid together. The past history of what had been achieved, or not achieved, had to be set aside with our eyes on the prize.

The FOH issued a short statement to the media after the meeting designed to encourage more supporters to pledge:

> There was unanimous agreement to a number of critical issues that will allow the Hearts family to move forward as a unified force in order to prepare the best possible bid for the fans to own Heart of Midlothian Football Club.

In the meantime, the group would like to encourage all fans of the club who wish to assist in bringing this about to make their pledges via the Foundation of Hearts website.

Independent Chair Ian Murray said after the meeting, 'We had a very productive meeting this evening with all the groups representing the fans. There is a lot of very hard work to do but the message from tonight is clear – it's in the hands of the fans of this great club as we go forward with one voice. I would encourage all those who can to make a pledge.'

The next meeting would take place the following Thursday evening at the office of FOH Director, Brian Cormack, at 23 Melville Street in Edinburgh. This would become our home ground for meetings. The steering group would meet at 6.00pm, then we would meet as a larger group combining with FOH an hour later. In all my communications I continually emphasised that our timescales were tight and, as a result, always welcomed thoughts and ideas in advance of meetings if members couldn't attend. I would rue this process in later weeks.

As all this was going on, Hearts was creeping towards the end of the season both in footballing and financial terms. The day after the meeting they went down to a 1-0 defeat at the hands of Dundee at Dens Park. There was a strange irony that if Hearts went into administration in the close season, the size of points penalty would be calculated as a third of the previous season's points total, so winning games wasn't really that beneficial. It was good for club morale and kept the tills ringing but could have been a footballing noose for the following season. There were also almost daily articles in the newspapers speculating about the possibility of Hearts going into administration.

On formally being announced as the new independent Chair, the inevitable occurred – my phone didn't stop ringing and my emails started to go a little outlandish. Many people wanted to get in touch and offer their assistance. This was fabulous but there was a delicate balance to strike between keeping a focus, gaining as much insight and expert advice as possible and sweating everyone connected with the club.

After the initial meeting, it was important to try and speak to as many of those involved as possible outside the rigidity of the formal meetings. A lengthy conversation with Richard, followed by an even longer download from Alex gave me a good background to what needed to be done.

I was also surprised by the instant media interest. This was partly due to the relationship Lawrence had built up over years but also because many of the media were sympathetic to Hearts. Some were supporters like the rest of us. They were willing to help where they could and none more so than Stuart Bathgate from *The Scotsman*, whom I met in my first week as Chair. He would be incredibly helpful alongside Brian McLaughlin at BBC Sport Scotland.

But some of my fondest memories were meeting with those that had graced the Tynecastle turf. The first such meeting was with Hearts record appearance holder, Gary McKay. He had been on the fringes of FOH for some time and wanted to both share his experiences and offer his services. We met in Costa across the road from my flat on the Wednesday evening after my appointment. We talked for over two hours about the history of FOH, the politics of Hearts and what he was able to do to help. I was always left with the impression that former players like Gary just loved the club. He cared for it deeply and wanted to see it doing well. He vouched for and suggested a number of people that were involved in the campaign to prevent Hearts from moving to Murrayfield that may be useful for FOH. Gary and others would need to be utilised in the coming weeks and months.

We knew that the involvement of Hearts hero, John Robertson, in the share issue was fundamental to its success. We would need all former players, managers and familiar faces to help get the FOH message across. Their ability to connect with the fans was something that no other individual or group could do. Pretty much all I could think about, though, when talking to Gary were his two famous wonder goals: one against Clydebank in the last home game of the 1985/86 season when we touched the championship trophy; and his thunderbolt for Scotland away to Bulgaria in 1998 that sent Jack Charlton's Ireland to the World Cup. He's a cult hero in Ireland as a result.

All these connections would prove critical. We didn't know at the end of April that Hearts would be a matter of weeks away from administration but we were all pleased that we had a plan that just needed to be executed.

Would we have enough time?

CHAPTER 8

Founding the Foundation

FOH HAD BEEN around for a number of years. It was created as a non-profit organisation in 2010 by a group of local businesspeople, all of whom are lifelong Hearts fans. They all shared a passionate vision for the future of the club which was based on bringing Heart of Midlothian back to the people who are truly adoring about the club – the fans. They knew the club was in financial trouble and that the Lithuanian owners had lost interest.

The sole purpose of FOH was to own a majority shareholding in Hearts. This would be achieved by a membership scheme that supporters would automatically join by making a regular financial commitment. The proceeds from these commitments would be used to generate a capital sum and a regular income to buy the club.

After the agreement to use FOH as the vehicle for preparation of a bid, I would become the independent Chair. That would mean the founding Directors of Edinburgh insurance business owner Alex Mackie, East Lothian Councillor Jamie Bryant, Edinburgh property developer Brian Cormack, tradesman and fan guru Garry Halliday and former Hearts player and cult hero Donald Ford would be joined by all the Hearts supporter organisations represented in the steering group: the Federation of Hearts Supporters clubs (FHSC) Vice Chair Henry Snedden; the Heart of Midlothian Shareholders Association (HMSA) Chair Bill Alves; the Heart of Midlothian Supporters' Trust (HMST) Chair Jane Lewis; Hearts Youth Development Committee (HYDC) Chair Calum Robertson; and Save Our Hearts (SOH) representative Dougie Masterton.

A number of people informally connected to FOH had been providing varying degrees of support since its inception in 2010. PR and marketing expert Alastair Bruce through his company, Shaw Marketing, had been offering a great deal of professional support and Stuart Murray from law firm Shoosmiths was attached as the FOH corporate legal advisor. Robert Wilson, former partner at Deloitte and the first Chair of the Scottish

Premier League was counselling with his vast experience in both business and football. One of Edinburgh's most respected corporate finance professionals, Kevin Windram, and future FOH chair, Stuart Wallace, who worked as a partner at PricewaterhouseCoopers, had been providing tax advice. There was also a certain successful Edinburgh businesswoman and entrepreneur, Ann Budge. She had been attracted to the FOH project from the beginning and was providing some guidance, advice and support.

Although she had been invited to join the FOH Board on several occasions but had declined, she did bring in Robert Wilson and Alastair Bruce to help with strategy and marketing. She thought that by introducing them, she could back off. However, they both agreed to get involved *only* if she stayed. The initial approach from FOH to Ann came out of the need for them to get technology expertise to build a user platform. It was never about resources but about her IT background. Ann explained:

> When the original founders of what is now FOH first got together, they discussed who they might approach for advice and help! Gary McKay knew my daughter and myself slightly and knew we were Hearts supporters so he mentioned me to them. Alex Mackie then wrote to me. I wish I still had his hand-written letter, asking to meet for a coffee to discuss the plight of Hearts. I was intrigued and went along. I agreed to attend a few other group meetings and somehow found myself involved.

All these professional consultants were crucial in helping to drive FOH forward in the short two-month period we had given ourselves to present a credible offer. I appreciated the amount of work FOH had done over the years to get them to the point of being able to deliver an ownership vehicle. The problem was that the circumstances of the current plight of Hearts would not necessarily be a comfortable fit with what was in place. It had been effectively dormant for a long time. The reason it stuttered was by no means anything to do with those involved. They had the foresight to set something up long before it was required. It was merely a consequence of requiring the crisis to germinate the idea of supporter ownership in the minds of the fan base. I don't think any fan would deny the club was in a financial crisis but it was only when the dark clouds gathered over the club in November 2012 that people believed it to be real. The crisis point was when FOH became required the most. It was the emergency that would ultimately lead to its success. I absolutely believe that had Hearts not been in a life-threatening position, FOH would never have been required, let alone been successful.

We all knew that there was not going to be an easy way out of this crisis. The last few months had shown that. There were hardly queues of suitors lining up outside the front door. The only option that would allow us to be masters of our own destiny was that of supporter ownership. It was originally devised in 2010 by Garry Halliday and Jamie Bryant. After the death of a close friend they decided they wanted to do something in his memory that would help secure the future of Hearts. Jamie and Garry had the idea that you could raise money from the fans to wrestle the club away from the Romanov regime. Jamie and Garry thought they would run this idea past some businesspeople and through a few contacts got to Alex.

Alex had come to prominence with some of the Hearts support the previous year when he challenged the Romanov regime at the Hearts Annual General Meeting (AGM). I don't think the Romanov regime ever forgave him for that challenge.

Their initial idea was that they would get 8,000 Hearts fans to give £3,000 each. That would raise £24m to purchase the club. Alex initially said he couldn't get involved in that idea as it seemed overly ambitious and to get 8,000 individual fans to stump up such a lot of money just would not be feasible. After a sleepless night, Alex made contact with Garry and laid out that he didn't think the initial idea from Jamie would work but that he was happy to assist in looking at the figures and coming up with a more realistic proposition.

Garry and Jamie always gave the impression that Alex was hooked on the idea from the outset. This couldn't have been further from the truth. Alex just didn't see how it could work. However, the deciding factor for Alex was that they had given the impression they had access to Sergejus through the involvement of their colleague, Brian Cormack. That was music to the ears of Alex. He had been attempting to get access to information about the club since their altercation at the AGM the previous year. Access to Sergejus was impossible for Alex after that AGM.

Alex didn't have a problem with the general concept. He and his family built up their own successful Edinburgh-based insurance business. One of their most successful products was to allow those clients who could not afford to pay a large insurance premium as a lump sum to pay it by an interest-free monthly direct debit. That idea was injected into the conversation and seemed like a more credible way forward. That was really the start of the long FOH journey and how fan ownership could be achieved.

FOH wanted to get away from a model that facilitated individual owners pursuing a short-term strategy for instant profit or personal gratification. That had only damaged Hearts over pretty much every period of its history. That had to be changed. The idea was that the only people able to do that were the supporters. Supporters owning the club directly would allow decisions to be made that looked to the longer term. Never again would the club be jeopardised by allowing owners to plough money into the playing squad for short-term gain. Any investment in the team to improve the fortunes of the club would involve significant investment in the youth academy. That would provide a conveyor belt of talent and saleable player assets. That is where the additional investment in the team would come from and how sustainability would be achieved.

There is a balance to be struck as a football fan and that would have to be addressed. On the one hand, supporters wanted a rich owner who would plough in as much money as it would take to win trophies and succeed in Europe. On the other hand, they yearn for a return to a local club that benefits the community and represents their values and aspirations. That was an equilibrium we would have to take head on. Historically, at Hearts, chasing the Holy Grail has only ever created instability.

One of the most contentious, complicated and, if we are all being honest, deeply mind-numbing parts of the process would be the governance structure. I've never liked governance. It is arguably the single most important element in any organisation and doubly significant for a football club that has to be accountable to tens of thousands of passionate supporters. It would be the part of the FOH project that would drive everyone to insanity and back.

There was nothing inherently wrong with what was in place at FOH but the existing governance structures didn't seem fit for current purposes. It was written at a time before the circumstances of Hearts' position were known. The thorniest issue was how you would balance the ownership of Hearts with the actual day-to-day operations of running a football club. There was a common misconception that the FOH would run Hearts. That was never the case and never could be the case. They were separate organisations. Ownership didn't equate to operating. The hardest message for FOH to communicate was that fan ownership was different from fan-run. If it did mean fan-run, we would merely be replacing one type of dictatorial ownership with another. That wouldn't work in the context of supporter ownership. We had to develop a new model that would survive the test of time.

It had to be transparent enough to give the supporters confidence that they could invest in FOH. That meant that there could be no automatic right for any FOH Director to be a Director of Hearts. That wouldn't work. There had to be clearly defined Chinese walls and a governance structure containing distinct roles and responsibilities for each organisation.

We had to try and understand the existing structures. To that end, the supporter groups met with Stuart Murray from Shoosmiths to gain a knowledge behind the original formation of FOH. Following that meeting, many discussions and debates took place as to how we could remodel it. It wasn't about starting from scratch but adapting to the original circumstances. The FOH had a distinct advantage in that it was formed before the club went into administration. In normal circumstances, it is after an administration event where people hastily come together.

Henry Snedden was given the unenviable task of reviewing what FOH had in place in terms of governance and how it could be made fit for purpose. He was also looking with a fresh pair of eyes at the public facing information through the FOH website. One of Henry's undoubted strengths is his ability to be honest and direct. Henry produced a lengthy critique that showed the current FOH governance framework and website were 'not fit for purpose'. His primary concern was that he felt that neither the website or the articles of association would be easily understood or make an instant connection with the majority of Hearts fans. We had to get our message across to them first time. There wouldn't be any second chances. It was going to be a one-shot campaign appeal and we couldn't afford to get it wrong.

As it turned out, Henry's initial concerns were entirely justified. As a result, the FOH website and original governance documents were never released to the wider fan base. He was correct and we didn't have time to be massaging egos. We had to get on with it. It was a huge body of work but gave us a direction that was critical to making progress.

Henry's analysis on the legal and governance position was never universally accepted. We had to force this through. It created a long exchange of emails between Henry and one of his Hearts idols, Donald Ford, whom we never met face to face. Donald took umbrage at the changes that Henry was recommending. Donald had played a huge part in the founding and development of FOH in the early years but aside from giving us his name to help market FOH, he didn't really get involved after I took up the Chair. To be fair to Donald, he too didn't have the flexibility of time to devote to the FOH cause and was based in Carnoustie. We had moved forward considerably since his hands-on involvement. I guess this was the genesis of his concerns.

Whilst I will bemoan the very existence of governance until the end of this book, I can't emphasise enough that nothing would have happened with FOH had it not been resolved. You just couldn't have a situation where the members of FOH in a 'one member, one vote' scenario could dominate the Hearts Board and sack the manager after every bad result or misplaced free kick. We also wanted to design a governance structure that retained and attracted the key professional skills necessary to properly operate and manage a membership organisation of thousands of people who would be paying millions of pounds every year into FOH coffers.

The one enormous upside to the current FOH structure was that 2,400 supporters had already pledged to give a regular amount. All we had to do was convert those pledges into actual contributions and grow them.

Then there was the name. There was no legitimate reason not to keep the FOH name but the appetite to try and have a fresh start was strong. In all my time in business, politics and organisations, it has always been the name that causes the most discussion, debate and angst. The founding FOH Directors were rightly keen to retain the name, but they did concede that a distinct and marketable campaign title may be required to raise the funds. That marketing campaign became 'Own the history. Shape the future.'

Despite the sheer volume of work, the interest from everyone connected with Hearts, the intense thirst to feed the media and the growing number of issues to resolve, we all felt quite positive. I remember vividly Garry saying at the commencement of our second meeting that he was looking forward to playing his part in delivering a 'historic moment for Hearts'. That's what was driving us all. And it was this sentiment that motivated us towards focusing on explaining our road map to the fans in a way that would try to capture the imagination. It was paramount that they quickly bought in to the new FOH model and the process for buying the club. After all, they would be the new owners.

All the internal work that was going on was crucial but it would only work if we were able to persuade the fans about the importance of pledging. It was paramount to be honest with them about what Hearts will look like next season, the season after and into the future. We had to manage their expectations whilst providing a positive case for fan ownership and what that would mean for the club. Inevitably the supporters would want to know if we would match the recent success of three Scottish Cups in 14 years. In historic terms, this was quite a good success rate for Hearts. Will the fans be able to see Hearts compete as the third best team in Scotland by participating in Europe competition at least three years out of every five? These were not unreasonable expectations, but we had to walk a very fine line between inspiring the fans about how positive the future could be whilst being honest that the journey to achieving those expectations would be a very long road.

I did have a fear that the relationship with the supporters would be coloured by recent events. Bear in mind that some fans were still smarting over the share issue. They were asked to bail out the club in their hour of need rather than it being a genuine attempt to invest in its development. The £1.2 million that was raised was seen as a donation to the club and nothing else. It didn't help that participants had not yet received their share certificates. That was only six months previously and they were again being asked to pledge more of their hard-earned cash. Explaining how the FOH funding would work, including any incentives, and how secure and needed it was would be central to any marketing strategy. Part of the ongoing problem was that we still didn't have an indication of what level of funding would be required to buy the club. Romanov had only ever publicly stated he wanted over £50 million. He was surely not serious when he stated that price. His valuation was well off. It would be worth nothing if it wasn't saved. While there is always the emotional attachment in buying into Hearts, as witnessed by the share issue, we would have to be clear with the pledgers what they were buying through the FOH. Was it simply the case that they would be solely financing the capital purchase of a controlling interest or would they also be funding ongoing working capital? Would it be both? The recent history of Hearts also posed the question – would the pledgers be confident in the people they were entrusting their cash to? These were all big questions for FOH.

This is why the governance discussion and model were so crucial. Would fans want to be a 'member owner' that contributed to owning the club or would they rather be a shareholder that actually owned a percentage? Would it be a combination of both or neither? We would have to do a lot of work trying to understand what the fans would want in return. There would not be an easy answer, nor would the chosen direction please everyone. The thing that we were all learning rather quickly was that if you tried to please all of the supporters, you were likely to end up pleasing none. The only plausible strategy in making these big decisions would be for the sole focus to be on what is in the best interest of the club and having a robust justification for why these decisions were taken.

Much to my frustration and annoyance, I was taken aback that some fans were already of the opinion that the supporter groups were going beyond their remit and didn't represent all the supporters. A simple mathematical calculation would have shown that the largest group of fans were the fans not represented in any of these groups. This is absolutely correct but in the absence of any other mechanism to involve representatives of all of the fans, I couldn't see how this could be resolved. It was the best we had. We did, however, guarantee that regardless of who was making the decisions, the governance would guarantee the fans a real and tangible say in both the future of the club and at representative level on the FOH and Hearts Boards. These were complicated and controversial subjects. I just had to keep reminding everyone that time was our enemy and we had to work with what we had in front of us.

Contentious discussions were never very far away at the FOH Board to the extent that I asked a member of my own parliamentary staff team, John Griffiths, to come and take formal notes of the meetings and act as a 'witness'. One such discussion was how we should interact with the Lithuanians. They were still the owners and if we wanted to negotiate an affordable purchase then we would have to maintain a strong and productive relationship with them. Some in FOH didn't think that was the best strategy and we should be vilifying them in the public domain for taking our club to the brink of extinction. The argument for that would be to unify the fans to lever them out. I was firmly of the view that we should not be creating any enemies or potential negative media stories. The Lithuanians would have to be our friends if we had any chance of producing a bid and having it accepted. We may also need to use the club as a conduit for FOH. They had a database of Hearts supporters that topped 48,000 and that, in itself, was worth its weight in gold. If we could access that we could talk directly to the people that we needed to pledge. We did get an undertaking that the supporter database would be accessible to FOH but only in the event that a viable bid document was received by the Board. After all, it was in the interests of the club and its supporters to provide this access.

We also couldn't risk compromising Fiona or David. We needed them to assist us and give us access to club information. In response to the debate about the strategy towards the current owners, Fiona thought it would be helpful to restate the club's formal position, which remained from the day FOH was created. She read a statement that said:

> The Board of Heart of Midlothian FC remains receptive to receiving a for-mal realistic bid from supporters for a minimum of 51 per cent of the share capital of the club. The current Board of Heart of Midlothian PLC. is the correct body to which any bid for the club should be made. The Directors of the club are then responsible for advising the main shareholders (UBIG) and creditors (UBIG, ŪKIO and potentially HMRC) of the validity of the bid and, as importantly, the organisation making the bid.

She helpfully informed us that the club understood that there was only one group that could justifiably claim to be the organisation representing sup-porters and that was the restructured FOH. This was music to my ears and a giant step forward.

Fiona was correct to clearly give her opinion that it was best to avoid unnecessary conflict with the owners. She explained that their business cul-ture would reject any accusations of divisiveness, failures to assist, failures of responsibility on the part of the club or, for that matter, any other people and organisations connected with the club. That would make any bid and purchase more difficult to achieve. She was never wrong.

Fiona was a key ally for FOH in those initial stages. After advising us about how to approach the relationship with the current owners and, by associa-tion the club itself, she endeavoured to clarify some of the issues around the current financial situation and what could be done to assist with the bid.

Then came her honest assessment of the situation from the perspective of Hearts. The reality was that no realistic bid had yet been submitted to the Board. There was a growing realisation that FOH were now serious about a bid by 30 June. That was viewed by the Lithuanians as being in everyone's best interests. I could see why the club insisted on a deadline. It was a 'put your money where your mouth is' challenge. It also came hot on the heels of a statement on ūkio Bankas from Lithuania.

The Lithuanian authorities, at that time, were understood to be keen for matters with ūkio Bankas to be settled soon and that created a race against time to prevent Hearts being sold off to the highest bidder in a fire sale alongside other ūkio assets. The liquidator wrote:

> On 2 May 2013 Kaunas Regional Court started the bankruptcy proceed-ings against AB ūkio Bankas. According to the court decision, the company UAB 'Valnetas' has been appointed as administrator of AB ūkio Bankas.

After assessing the interim report on the financial standing of ūkio Bankas presented by its temporary administrator, according to which the Bank's assets are less than its liabilities, the Board of the Bank of Lithuania (the national bank) applied to court on initiation of bankruptcy proceedings against this credit institution.

That ultimately meant only one thing for ūkio Bankas:

Taking into account the finding presented by the temporary administrator of ūkio Bankas, that the liabilities of ūkio Bankas are less than its assets and that there are no real possibilities to restore stability and credibility to its operations, the Board of the Bank of Lithuania recognise the bank as insolvent on 18 February 2013 and took a decision to permanently revoke the banking licence issued to this bank.

Around 50 per cent of the club's shares were owned by UBIG, the Lithuanian investment holding company that owned ūkio Bankas. UBIG had gone to the Lithuanian government to declare itself insolvent but at this time it had not been ratified by the relevant court. The result was that legally no party could have bought the club by going to Valnetas unless they just bought the main assets and not the actual shares of the club.

At this time, we all knew the club was living day-to-day but we didn't know what, if any, contracts were in place for the huge debts. We were given information that showed the club had agreements in place with its main creditor ūkio Bankas (in liquidation at that time) and main shareholder and significant creditor UBIG (*not* in administration at that time). In the case of ūkio, an agreement was in place until December 2015 and as such the club concluded that 'there is no concern about the (£15 million) loan being repaid in the immediate future'.

That didn't make comfortable reading for me. Any agreement that was in place with ūkio could have easily been disregarded given their circumstances. The ūkio administrator was responsible for maximising the resources available to pay off its creditors and that would have included debts owed to them by Hearts. The remarkable thing was that I was told the Hearts Board had no reason to believe there would be a change to the existing terms and if there was it would be a 'beneficial change for both parties'. I couldn't see how that could be the case. They used this to insist that the debt should not adversely affect the level of any FOH bid. That seemed ludicrous to me.

Given ūkio was being liquidated, they could call in their debt and the security on the stadium asset at any time, but they couldn't dispose of the entire club without negotiation with the majority shareholder (UBIG) or unless they were in a position to repay the debt.

It was important on the back of this to get some kind of financial prospectus and information pack from Hearts. How could FOH, or any potential bidder for that matter, produce a credible proposal without such information. Fiona agreed that she would prepare a full data pack within the week. I would have to sign a non-disclosure agreement. That was progress despite my continued reservations that the information would not provide the clarity we needed.

FOH was making progress. We agreed a large number of action points and reaffirmed the aims of the working groups. The main focus for the coming days would be to update the current 2,400 pledgers and devise a marketing and communications strategy for increasing those numbers. A lot of work would have to be done to convert them into actual cash payments. That would involve a wholesale revision to the FOH website, governance and public facing social media channels. The mantra was pledgers, pledgers, pledgers. That was all that really mattered.

Events had continued to move forward at a rapid pace. The coming together of the fan groups sent a message that there was now a positive and clear aim of bringing the ownership of Hearts into the hands of the fans. The Hearts Board had moved their position quite substantially to recognise FOH.

We were honest with the fans that this would not be an easy road, and the journey would take time. The rewards, though, would be historic. Hearts supporters had demonstrated time and time again that their loyalty and commitment to the club was unquestionable.

There had been a lot of maroon water under the bridge since FOH was first established in 2010. In early May 2013, it was rejuvenated and preparing a bid that had the potential to allow it to achieve its initial objective – a majority shareholding in Heart of Midlothian Football Club owned by the supporters – distinguished by values such as integrity and transparency. I believed we could achieve that and I was determined to make it happen...

CHAPTER 9

Budgein' the Figures

THE FOH WAS up and running. We had a target date to bid for the club. We had a united group of supporter organisations and a rough plan. The main task would be to harness the power of the fan base by communicating the vision and purpose of FOH. We would have to reiterate the dire situation at Hearts whilst selling the benefits of supporter ownership. This was now in our hands. There would be no credible alternative to save Hearts. FOH was the only show in town.

FOH being the only option was going to be a complicated sell to both the fans and the owners. There were a number of potential suitors who had expressed a very public interest in pursuing a purchase. The fans had been fed a diet of hope from those groups for a number of months. The most prominent were Italian Angelo Massone and a group of Norwegians who were being represented in Scotland by an organisation called Crest Sports run by a Kai Isaksen. There was also the inimitable Bob Jamieson and others.

Of course, Lord Foulkes and I were still in constant contact with Barry Cole and his colleagues, and we always hoped that one of the plethora of leads we had may come to fruition but it was unlikely. I recall reading Jambos Kickback shortly after the initial FOH statement on my appointment and it was peppered with comments such as 'Don't worry, the Norwegians will come in and save the club' and 'FOH won't work as there are too many others looking to buy the club'. This was a real danger. To be fair, Jambos Kickback was exceptionally helpful. Ron Ross, who co-runs the site, fast tracked a username and password for me. 'Ian Murray – FOH Ind Chair' would be used to communicate through the forum. I posted as much as I could on there. I also did live Q&As and got them involved in pretty much everything FOH was doing. It was a superb resource for finding out what supporters were thinking and saying. It wasn't always positive. I never expected it to be. It was, however, crucial. They weren't just a great information outlet, but they raised tens of thousands of pounds for Hearts over many years.

Their part in keeping Hearts afloat and rebuilding should never be underestimated, despite some of their more challenging posters.

What we decided to do as a group was fourfold. Firstly, to set up a marketing group to update the existing 2,400 pledgers, creating a plan to communicate with the wider supporter base to increase these numbers and develop messaging for FOH. Secondly, to create a governance group to look at making FOH fit for purpose, including all the necessary legal documentation. Thirdly, to form a finance unit to research the best way to convert pledges to direct debits, assist in the formation of financial projections and look at tax and regulatory matters. Fourthly, to construct a small bid group that would generate the offer for the club and take forward the negotiations with the Lithuanian owners.

We were all very impatient. We wanted to complete everything the day before yesterday. There was a danger that if we went too fast too soon, we may get things wrong and lose the trust of the supporters. We had one chance at getting this right. Running before we could crawl could jeopardise the entire project. That led to the postponement of the idea that we would hold supporters' meetings to outline FOH. We weren't ready and the number of questions that supporters would rightly raise would not have adequate answers. We decided to concentrate on communications.

I asked for volunteers for each of the working groups but wanted to put together as strong a team as possible. The marketing group consisting of Bill Alves, Alastair Bruce, Lawrence Broadie, Garry Halliday and Dougie Masterton. They set about developing a communications plan for the supporters. A more eclectic bunch you couldn't find for the marketing group but each and every one of them brought different skills and a range of perspectives. Garry was always seen as the voice of the fans, Alastair the professional marketer, Lawrence for campaigns and media experience, Bill for his angle from the existing shareholders and Dougie Masterton from his previous experience of how the SoH campaign communicated with fans back in 2005.

The initial media generated a huge amount of traffic to the FOH website. The preliminary 2,400 pledgers had swelled to 3,200 by the time we sent the first communication. It was a clear and concise message. The club was in severe trouble. The fan groups had all come together through FOH to prepare a bid for the club. Their pledge was an integral part of that process. We would be putting in place a system for that pledge to be drawn down in the near future. Critically, we were asking the 3,200 fans, who had already committed to the project, to become ambassadors for spreading the word.

The very fact they were on board already meant they at least considered owning the club and were willing to commit their funds to achieve that.

It was utterly remarkable that of the 3,200 emails that were issued to this group, only three unsubscribed. Hibs fans in disguise perhaps? The geographical spread was also very significant. Obviously, the vast majority came from Edinburgh, the Lothians and Fife but there were also a large number of pledgers from all over the United Kingdom, Europe and further afield.

One of the questions we were constantly asking ourselves was what our target was for the number of pledgers, how much they would be willing to give and how that could be formulated into a bid for the club. There was some information available as the initial FOH website allowed individuals to select the monthly amount they would be willing to pledge. The average from the 3,200 was just over £15 per month. I did a rough spreadsheet based on the fact that there were 8,500 current season ticket holders and 4,200 had participated in the share issue the previous year. That should give us some guide as to the potential of what could be raised. When I look back at that spreadsheet (or figures on the back of a cigarette packet), it seems to have been pretty accurate. I thought we could get 5,000 pledgers at £13.50 per month with another 500 at £500 per year (£41.66 per month) and a top end of 50 people at £5,000 per year (£416.66 per month). That would give a total annual contribution to the FOH cause of just over £1.3 million per annum. We decided that we would move forward with an annual revenue raising target of £1.5 million. That would break down to approximately 6,000 individual pledgers at an average monthly contribution of £20 per month. Any large net worth contributions would be a bonus.

Given that ūkio Bankas was already in liquidation and UBIG would be following shortly afterwards, we had to try and determine what the ūkio liquidators would accept for their 29.9 per cent stake. That stake was part of the security on the £15 million debt along with the stadium and other assets. We would have to get an undertaking that the 50 per cent of Hearts shares that were held by UBIG would come across to FOH as part of this deal. Given there was no security on debts owed to UBIG, nor any inherent value in their shares given the secured position of ūkio Bankas, that, whilst a problem, was not insurmountable.

The price that we were willing and able to pay for Hearts would be something the bid team would have to analyse and prepare. Remember, at this stage in May 2013, the club was not in administration and was still operating as a going concern.

That led to the formation of a formal bid team. It was agreed by the FOH Board that it would be beneficial to have this team sit outside the new FOH structure. It would be best if it was led by someone who was not on the FOH Board and be populated by people with suitable corporate and business experience. It was obvious that the bid team should be a continuation of some of the specialist advisors that the FOH had been utilising. It was agreed that I would approach Ann Budge and ask if she would lead this team.

I first met Ann shortly after being appointed Chair of FOH. She had been involved to a greater or lesser extent in the project since 2011 when she was introduced to the idea through her expertise in technology. I was keen to introduce myself, get her views on what she thought was the best way forward, if she would be willing to continue to advise, and would be willing to head up the bid team. I met with her in Café Andaluz on George Street in Edinburgh. She was a total breath of fresh air. I had done a little research before our meeting and I was expecting a ruthless businesswoman who has had to work twice as hard as any man to get her to the top of her profession. I was instantly struck by the combination of her enormous experience and formidable business knowledge alongside her friendly approach, calmness and warmth. She also had a visible passion for Hearts that had been cultivated from taking her daughter, Carol, to games. She married into Hearts through her former husband. He had started to take her daughter to the matches when she was about eight years old. That was in the very early 1980s. Some 12 years later, Carol bought her a ticket saying, 'Its high time you came to Tynecastle. You don't know what you're missing.' From that moment on, Ann was hooked on Hearts, despite every other member of her family supporting Hibs!

As I saw it, one of her strongest attributes was her ability to set a strategy and appoint the right people to fulfil it. Two such people she involved who would be key players in the success of FOH were Robert Wilson and Kevin Windram.

I was keen to hear Ann's take on the FOH strategy and people involved. I knew she had been a regular attendee at previous FOH meetings. She would have an opinion on the people sitting around the table and if that combination could deliver a successful outcome. I had developed some of my own views in the few direct interactions I had with the group and the conversations with others. There were obvious tensions between FOH Directors that needed to be addressed and it was clear that there was historical baggage that some were intending to carry into every discussion. The politics of FOH were more complicated and deep-rooted than that of Westminster and that is saying something. Given her talent at surrounding herself with the best people, I would need the help of Ann to understand and resolve these issues.

My meeting with Ann was very successful. She was delighted to continue her advisory role and committed to leading the bid team. This was very much her 'cup of tea'. This was about pulling a business plan together and working out a strategy – all the things she was most comfortable with. It wasn't really about football, per se, at that point. It was about an exciting project. She also wanted both Robert Wilson and Kevin Windram on this team. In addition, myself, Brian Cormack and Henry Snedden would represent the FOH Board. Ann would chair the bid team and be given a free hand to adjust it as she saw fit. I would be the Vice Chair should Ann not be available. It would be professionally supported by a close friend of Robert's, John Reid, who was a Partner at Deloitte LLP and an expert in company restructuring. He could assist in the analysis of the current market conditions in preparing a realistic bid and the shape of it.

The bid team worked very well together under Ann's guidance. Robert was superb at asking challenging questions and testing proposals to breaking point. I was a big fan of Robert. He was a huge thinker and had one of the sharpest brains and brightest intellects of anyone I have ever met or ever will be likely to meet. He was resolute, a dyed-in-the-wool Hearts fan and placed everything he did on his considerable credibility and undiminished integrity. He was direct and always honest. If he didn't like or wanted to question something, he would be robust. One of his main qualities though was to challenge, debate, hear an opposing point of view and then change his mind as an outcome of the discussion. That was what made his advice so powerful. Having someone of the calibre of Robert on the bid team and advising FOH was a real coup.

Robert had been involved in the FOH as an advisor since 2011. He was recommended to Ann by a mutual friend. He had been recently diagnosed with Motor Neuron Disease (MND) and had taken early retirement as a Partner of Deloitte to spend more time with his family and friends. Ann approached him to assist with FOH strategy. He got involved without hesitation.

MND is a terrible condition. It describes a group of diseases that affect the nerves (motor neurons) in the brain and spinal cord that tell your muscles what to do. With this condition, messages from the motor neurons gradually stop reaching the muscles. This leads the muscles to weaken, stiffen and waste. MND can affect how you walk, talk, eat, drink and breathe. It is terminal and there is no cure. Although the disease will progress, symptoms can be managed to help achieve the best possible quality of life. However, MND affects everyone differently and Robert didn't know how it would affect him or how quickly. When we first met in early May 2013, he was still independent, but his mobility was weakening, and you could see his health deteriorating. Over the next few months, he would be confined to a wheelchair and rely on his wonderful close family to deliver and collect him from meetings. Despite this, it never affected his sharp intellect and he was a powerful force behind FOH and the rebuilding of Hearts.

Sadly, Robert would pass away of the disease a few short years later in August 2016 whilst serving on the Board of Hearts. One of his legacies, and there are a glittering number, would be the pivotal role he played in the saving his beloved team. His contribution to the success of FOH and indeed to the rebuilding of Hearts should never be underestimated or forgotten. In paying tribute to Robert. Ann said:

> Robert was one of the main driving forces behind FOH. He became my closest confidante, helping us to develop the strategy and indeed helping us put together the financial plan that would lead to the success of the offer.

And he certainly was.

One of Robert's critical interventions was his professional evaluation of the complicated ownership situation at Hearts. After a detailed meeting with him and Ann in the Sheraton Hotel in Edinburgh, he produced an analysis that would determine the road map to a bid for the club. The road map concluded that FOH had to plan on the basis of an administrator seeking to realise as near to the value of the one major asset – the stadium. That would be given a rough valuation of circa £5 million, although there is always a possibility in property assets of securing it for less than that if there are no other interested parties. Based on that, he concurred that there was an urgent need for the marketing group to focus on both immediate one-off donations as well as regular monthly contributions. There should be a publicly stated short-term fundraising target of £5 million to focus attention.

Clearly, the £5 million target would be an enormous challenge and we would need to explore all avenues of potential capital funding in addition to the fans' regular contributions. Those avenues would leave no stone unturned and include the consideration of an approach to the City of

Edinburgh Council to see if it would be possible for them to extend a loan to FOH for the purchase of the stadium. That loan could be paid back over time. This would have significant political implications for the Council, but it would sit alongside an economic appraisal showing the serious potential economic downside for the local Gorgie community and wider Edinburgh area if Hearts disappeared. The bid team was of the view that a credible proposal could be put to the Council and that was what would be done.

As well as the Council, we would explore the potential for business loans from the traditional banking industry. These would prove more complicated as FOH had no trading history and football was not an industry that was favoured by any of the major banks. They had all been burned both financially and politically from previous dealings with football clubs. They were hugely nervous about getting into that sector again. However, a simple property mortgage may have been a possibility and that would be explored.

Then there were private individuals and investors. Could we persuade a wealthy individual to take the risk on helping FOH with a capital sum that would be repaid over time or was there any possibility of finding an organisation or business that would simply lend FOH the money on commercial terms?

This type of capital raising model was something that Barry had advocated previously and one in which he and Ann would briefly discuss as a feasible way forward. Barry also had constructive conversations with John at Deloitte.

But there was a major stumbling block in all of the financial discussion. It would be relatively easy to put together a proposition that sought the £5 million capital sum on a commercial basis. The terms may not be as generous as for sectors or businesses that would be assessed as more secure but was it achievable? You lend me £5 million repayable over ten years at a negotiated interest rate. If FOH defaulted on those repayments, the stadium would be secured against the debt. Therefore, the loan would be secured against the assets. The bigger problem was that of working capital for Hearts.

The financial position of the club in May 2013 was not positive. The projections that had been provided to us by Fiona showed that there was a revenue requirement of approximately £1.5 million per year. That would mean that should FOH take ownership of Hearts, it would have to find £1.5 million in the first year to keep it afloat. That would be on top of any repayments required to repay the £5 million capital loan to purchase the club.

The breakeven was £1.5 million more than Hearts was generating. Kevin, being a professional in corporate finance, had taken on the task of poring over the club's finances. Kevin's examination of the figures confirmed that FOH would have to find £1.5 million in the first year and there would be a cash flow problem that would crystallise as early as the end of August 2013. He also made the assumption that the revenue of the club would fall as it was likely that administration would happen resulting in a points deduction and probable relegation. It was important not to sugar coat the circumstances the club were in. All revenues had to be based on being in the second tier Championship League and not the Premiership, perhaps for more than one year.

These figures were not overwhelming for the bid team or FOH. We knew we had to generate up to £1.5 million a year in revenue and that we had to develop a long-term plan for Hearts over the following three to five years. That plan would look at how to grow revenues, place the club on a solid financial footing and make it break even without the additional support of FOH contributions. We fundamentally believed it would be possible to cover the additional working capital requirements of some £1.5 million per annum over the first three years from monthly FOH contributions whilst a sustainable model was being implemented. It would be a tall order but the working capital requirements would be an unquestionable element for any purchaser of the club. The figures were there for all to see and confirmed to us by Kevin. Any bidder for Hearts who did not recognise this requirement would be short-lived. The question for FOH was whether those fans who pledged would be content for their monthly contributions to be used to plug a hole in Hearts finances for what may be a lengthy period.

What Kevin was also able to do was provide some clarity about the factual position. There had always been an element of guessing by piecing together annual accounts and talking to those at the club, but nothing was ever clear enough for a formal bid. We were able to confirm that, at that time in mid-May 2013, Hearts' debt stood at £24.7 million. This consisted of £15 million to ūkio Bankas, secured against the stadium, and a call on 29.9 per cent of Hearts shares from UBIG's total 79.9 per cent. The stadium and 29.9 per cent would be called in as ūkio Bankas was in liquidation proceedings. On top of this, £9.7 million was due to UBIG who were holding 50 per cent of Hearts' shares.

Kevin was also able to confirm that the debt Hearts owed was secured until June 2015 on an interest only basis at £45,000 per month. The club Board were negotiating with the liquidators of ūkio Bankas a debt write-off/

write down to maximise their 29.9 per cent shareholding. In essence, it was worthless whilst there was a risk that Hearts would fold.

We heard a rumour that the current owners were looking at this as a way to negotiate a complete debt write off to allow the shares to be transferred to them. This would be a tall order for them, but it did give us some figures to work from in terms of the value of the club overall. They were looking to put in a cash injection of £1.5 million to cover the club's funding shortfall for the financial year from 1 June 2013 to 31 May 2014 in return for a proportion of UBIG's worthless 50 per cent shareholding. Therefore, the existing club owners could plug the annual £1.5 million funding gap for half of UBIG shares and then use that as a price indicator for the £15 million debt they were owed. In essence, you'd get the club for £3 million in that scenario.

The bid team also made the decision that it would be prudent to deal directly with the Valnetas and UBIG rather than the current Lithuanian owners. They would soon be gone.

A recurring debate was whether any FOH revenue streams could be directed to the club to prevent it from going into administration. This had to be discounted as an idea. It would be impossible and almost immoral to ask the fans again for more financial support merely to prop up the club and its current owners. Everything would be done by both the club and FOH to avoid administration, but it would not be a reasonable proposition if administration was a matter of 'when' rather than 'if'.

The major positive was that things were starting to develop on the way forward. By mid-May 2013, FOH had amassed 3,300 pledgers at an average of £21 per month. We were more than half way to our 6,000 target and these numbers were growing at almost 200 per week. Given the marketing plan hadn't really kicked in as yet, we were pleased with progress.

A major part of the strategy was to set up a short life working group that would look at how to convert these pledges to cash. The group would be led by HYDC's Chair, Calum Robertson, and have Andy Grant for his financial experience, Alasdair Bruce for website and technical assistance and Alex. Henry was also a member of this group but only to lend support to Calum in our efforts to persuade Alex to drop his idea of standing orders and to seriously explore the GoCardless concept. Once these objectives were achieved, Henry took a backseat. He was busy enough on the legal and governance matters. It would be supported by Richard as he had done this with

St Mirren (although never got to the point of drawing down pledges) and involve FOH bankers, Clydesdale Bank.

If I thought that governance was going to be a long, controversial and drawn out problem, then this process was certainly the worst by a considerable margin. The frustrating aspect was that there weren't really very many options available and these options were further limited by the need to make the process as automated and simple as possible. We couldn't deal in cash for obvious reasons, so it came down to either a standing order system or direct debit. I never thought a debate about which payment method to use would generate such heated and deep-rooted views. In hindsight, I don't think the issue was actually anything to do with which system to use. It seemed that this was the area on which the tensions in the FOH Board were channelled and magnified.

It really did lead to all sorts of problems to the extent that outside journalists got involved. I guess they were being briefed privately and some were using their contacts to push their own views. It certainly didn't help that Richard, who had made an undisputable pitch for an online and automated direct debit system, was on the Board at St Mirren.

One of the early instances that I had to deal with was a very public spat on social media between *The Guardian* sports reporter and avid Hearts fan, Ewan Murray, and SDS about the involvement of Richard as their representative. I've never been able to find the genesis of such angst, but it seemed to rotate around Richard's Directorship at St Mirren and whether that was a conflict of interest. Regardless of the arguments for and against such accusations, we were comfortable with his involvement and grateful for the vast knowledge he brought to FOH. He had recent experience in trying to achieve a similar supporter ownership objective for St Mirren fans. Richard was solely involved to help FOH prepare their bid by giving up his own time in order to provide strategic counsel to FOH and, for that matter, all other clubs in Scotland who may want to examine this as a potential route.

There was a turgid and often heated discussion where it was agreed that any system had to make it as simple as possible for fans to pledge, be cost effective, allow lump sums, allow control to draw down funds at a specific date and allow funds to be easily returned. The GoCardless scheme was introduced to the group by Richard and it seemed to be exactly what we were looking for. Alex was hell bent on an alternative manual standing order system, his argument being that it gave the user maximum control over the amount pledged, cancellation, reinstatement and low cost. There was no argument as to what each system delivered, and it was the case that GoCardless was unproven in the football arena. I never thought it possible that we could have a situation where we were aiming for 6,000 members and we would have to securely store individual paper forms! To give comfort to both the FOH Board and GoCardless, Calum and Lawrence hosted their senior team for a match at Tynecastle. It would allow them to get a much better idea of what we were trying to achieve and also provide FOH with the confidence that this could be done. The system was already being used by *The Times* for subscription purposes and other major brands. We just needed it to work on a much larger and faster scale for FOH.

It was agreed that Calum would produce a report on the use of GoCardless. Some within FOH remained resolute that standing orders were a far better option. We all disagreed. However, once the working group had fully explored the evidence and the various alternatives, it was clear that the 'fall out rate' from standing orders would be much higher. The outcome was that the GoCardless direct debit system would be put in place for UK bank account holders. There was going to be an issue with international supporters, but Andy had used the PayPal recurring payments system before, so we adopted this for that purpose. We would have a very small number of other mechanisms for those that did not have a bank account or online access. That way we could automate the process of turning the pledges we had received into monthly cash amounts.

The process the FOH Board and working group went through to make this critical but simple decision was extraordinary. The chemistry of the FOH Board was not good. To say it was often fractious was an understatement. All the advice and stories Lawrence had told me about previous meetings were all now being played out in front of my eyes. To a certain extent, it wasn't helped by the growing number of people attending FOH Board meetings. Some of the working groups had, not unreasonably, sought other assistance and they were attending Board meetings to give their feedback. Often, though, they would take one of the two sides that formed: the 'founding five' Directors of FOH or the five new FOH supporter group Directors. It was like a five-a-side grudge match every meeting.

I had to constantly remind everyone that all eyes had to stay on the only prize which was to save our beloved football club. Raking over the coals of previous meetings and communications going back years was neither constructive nor productive. In fact, I am sure meetings would have lasted half the time had we kept discussions focused on the points in hand.

It was sometimes easier to take action points out of the formal Board process. Henry had finalised his report on the governance, legal and existing website. He recommended that everything had to be radically overhauled and simplified before being released to supporters. We wanted to publish and release formal documents at the beginning of June and try to get the direct debit system in place by July. That was not going to be easily achieved at the Board and it had to be done quickly. Given the impasse on these issues at the FOH Board, myself and Henry met in the Beanscene coffee bar one Sunday morning and between us, with the help of Henry's dilapidated laptop, we wrote the framework of the revised aims and objectives and material for the website. These would be circulated and discussed at the next FOH Board meeting.

I couldn't believe we had just got it done. Henry was so good at wanting to get things done. He also had 50 years of being a fan and that drove him. He wanted to ensure that there were no hostages to fortune in any public communications or documents released by FOH. His attitude was that if someone asked him if they should give their money to FOH, he would want to be able to confidently reply, 'How could you not?' He wanted to secure the future of the club and the best chance of that being achieved was through FOH.

We now had a members' agreement, revised website, draft aims and objectives and alterations to the existing governance documents. I don't know what they put in the coffee at Beanscene but Henry and I managed to do months of work that had been stalling the discussions at the FOH Board in one long afternoon.

That was where the interconnection with the collection system and the website was developed. We considered it essential that the FOH website needed to deliver a short, sharp and clear message outlining our aims to all Hearts fans. Vitally it had to encourage them to instantly sign up to make donations online. This meant being able to click through to a direct debit option directly from the website. GoCardless would allow that process to happen with a bit of technical wizardry from Alastair's web development team at Shaw Marketing.

Throughout this process, Lord Foulkes and I were still working away in the background to ensure FOH had the best chance of success. We also wanted to verify the processes that were in train with ūkio Bankas, UBIG, the Lithuanian institutions and the footballing authorities. To that end, we met with the Lithuanian Ambassador again in Parliament and impressed upon her that the situation for her country would be very negative if they were to let Hearts die. She understood the significance although never gave too much away: the ultimate professional diplomat. We made representations in the strongest possible terms and hoped that these would be fed back to the relevant people in Lithuania. We were absolutely sure they would. She was fabulous.

We had been keeping stakeholders informed of progress which led us to the SFA Chief Executive, Stewart Regan, and SFA President, a certain former Chair of Hearts, Campbell Ogilvie. We went to Hampden late one Friday afternoon in mid-May 2013 to seek clarity on how the footballing authorities would treat this process and if there were any levers they could pull to help. It was a strange experience. I had never been in the SFA corridors of power before and didn't really know what to expect. I remember pulling into the Hampden car park with Lord Foulkes and thinking back to the previous year when we hammered Hibs to win the cup.

To be fair, Stewart Regan and Campbell Ogilvie listened intently to the current position at Hearts, the plight of ūkio Bankas and UBIG and the plan by FOH to take it into supporter ownership. We also discussed who would be a 'fit and proper person' to own a football club and how those rules would interact with some of the potential other purchasers. Their conclusions were that they would have to wait and see developments but there were rules and regulations on what happens to member clubs who enter administration and/or liquidation. Until that insolvency event, they would not be in a position to make a judgement. I did feel as though they were all still very sore from the Rangers experience and they would take a very cautious and rules-based approach to anything that would happen to Hearts. I suppose that was always going to be the case. We couldn't blame them for that. They did emphasise, however, what we already knew – that it would be in the best short- and long-term interests of Hearts to complete the 2012/13 football season in full as that would make the situation easier to resolve.

There was huge interest in what FOH was doing. The press and media calls were being fielded expertly by Lawrence. We were controlling the story so that we could maximise the pledges coming in. I was surprised at the response I got when I attended the Sports Writers Annual Dinner in Glasgow. Everyone from Gordon Strachan to Archie Macpherson was keen to ask about the progress FOH was making and to pass on their good wishes. The only fly in the media ointment was the FOH Twitter feed. Too many people had access to it. That meant we didn't have it under control. It all came to a head when the official FOH feed tweeted out an advert for the annual Hearts Willie Bauld Memorial Dinner. We received a very large number of complaints as FOH was seen to endorse a male-only event, an event that hit the headlines the year before for not allowing women to attend. Lawrence and I had to sort this out but, again, it knocked a few noses out of joint.

Just as well then that I got a good news text from David late in the evening on Saturday 18 May, after Hearts drew one each at Aberdeen on the last day of the season. Hearts had made it to the end of the football season. It simply said, 'Good news today Ian. SPL it is for next season.' That was fundamental to Hearts survival as they weren't yet in administration. The players and fans could go away for their summer break, but would they have a team to support at the start of season 2013/14?

CHAPTER 10

A Pint for £2.50?

HEARTS HAD MADE it to the end of the Premier League campaign, but no one was under any illusions that the closed season would be tough. The club management, supporters, players and staff were all hanging together. This togetherness was one of the few positives.

We were into June 2013 and working very hard to convert the maximum number of pledges by the start of July. This would coincide with the submission of our bid. At the start of June, we were all buoyed by the news that we had broken through the 4,000 barrier. To celebrate, Lawrence came up with the idea of inviting all four goal scorers from the 2012 William Hill Scottish Cup Final win over city rivals Hibernian to pledge to support the cause.

We were absolutely delighted to announce shortly afterwards that Rudi Skácel, Danny Grainger, Darren Barr and Ryan McGowan had given their backing to FOH by becoming pledgers themselves. It was a massive boost. The power of the 2012 Cup win was immense and the impact on the marketing campaign of having hero Rudi Skácel could not be quantified. It was a master stroke of marketing that really saw pledges fly. It was almost as influential as members of the famous 1998 Cup winning team. The press ran headlines, 'The French Connection backs the Foundation'. It was another positive twist when two of Hearts' great Cup heroes pledged their support. Stéphane Adam, who netted the decisive goal in the 2-1 over Rangers, had been joined by compatriot and idol goalkeeper, Gilles Rousset, in vowing their unconditional backing.

To coincide with this news, we decided to go forward with the organisation of a large fan meeting. This would take place on Friday 14 June. We would hope to have some Hearts stars of the past in attendance to help with the message. Alongside this, all FOH Directors were dispatched around the country to get the message out to as many supporters as possible.

The drawdown of pledges by the creation of a direct debit scheme was also in full flow. The work was now a technical exercise and was in the hands of Alastair, Darren and Gordon Murray from his team at Shaw Marketing. In just a few short weeks, we had reached a milestone in the history of our club.

We still had our target of 30 June to submit a formal offer for Hearts and this would be followed in early July with the first drawdown of formal pledges through the GoCardless system. We had set ourselves a very ambitious target of launching the system on Wednesday 19 June – ironically, although we didn't know this at the time, the day Hearts went into administration.

Discussions with other groups were also ongoing. A consortium emerged led by former SRU Chief Executive, Gordon McKie. It was very interesting indeed. They were keen to provide the capital sum to buy the club in partnership with FOH. We would then use the revenue generated from pledges as working capital to keep the club on a break-even basis whilst it was rebuilt. Their investors were also comfortable with looking at supporter ownership in the longer term. Gordon was great to deal with. He was always straightforward. He did most of his initial dealings through long term Hearts fan, Stephen Paterson, who was the corporate finance director at Haines Watts. His colleague and ardent Hearts supporter, Fraser Kerr, was also involved. This was a serious team with serious ideas and the resources to make a credible bid for the club.

I always maintained that one of three outcomes was possible: FOH could buy the club; FOH could do it with someone else; or someone else could buy the club. I, along with the FOH Board, was obviously championing majority supporter ownership but we would have settled for whatever was in the long-term interests of the club. We wouldn't stand in the way of that. Gordon knew this and so did the others who were serious about making a formal bid. I met Gordon on a number of occasions and he even presented his idea to the FOH Board. We had a straightforward attitude that we didn't have all of the wisdom and if there were other interested parties then we would assist them. This was about the future of the club, not about FOH.

Another important aspect of the process was getting access to the club's extensive database. They had over 48,000 active email addresses of people who had recently bought a ticket or interacted with the club in some way. Getting the FOH message out to them would give the pledges a significant boost. The sticking point was that the club didn't want to be favouring one potential bidder over another. David was keen to do it but we had to negotiate how. After a number of discussions, we agreed a way forward. The club would have to control the statement but could put it out jointly from FOH and the club. This would achieve two objectives: firstly, it would encourage fans to continue to support the club in the normal way by buying season tickets and merchandise and, secondly, it would endorse the FOH as having the best interests of the club at heart. The message would encourage supporters to go to the FOH website for more information. If we could have the GoCardless system up and running by the time the email was sent, we could gain a large number of new pledgers.

This would be accompanied by a magnificent information booklet that Alastair and his team worked up. I'm not sure who came up with the marketing strapline, 'Own the history. Shape the future.' but it was inspired. If I was pushed, I would give the credit to Garry Halliday. It summed up perfectly what we were asking the supporters to do.

The front of the brochure had a black and white grainy photograph of Hearts captain, Freddie Glidden, lifting the Scottish Cup at Hampden in 1956. That was the proud history we were proposing the supporters owned. It was right to raise the excitement levels of those interested in participating in the project through emotive pictures of Hearts' past successes and messages of support from heroes from bygone eras like Donald Ford. It also laid out clearly what we were for. The FOH had seven key principles of supporter ownership:

- Democratic member control
- Voluntary and open membership
- Member economic participation
- Autonomy and independence
- Education, training and information
- Co-operation among co-operatives
- Concern for the local community

The brochure contained a quote from each of the FOH Directors about what Hearts meant to us. We were trying to demonstrate that all fans were in this together. We wanted to communicate the message that the next steps in the history of the club were going to be taken by all of us together. It was only togetherness that would ensure that the next time we all sang 'This is my story, this is my song', we would have written a new chapter in the story of Hearts.

My favourite quote was given by Jane Lewis. She wrote:

I became involved in the Foundation of Hearts because I couldn't sit back and watch the club I love go down the tubes and wonder if there was something I could have done to prevent it. No great changes are ever made by people sitting on their hands and hoping for the best... There is no white knight, so it is up to us, as supporters, to go into battle for our club.

Jane's comments really hit home to me when I was lucky enough to play on the hallowed turf. The UK Parliamentary Football Team had arranged an end of season charity match against the Scottish Parliament. We played it at Tynecastle. That was all my dreams coming true but all I could think about was what Jane had written for the brochure. What if, in actual fact, the last football match to be played at Tynecastle was this one? It wasn't worth thinking about. Whilst others were warming up and preparing excitedly for the match, I just looked around the empty stadium and up to where I had sat with my brother since the Wheatfield stand was erected: section F, row 11, seats 21 and 22. I just stared at it and replayed some of the most wonderful moments we had experienced from 'our' seats. It was quite an emotional few moments. We lost 3-2 and I was as jealous as I had ever been that my Scottish Labour colleague, Neil Bibby MSP, scored a couple of goals.

After that game, the gravity of what I had taken on hit me hard. I was very pleased with the pace of progress but we were not in control of what was becoming an increasingly complicated process. It seemed like every time we managed to take a few steps forward we would take a couple back.

However, we did have a major breakthrough with who we were dealing with in Lithuania. The Romanov regime was all but finished. We would deal directly with Valnetas who were seeking to sell Hearts on behalf of ūkio Bankas. We had got information from the Lithuanian Ambassador a few weeks previously. I received an email from the law firm in Lithuania working on the bankruptcy of ūkio Bankas and directly on the Hearts project. Deimantė Korsakaitė would become a significant player in the saving of Hearts and it was superb to have a person to communicate with directly.

My main questions to Deimantė were around timescales and if they were going to sell the assets of the club for a lump sum. I also needed to know if they would be accepting of a fans' bid that paid for the assets over a period of time. She recommended that FOH provide alternative bids with the two options. She would then discuss and assess the bids with the bankruptcy administrators team.

She did advise something absolutely critical. I inquired about whether she had control over the club's shares. Her response was to the point, 'We do not have the control over shares.' That meant she was merely looking to maximise the value of the stadium they had a security over and that would leave FOH with two options: either an agreement is reached and the shareholders (UBIG) cooperate with ūkio Bankas and sell their shares; or we would proceed with the sale as an asset deal meaning sale of the club as a going concern.

Deimantė concluded, 'The issues are yet not clear.' What was clear was that she didn't technically have the power to sell the club. That power still resided with the Board of UBIG. It was all over for UBIG but that didn't necessarily make the situation for Hearts any surer.

The legal position of UBIG hadn't been settled. This would buy us a little bit of time. Robert had been proven right. All of this process would be dictated by the value of the single stadium asset and the shares would have to follow.

In early June, we set some pretty ambitious milestones in order to push the project ahead. The most challenging of those ambitions was to convert the existing pledgers to monthly direct debits via the GoCardless system and take the first payment on 4 July. I knew this was going to be tight but if we were going to submit a bid by 30 June, we would have to build considerable confidence in FOH and the financial resources. After all, none of this process was going to be cheap to achieve. Legal fees alone would be substantial.

There was another unknown factor: the club could go into administration at any time. There were rumours that HMRC was on the verge of submitting another winding up order after Hearts failed to settle a £100,000 tax bill. The £100,000 was the outstanding amount from one of the annual scheduled payments of £500,000 that Hearts agreed with HMRC late in 2012.

There was a big problem looming with these decisions. What would happen to any cash collected if FOH were unsuccessful in purchasing the club? This question vexed us as the FOH Board. As soon as money started to come in from supporters, we would have to be accountable for it. We would also have to look at spending some of it. What we were asking of pledgers was to provide us with funds that would be used for the financing of the purchase of the majority shareholding in Hearts and, in the short- to medium-term, the funding support would be reinvested in the club for purposes to be determined by the members of FOH, for the betterment of Hearts.

These were two very restrictive purposes. They did not include using any of the money for the process of buying the club. All contributions were obviously an indicator of how much we could afford in terms of the bid, but they would also enable us to determine the level of additional funding for the day-to-day operations. Hearts had a massive financial black hole to plug. But we were conscious that we couldn't just spend the supporters' money on other things. We were getting a lot of pro bono support from some of the best professionals in the country, but we would have to spend some money in order to get any deal over the line.

These Board discussions were robust but very necessary. The fundamental principle was that any money the supporters contributed was for FOH to buy Hearts. We were not in a position either constitutionally or morally to fritter away large sums of other people's money if we were not going to be successful in that sole aim. Some on the Board rightly pointed out that the process of any bid and trying to achieve the sole aim would involve expenditure and this would be acceptable as long as we were upfront from the outset.

Did we need a proposition that indicated we could use initial funds for other legal and administrative costs should it be necessary? Should we say that we would go back to the pledgers if a deal is unsuccessful and give them options to have their money returned or donated to the club or an associated organisation like HYDC or Hearts charity, Big Hearts?

It was agreed that these were unnecessary complicating factors at this stage. The message to supporters had to remain clear. The only message should be that the aim is to purchase a majority controlling interest in the club and operate it sustainably. The rest, at this stage, would be detail that would merely distract from that message.

We pressed ahead with the objective that should the FOH be unsuccessful in achieving the ownership of the club, all funds would be returned minus any nominal bank transaction costs. This would be written into a members' agreement that would be issued to all pledgers. Given that we made this decision, it was decided that we would not draw down funds until we knew a deal was possible. However, given we were set up for the bid to go in we kept the pencilled 4 July drawdown date as a critical target to have the technical infrastructure ready. I did tell the supporters in a newspaper interview that:

> I can guarantee that, unless we are handed the keys to the door of the main stand, every single penny that has been pledged to us will be refunded.

If we were to maximise the understanding of FOH, the best way to answer many of the questions from fans about the future was to ensure that they knew that FOH was about them. It was a membership-led organisation in which every member was equally entitled to contribute. The make-up of the FOH Board would always be determined by a 'one member, one vote' system regardless of contribution. It had to be acknowledged that all the members would decide the direction of FOH. We were merely setting up the initial organisation to enable a successful bid but, in the future, it could be changed by its members. As an example, many had suggested they may be more inclined to give more if they got something back in terms of a percentage of shares etc. That was a discussion for the future but those democratic processes would have to be locked into the governance structure.

We were making great strides but there were always distractions. Some members of the FOH Board would overreach our remit. It took a number of weeks to try and prevent a lot of time being wasted in a negotiation with a potential benefactor to bring Rudi Skácel back to the club. It would not have cost the club or FOH any money, but it was just something that we shouldn't have been getting involved in. It was not the job of FOH to be considering such issues even if the anonymous funder had approached some of our Board members. There was also the irony, which wasn't lost on most of us, that before we even owned the club we would be interfering in the selection of players. The huge row we had as a Board to try and get this issue off the table nearly cause irreparable damage. Everyone was just trying to help, and we would be flooded with these types of issues in the coming months. I can't believe we were arguing over a player coming back to Hearts when there may not have been a club in a matter of weeks. It reminded Bryan Jackson of his time as Administrator of Dunfermline when he was about to lock the doors for the last time whilst someone was demanding a meeting about what pies they should use for the following football season.

As the FOH were progressing the plans for the formal bid, the club was preparing for the new football season. The manager, Gary Locke, who had been brought in that February following the departure of John McGlynn, was given a contract to the end of the following season. It was a poisoned chalice for Gary, but he gave everything and then some more to try and get a successful team on the pitch. I felt sorry for Gary as I was getting calls, emails and texts almost every other day from players and people associated with the club asking for more information on whether an administration was imminent. I struck up a fruitful relationship with former Hearts player and supporter, Allan Preston. He cared deeply for the club and was trying to help as a football agent. He had recommended Danny Wilson to Hearts but the deal was hanging by a thread. He did eventually sign but just a few days before the club would go into administration.

I felt sorry for the staff and the players at this time. We all tend to forget that players also have to pay their mortgages and a club going into administration can result in their contracts being declared void. Allan was a wise counsel on these issues. I was always grateful for his support.

The number of people who were willing to help was incredible. They weren't just giving support to me and the FOH but also to the club. It was extraordinary that in the space of under four years, the wage bill for the playing staff had gone from around £12.5 million to just under £1.5 million per year. That couldn't have been done without the dedicated Hearts family of people like Chief Scout, John Murray, the management team led by Gary and agents like Allan. They cared and that made up for the lack of resources.

You may find a wage bill for Hearts of below £1.5m astonishing. I know I did. However, without that process having been carried out over a number of years before administration, the impact of the formal administration would have been much more severe.

Gary would have to try and build a squad capable of competing in the Premiership. He would also have to contend with a 15-point deduction if an 'insolvency event' occurred at any point up to the end of the following season. The cards were stacked against him. That was compounded by another transfer ban imposed after Hearts failed to pay all their players' salaries at the end of May 2013.

We were making swift progress since I became Chair of FOH just six weeks previously. The focus of everyone associated with Hearts was engaged on ensuring the club was saved. Despite the several hundred emails between the members of the FOH Board, the undoubted strife, character clashes and conflict between founding Directors and the supporters Directors, the various groups were publicly working together harmoniously for the first time and, just as importantly, the club had shown a new receptiveness towards us.

The momentum was growing as we achieved new pledge milestones every week. That provided a real sense that we were preparing to enter a crucial phase in terms of converting pledges to cash and beginning the process of making a formal offer.

We had never really publicly verified what we were trying to do. We were set to test that at the fan meeting at Tynecastle on Friday 14 June.

Hearts Chairman
The Right Honourable
The Lord Foulkes of
Cumnock welcomes new
Hearts owner Vladimir
Romanov to Hearts.
© Edinburgh Evening News

Chairman George Foulkes with Chief Executive Phil
Anderton introducing George Burley as the new Hearts
manager. © SNS Group 2008 - All Rights Reserved

Hearts qualify for the Champions
League after a 1-0 win over
Aberdeen that secures 2nd place
in the Premier League. Romanov
with goalscorer Paul Hartley. © SNS
Group 2008 - All Rights Reserved

Hearts fans attend the first FOH meeting at Tynecastle on
14 June 2013. © Edinburgh Evening News

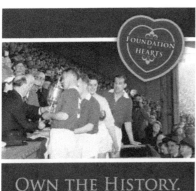

The front page of the FOH fans brochure. Courtesy of Foundation of Hearts

Ian Murray from FOH and Trevor Birch from BDO at Tynecastle shortly after Hearts went into administration. Courtesy of Foundation of Hearts

Hearts legend Dave McPherson with Ian Murray and Garry Halliday promoting FOH at Tynecastle. Courtesy of Foundation of Hearts

Hearts hero Rudi Skácel helping to promote the FOH cause after it was launched at Tynecastle a couple of months previously by FOH Chair Ian Murray. Courtesy of Foundation of Hearts

Ian Murray on the pitch with Eilidh Child and Scott Wilson at half-time in the Hearts v Aberdeen match on 24 August 2013. Hearts won 2-1. Courtesy of Lawrence Broadie

Actor and Hearts fan Ken Stott supporting FOH from New Zealand where he was filming *The Lord of the Rings*. He is shown in costume here as Balin. Courtesy of Foundation of Hearts

Actor and Hearts fan Ken Stott supporting FOH from New Zealand where he was filming *The Lord of the Rings*. Here he is not in costume. Courtesy of Foundation of Hearts

The week prior to FOH being named preferred bidder, the *Edinburgh Evening News* runs a front page to plead with Angelo Massone to stand aside. © Edinburgh Evening News

Craig Levein lending his support to FOH in a press conference at Tynecastle prior to becoming Hearts Director of Football. Courtesy of Lawrence Broadie

Hearts fans who won the Man of the Match raffle team up with singer/songwriter Colin Chisolm (centre) to record a new version of the Hearts song. Manager Gary Locke (centre right) and his assistant Billy Brown (centre left) help with the 'singing'. Courtesy of Foundation of Hearts

Ian Murray appears track-side with BT Sport presenter Darrell Currie and commentators Peter Grant and Michael Stewart at the end of the Hearts v Celtic match at Tynecastle on 14 September 2013. Courtesy of Lawrence Broadie

Bryan Jackson (left) arriving at Tynecastle for the CVA meeting with his PR consultant Colin Wright (right) and Keith Anderson (centre), solicitor with Morisons LLP. © Edinburgh Evening News

Bryan 'Scrooge' Jackson speaks to the press after the successful CVA meeting and 'cancels Christmas'. © SNS Group

Ann Budge takes her usual seat in the Wheatfield stand after being named as the businessperson behind the financing of the FOH bid. © Edinburgh Evening News

The *Edinburgh Evening News* carries a full page advert for FOH for a donation to their local charity appeal. © Edinburgh Evening News

FOH unveils the 8,000th new member in a press conference at Tynecastle. Derek Shade is with Hearts star Dylan McGowan. Courtesy of Lawrence Broadie

Robbie Neilson and Craig Levein share a light-hearted moment with Ann Budge on 'Budgement Day' as they are appointed Director of Football and Head Coach. © SNS Group

Alim Öztürk scores the equalising goal from 40 yards against Hibs in a 1-1 draw at Easter Road wearing FOH-sponsored Argentinian-style away kit. © SNS Group

Hearts Directors Ann Budge, Craig Levein, Ian Murray, Robert Wilson, Eric Hogg and Kevin Windram thank the fans at half-time v Queen of the South on gaining promotion to the Scottish Premier League. © SNS Group

Chief Executive Ann Budge and SFL Chief Executive Neil Doncaster unfurl the Championship flag at Tynecastle v Rangers on the last day of the 2014/15 season. © SNS Group

Garry Halliday's 'plot ceremonies' become a reality as dozens of FOH members attend the first event where they were presented with their ceremonial plot on the pitch and a certificate. © Edinburgh Evening News

Former cup-winning manager Paulo Sérgio sporting the official Hearts third kit including the names of all 8,000 members of the Foundation of Hearts. Courtesy of Lawrence Broadie

Hearts open the Memorial Garden at Tynecastle, paid for from a generous beqest from the estate of a fan who had passed away. © Edinburgh Evening News

FOH Chair Stuart Wallace hands CEO Ann Budge a cheque for £3 million from the supporters towards the new £15 million main stand at Tynecastle. © Edinburgh Evening News

New main stand at Tynecastle partly paid for with a £3 million contribution from FOH members. © Heart of Midlothian Football Club

The new Tynecastle Park. Hearts will be 79.9 per cent fan-owned by mid-2020. © Heart of Midlothian Football Club

A collage showing generations of supporters enjoying watching Hearts created by FOH. The club was saved by the fans for future generations. © Foundation of Hearts

Thanks to a £200 donation by the Federation of Hearts Supporters clubs, we were even able to hire a projector and sound system!

There was huge media interest in FOH by then. The club was in trouble and we were having to embark on a very public campaign for pledgers. Stuart Bathgate at *The Scotsman*, Barry Anderson at the *Edinburgh Evening News*, Brian Mclaughlin at the BBC and Gary Ralston at the *Daily Record* were hugely helpful and supportive at this time.

The fan meeting was a sell-out of over 300 tickets. The interesting thing was that a couple of dozen Hearts employees also asked to attend. We filled four tables with them alone given the interest in what may happen next. They were very welcome. The uncertainty around the club would be affecting them more than most. Ann also attended.

I would chair the meeting and it would be officiated by Willie Hunter who was a regular at entertaining the corporate crowds at home matches. Friend of Dougie Masterton and regular at assisting with the Marketing Group, Iain McLeod, would make the presentation as that was his professional forte. The rest of the FOH team would be in attendance to circulate and answer questions. We would also have iPads for people to sign up their pledge. It went really well.

Willie Hunter introduced the evening. I made some opening remarks about who we were, what we were trying to achieve and why it was critical that the supporters backed the FOH. There was a good chance, despite all the noise about other bidders, that we would be the only show in town. I explained that Hearts was virtually 'worthless' and that the impending insolvency facing ūkio Bankas and UBIG could work in FOH's favour.

From a hard-nosed business outlook, the club only has value in terms of its history, its share in the SPL and the assets that it holds. The people in that room and all supporters were the only ones who valued the history, share in the SPL and the assets. The supporters were in a tremendous position to buy the club.

Donald Ford could not attend but supplied a written statement that Willie Hunter read out. It hit all the right buttons:

> Across the entire breadth of the professional game in Scotland and, of a much more serious nature, within Tynecastle Park, recent events have dramatically underlined the frailty of Scottish football. It was against this background of desperately needed change that the Foundation of Hearts was created.

The thinking and planning which has been under way within the group has been comprehensive, exciting and, potentially, life changing – in terms of both diehard Hearts fans and the entire structure of the professional sport in Scotland. While removing the club from any further management by overly optimistic owners has been the Foundation's principle aim, a lot of excellent ideas have also been discussed which will be put to member clubs regarding the future state of the game in Scotland.

Most importantly, here at Tynecastle the position is now dire. The facts are that the company has been technically insolvent for several years and recovering the deficiencies of cash which have built up is impossible. In the current market place, *no* increase in income will ever be enough to make the slightest dent in the amount by which the debts of the club exceed its assets. In the current financial climate, borrowing from banks is both non-negotiable and unsupportable. The *only* possible solution is for a 'new' concern to take over control and run Hearts on an affordable annual budget.

If the Foundation plans can reach a stage of maturity with the clubs' supporters which would allow this to go ahead, there is an opportunity to a) revolutionise the ownership and running of the club b) begin the establishment of a wider base of youth football in Edinburgh and the Lothians to increase the feeding of the best players to Tynecastle and – crucially – c) present and urgently discuss the possible restoration of the game within Scotland to other member clubs before any more time is lost.

Much time has been – and is being – spent on the structure of a possible fan 'buyout'. This is clearly important, but the new shape of ownership still needs to display leadership as well as enjoying (and being aware of) input from the many groups which make up the HMFC support. While the new ownership should encompass *every* Hearts supporter, it is still essential that there should be integrity, honesty and leadership shown by the Board of Directors which is eventually appointed to restore fortunes at the club.

This is a defining moment in the club's long, illustrious history – and time is short. There are no guarantees that Foundation of Hearts can provide a magical solution to the current position of the company. With the right structure, courage and sound principles in both the financial and football development aspects of the club, however, the Foundation does have every chance of working. It is up to Hearts' supporters everywhere to grasp this – perhaps one and only – opportunity.

Iain then presented his PowerPoint presentation. He pulled every heartstring in the room. However, it was his final slide that really got to the point. We had all seen the presentation at the FOH Board and signed it off. Iain had slipped in a last slide of his own though. I was glad he did. He paused and looked around the audience and then dropped the bombshell. The last slide had a large pint glass full of beer emblazoned across it. It had the words, 'Would you let your club die for the cost of a pint of beer a week?' Suddenly, the £10 per month minimum pledge was put into context. It was a relatively inconsequential amount of money to help save Hearts.

I did the question and answer session and tried to respond to every point that was made. I was completely honest when I didn't have the answer and made that clear. My favourite question of the night came from an older man who I had noticed was listening intently all evening. I worried when Willie pointed at him to give his contribution. He said, 'I would like to take exception to something Iain McLeod said in his presentation.' I gulped. The evening had been going so well and I was about to get asked a question that we hadn't expected that had the potential to derail us all. Thankfully, we had asked the media who wanted to attend to stay for the start of the meeting but to leave before the main event commenced. 'Thank goodness' was my thought at the end of his question. I nodded at the gentleman in anticipation of what he was about to say:

> He challenged us to save Hearts for the cost of a pint of beer a week. Where the hell is Iain McLeod getting a pint for £2.50 because I would like to know.

The room erupted into laughter. We ended on a joyful and poignant note. Everyone left with the bit between their teeth and some homework. Pledge and spread the word. It was a fortuitous meeting as, within days, Heart of Midlothian Football Club would be plunged into administration with its very existence in doubt...

CHAPTER 11

The Tip into Administration

WE ALL GO to football matches to see goals, incidents and entertainment but, as a result of the supporters' efforts by backing the club financially, the biggest victory of season wasn't ever going to be on the pitch. It was the victory of keeping the club alive. Anything else would have dragged the club below the waterline. The club would have died. Playing in the top division was critical financially, but it was also psychologically important.

On Thursday 13 June, the day before the FOH fan meeting, David Southern was at a Scottish Professional Football League (SPFL) meeting at Hampden Park representing Hearts in league restructuring discussions. Remember them? That morning, a statement went out to say the entire Hearts squad had been put up for sale to try and secure funding to keep the club afloat over the summer. On leaving the league restructuring talks, the media were packed in the reception area at the National Stadium and it wasn't restructuring of the league that was on their minds.

The Hearts Board had issued a statement that included:

The Board had planned to bring income in through the sale of players while considering the financial forecast for next season, but now this will need to happen much earlier in order to preserve the business.

The statement said they required £500,000 in additional cash to keep the club going over the summer. That equated to 2,000 more season tickets.

The Board claimed it was as a result of other revenues 'drying up', with season ticket sales about half what they were at the same time the previous year. The problem was that supporters were reluctant to part with several hundred pounds when there was no guarantee that the fixtures would be fulfilled. It was a vicious circle. This was the backdrop to the fan meeting the following day.

Hearts was a bigger story than league reconstruction. David knew the club was in a difficult place and reinforced that message to the media.

He said that it was doubtful they would be able to pay players wages that were due at the end of the week. He added that Hearts actually needed to raise a 'significant six-figure sum' before the weekend. This was obviously in response to the payment due to HMRC that was subject to the speculation about another winding up order.

David had a good relationship with the sports media. He had worked with them over many years and was seen as being both straightforward and honest. David was long enough in the tooth to know these would be the headlines on the news programmes that day and into the written media the following day. That could not be avoided. This story was big, especially with what had happened to Rangers and the fact that no club was too big or important to fail.

David felt like the last person standing at that point. He had had little contact with Lithuania in the last few weeks which in itself told everyone all they needed to know. David understood that while he and his team had slowed the prospect of administration on frequent occasions it was surely only a matter of time. The 'if' had been replaced with a 'when' and the 'when' was becoming more and more imminent by the day.

In any potential administration, the thoughts are always for the staff and all those who were at risk of losing their jobs and livelihoods. They had all worked so hard, often not knowing when and perhaps even if they would be paid. Their support for the club was unconditional and that attitude rubbed off on many, including the supporters. It created solidarity between everyone that was associated with Hearts.

David as Managing Director, and the person who was in the stadium day in, day out, had arranged to meet the staff. The speculation in the press was not fair on them and he had to make sure that he imparted all he knew to them. The problem he had was that there had been no contact with the owners in Lithuania despite repeated attempts for information.

In the late morning on Friday 14 July, David was taking call after call on the situation. Most were recognisable numbers and names on his phone. Just before going in to talk with the off-field team at the club, an 'unknown number' called. He clicked it to message and went in to meet the staff. He tells me that they spoke for almost an hour about everything from what could lie ahead in the coming days to the worst- and best-case scenarios. All through this, his phone was ringing silently in his pocket. On returning to his office after the meeting, he noticed eight 'unknown number' missed calls.

He hadn't sat down when it rang again. The call was from Hearts lawyers, HBJ Gateley Wareing (HBJ), one of the top law firms in the country. The call triggered five mad days that would see the club go into administration and end up in the hands of specialist football administrators Bryan Jackson and Trevor Birch at BDO.

But even this process wasn't straightforward. David was taken aback by what he was being asked by the administrators. He was asked if he could go to the offices of administrators KPMG, who were the favoured administrators of the Lithuanian regime, and sign the papers to confirm the administration. David nervously laughed thinking that they had mistaken him for a Board Director. They hadn't. They had been advised by the Board that he'd do it. David has always stated that there was not a chance that he would be responsible for signing the papers that would put the very future of Heart of Midlothian Football Club in jeopardy.

He explained politely to the club's lawyers that the people working at the club had done everything to keep it afloat and it was him and his small team that had glued it together. David resolutely maintained that not one of the staff at the club was going to put their name to a situation that they had warned against on many occasions over many years. The owners were responsible for the current plight and if they wanted the administration papers signed then they would have to get themselves to Edinburgh to sign them.

In theory, it is just an administrative court process. It was always going to be signed. It was not going to be signed, though, by those that had worked tirelessly to save Hearts. It wasn't their responsibility. It may have been symbolic, but it was an important statement to make.

David received a call shortly after from one of the club's Directors asking him to sign the papers and again he explained why he wouldn't. He felt it would be a huge slap in the face to everyone who worked at Hearts, frequently with delays to their wages. Everyone at Tynecastle was so emotionally invested in the battle to keep the club alive, and it may just have been on a point of principle or a ceremonial refusal, but his belief was those that had been responsible for the position should put the final ink on the paper. As it was, a Director flew in from Lithuania on Sunday 16 June 2013 to sign the papers. This Director invited David and others for dinner that night. Not surprisingly, it had the feel of a last supper. The staff at the club were devastated, but that was nothing compared to the way the supporters were going to feel.

The Director flew back to Lithuania on the Monday morning never to be seen again. David and others had a lot of sympathy for many of the Lithuanian Directors who were employed at the club. They were genuinely trying to do their best and it was certainly not their fault that it had reached the end of the line.

On Monday 17 June 2013, the signed papers were lodged to formally place the club into administration. Such was the financial position at the Hearts that there were fears liquidation was the most likely outcome. Once the papers were lodged, the formal process commenced to appoint administrators. No one at the club was surprised. Shortly after discussions on who the administrators should be, Trevor, Bryan and James Stephen of BDO were appointed.

The Lithuanian Board of Hearts had requested KPMG take the court appointment as administrators. However, the Court of Session in Edinburgh appointed BDO, following requests from Valnetas. This is not an unusual situation. ūkio had the floating charge over the assets of the club and the main debt so could overrule the clubs preferred option. The ūkio administrator knew the track record of BDO. Bryan had done six football administrations previously. There was nobody better qualified. Hearts couldn't be in better hands. Bryan was well known for saving Dunfermline the previous year and had a string of footballing successes to his name. Trevor was a former Chief Executive at Chelsea and was heavily involved in the saving of Portsmouth FC. Pam Wilkins from the Pompey Supporters' Trust had been in touch to say what a brilliant job Trevor and BDO did to save them.

In fact, the solicitor for Valnetas Deimantė, had met with Bryan the previous month to discuss Hearts. She had been given his name through a variety of contacts. I suppose the Scottish administrators' world is quite small. She was seeking advice on putting Hearts into administration. They had this huge debt and she wanted to examine ways of getting it back. Bryan explained that the security that ūkio held over Tynecastle was only worth so much. Bryan advised her that if the security was worth, say, £5 million and a consortium was willing to pay them that price then why go through an administration process. It would be better to sell it as a going concern as that would be less costly, cause fewer political problems and be a much better proposition to a buyer. The only way you would want to place Hearts in administration was if they were going to run out of money and you wanted to keep the doors open. Liquidation would be a disaster as it would be a really distressed situation. She went away to think about these issues and said she would come back to Bryan in due course.

BRYAN WAS NOT overly keen to take on the Hearts administration as his experience of them was getting worse and worse. His previous two – Dunfermline and Portsmouth – were the hardest. He was loaded with work and didn't think the Hearts job would be easy. He reluctantly submitted a quote to Deimantė and it was accepted. In any normal appointment, it would have to go through BDO's company risk committee. The committee would examine the viability of the proposition and the potential for reputational damage to BDO. Bryan wasn't confident that it could get through this internal process as there had been no time to carry out any due diligence. Bryan didn't want to push it as, if it all went wrong, it would reflect badly on him and he knew from past experience how difficult these jobs were particularly as the footballing sanctions were increasing. The Rangers and Dundee administrations in previous years resulted in increased footballing sanctions whereas many years before Motherwell received no footballing sanctions for going into administration.

There was no reason why BDO would take this on but they did. Bryan thinks it was partly to do with BDO recently opening their first office in Edinburgh after their merger with PKF and the fact that it would be a good high-profile appointment, albeit risky.

I had a brilliant relationship with Bryan and his team. They really wanted FOH to succeed. I'm not sure if it reflects the personality of Bryan or indeed the sector he was working in but, on an occasion when I was having lunch with him, his mobile phone rang. Not an unusual occurrence. The amusing thing was his ringtone: the theme tune to *The Godfather*. Why would it be anything else?

On the same day that the papers were filed in court by Bryan, he had to take a really fraught and contentious CVA meeting at Dunfermline FC. He got it over the line. On his return to the BDO offices, there was already a large posse of reporters outside. Bryan had nothing to say to them. He hadn't drawn breath from Dunfermline. He genuinely had nothing to tell them. He hadn't yet been appraised by his Finance Controller.

Bryan later said his position at this time was 'as desperate as I have ever seen in football.' He tells the story of him going home after discovering the position at Hearts and sat in a dark room 'sobbing' whilst thinking about his retirement. He remembers saying to his wife, 'Yes, you were right, I should never have taken this job.'

He had 24 hours to come up with a plan. His sole job was to be the responsible person for the creditors of the club. There were 200 such creditors totalling over £28,424,336. The amounts ranged from £7 to £15,488,290 due to ūkio Bankas. Given the level of debt owed to ūkio Bankas, there was really only one creditor with any clout and that was the person that appointed him. No other creditors had any way of getting anything out of the administration. Critically, there was also £535,000 in football debt, which by the rules of football must be repaid in full by any new owners. Liverpool were due £47,000, while smaller amounts to the likes of Rangers, Livingston, Ayr United and Stenhousemuir would all have to be paid in full regardless of any outcome of the administration. Jambos Kickback raised a lot of money through events and made donations to some of the smaller creditors like Poppy Scotland and St John Ambulance to ensure they didn't lose out.

Bryan had a statutory duty to do his best for the creditors. One option for him would have been to acknowledge that there was no money and no way of generating money. Closing the doors and stopping trading would take out all the costs. Liquidating Hearts would leave the assets for sale. The proceeds of the asset sales would then be given to the creditors. That would have to be balanced by what it would leave behind. All the player contracts would fall so there would be no value in the playing squad and he would have been left with a stadium asset that would take years to develop. The controversy around that may even be too much for any developer. Hearts fans had recent experience of this with Cala Homes and it wasn't pretty.

Bryan's gut feeling was that liquidation would dissipate any value. If he could keep it open, it would preserve some value. If he could trade at break-even, it would be more valuable but how could he do that? If someone wanted to come along and fund the club for the processes of an administration, then that would be considered. Ironically, being in the closed season may have been a blessing in disguise as the club didn't need to pay the costs to put on games. They would have to pay wages but nothing else at this stage. That gave a little breathing space to an extent.

Bryan came up with a strategy. He knew that the club would normally sell 10,000 season tickets but had only shifted 7,000 to that date. If he could get the additional 3,000 sold within 14 days, he would not have to shut the club. There was nowhere else for him to go. He would announce this at a press conference later. The first question he got from the mass of the media was, 'Are you not trying to blackmail the Hearts supporters?' Bryan replied, 'Yes.' He had no other options.

In parallel with the appointment of BDO, internally at Tynecastle they created their own three stage operational plan to assist – 'Rescue, Recovery and Revival'. It was a bold move as the chances of Hearts leaving administration were not good. The overwhelming feeling from within the club appeared to be a bit of relief, as it may seem strange to say but administration provided some degree of certainty. Certainty that everyone at Tynecastle had not experienced in years. There was no certainty that the club would survive because there was no guarantee of that but at least with Trevor, Bryan and their team, they could work on a plan to try and rescue the club.

It may be sensible at this stage to provide a definition of what an administration process is compared to liquidation. A company goes into administration in order to package it for sale and to keep it alive as a going concern. Administrators, who are experts and independent of the business are appointed by the courts. They work with the creditors of the business to try to maximise their return. It often involves significant debt forgiveness, but the operations continue and it tends to save the business. A successful administration requires the creditors to approve the way forward with a legally binding Company Voluntary Agreement (CVA). More often than not, the main creditor required to approve a CVA are the tax authorities and banking institutions as they tend to have preferred creditor status and security over the main assets of the business – in Hearts' case, the stadium.

Put simply, a successful administration is about getting hold of the shares of the existing company into new ownership. The transfer of shares is for an agreed amount of money. That amount of money is then used to pay off the creditors. That pay-off can mean anything from one pence in the pound to ninety pence in the pound depending on the sale proceeds.

If a business can't be saved through a CVA process or there is simply no way of generating revenue, it goes into liquidation. This is again a judicial process but involves the appointment of liquidators who close the business and are tasked with the sale of its assets to generate cash to give to those who are owed money. The business is closed and creditors normally receive a small percentage of what their debt would be valued at.

The other major factor of a CVA process is that of HMRC. In order for a CVA to be successful, you require 75 per cent of the creditors of the business to support the proposed deal. If you can't get to this percentage the company is, in effect, closed and liquidated. HMRC have a policy that they will vote against any football CVA as they think the industry has not been dealt with properly and on a level playing field with other sectors. To put this in context, if the creditors debt to HMRC is more than 25 per cent there is no possibility of achieving a CVA. In the case of Hearts, the major creditors were ūkio Bankas and UBIG so the HMRC debt was relatively small at less than 10 per cent. However, it does mean that the room for manoeuvre with other creditors is restricted. That's what made the position when Rangers went into administration impossible to resolve. HMRC were the major creditor and were owed almost 100 per cent of the debt that brought Rangers down. Given HMRC would have voted against any Rangers CVA process, the club had no choice but to go into liquidation and start again. There are lots of column inches dedicated to that period in the Rangers saga, but the legal reality was that there was no way of saving Rangers in administration due to the HMRC policy position on CVAS.

On the morning of Wednesday 19 June, Trevor contacted David to introduce himself and ask that he join him and Bryan at their Haymarket office in the west end of Edinburgh. At 2.00pm, he went with Fiona to meet Trevor, Bryan and other members of the BDO team. Bryan had been clear that there needed to be an urgent examination of the company's records prior to making any announcements about what was likely to occur.

Everyone was acutely aware of the need for speed in this process given the uncertainty of the last few weeks and the proximity of the start of the new footballing season. The immediacy of the club's requirement was not lost on anyone in the room and once Bryan had been appraised of the financial and operational position of the business, he and Trevor would have to work out how best to create revenue streams that would give the club the best chance of survival. It was to be one of their toughest tests as the fans had done so much already, including raising over £1.2 million from the share issue and having purchased 7,000 season tickets, worth over £2 million, for the new season. All that money had gone. Not only had all the money gone but there was a paltry £7,000 in the bank account with no way, in close season, of generating any revenues beyond season ticket sales. Players hadn't been paid for May and non-playing staff hadn't been paid for the first two weeks in June.

There weren't even any quick player sales that could generate cash. All cash raised would go into a special administration account. BDO would take no professional fees unless a deal was done. Bryan knew he couldn't justify asking fans to put their money into the club and take out fees. This also took out the worry that any money would go towards the running of the club and not back to Lithuania.

Talks on the recovery plan continued all afternoon and into the evening. Bryan asked if David would continue running the day-to-day operations of the club which would allow him and his team to concentrate on the task of saving the club from liquidation. David and his team were already very emotionally invested in the club at this point and indeed had been for seasons prior to this moment.

They decided to try and engage with the supporters and, while in an ideal world staff would have been addressed by the administrators first, the need for revenue was so pressing that David called every supporters group to ask if they could attend a meeting that evening. He began phoning round the representatives of the main supporter groups and to their huge credit, almost every one of them were seated in BDO's office at Haymarket in Edinburgh by 6.30pm that evening. Anniversary dinners were cancelled, shifts were cut short and other excuses were made to friends and family by people that only wanted the best for the club. They stepped up yet again when the need was greatest. The club, and especially David, had worked with many of them over the years and they didn't hesitate once again. These supporters' organisations would all prove crucial to the saving of Hearts. I couldn't attend the meeting due to parliamentary responsibilities. Two hours later, the meeting adjourned, and everyone knew what had to be done. Bryan and Trevor had agreed to a series of headline targets with the supporter groups, designed to 'keep the doors open'. The 7,000 fans who had already bought season tickets would have them honoured. The drive was to sell a further 3,000 to keep the club afloat for the next few weeks or months. They needed three or four months of funding, between £500,000 and £750,000 to give them enough wriggle room to find a potential buyer. That responsibility was, again, in the hands of the supporters. In true Kitchener style, your club needs you... again. Oh, and if you have already bought a season ticket then please buy another and give it to a friend.

Bryan indicated that he thought the administration could take up to six months given the complicated ownership structure. It would end up taking almost 12. What he hadn't anticipated was what was happening in Lithuania. He knew nothing about what lay ahead. Even if he had been able to complete due diligence on Hearts, it wouldn't have told him what obstacles he would encounter in Lithuania or their attitude to a sale.

Henry Snedden recalled that he and his partner, Tracey, were celebrating her birthday and were out for lunch in Edinburgh when the call came through from David to meet in BDO's offices. Henry vividly remembers that

Bryan explained from the outset how perilous the situation was by outlining how little money the club had left in its bank account and then proceeded to outline the various options, which included cancelling the validity of all existing season tickets that had been sold to date and the very real prospect of liquidation within two weeks, unless the club, through its 'long suffering supporters', could somehow raise sufficient new money to keep the business turning over. He and Trevor explained that they needed to keep the business afloat for the next few months, while they talked to the Lithuanians to determine the options. I am delighted to say that the handful of supporters' representatives at that meeting managed to persuade Bryan (it didn't take much because he was clearly a sympathetic ear) that the Hearts fans would, once more, rally round and provide financial support for their club by whatever means necessary. Bryan was happy to accept their assurances and he was right to do so. He also made their support clear to the media.

They left the BDO offices later that evening fearful for our club's future but confident that, if they were going to get through this crisis, Bryan and Trevor were the right people to help it succeed. The people in that room knew that they both understood what a football club means to people (it's more than just a football team, it's a way of life!) and they had very quickly convinced everyone that they were going to do their utmost to help save our precious club. The next 51 weeks would show how much of a vital part they played in saving Hearts and it should never be undervalued or forgotten.

Henry has since been told by Tracey, who sat patiently in BDO's waiting room while that fateful meeting took place that, afterwards, he didn't say a word on the train home to Linlithgow. He had loyally supported Heart of Midlothian for over 50 years – was he really going to witness his club die? That and other similar thoughts churned over and over in my head over the months ahead and I am sure that I was not alone in this respect.

My conversations late that evening with Henry, Calum and David were sobering but we all knew what we had to do. The first stage was to sell 3,000 season tickets to supporters who had not renewed from the previous season and then take it from there. It was all hands to the pump and, although the search for a new owner was paramount, this had to be placed on the back burner whilst we fought for the short-term survival of Hearts. The club was also served with an immediate 15-point deduction for the following season. On top of this, the already imposed player transfer ban would stay in place until the club had exited administration. It was not going to be an easy ride.

We couldn't allow this administration process to turn into a liquidation. We had to find the funds to keep the club afloat.

The following day, Thursday 20 June, David told me he was in the office for 5.30am. He had been beset with the same affliction as all of us the night before – he simply couldn't sleep. He also knew that there would be a media circus that day and he was correct. He left the office just after 6.00am to nip round to the newsagent on Gorgie Road and even at that time there were already a couple of photographers outside on the pavement waiting for events to unfold. The nice thing for David was that they all took the time to wish him and the club well. At the end of the day, David had taken 83 calls, almost every one of them supportive and asking how they could help. Only one call was not supportive, from a former player. David hasn't ever said who it was.

That outpouring of well-wishers was not confined to those that were in the immediate vicinity of Tynecastle Park. David recalls that his phone started ringing from just after 7.00am. Word had trickled out the night before that there was to be a massive fundraising push from the administrators. The support was welcome and showed David that the Club could be saved and that it was worth the fight. But he was also very conscious that the staff were yet to arrive and the administrators were coming in to Tynecastle's small administration office shortly, probably wielding a very sharp and indiscriminate knife for the purpose of brutal cost cutting.

Rooms were set up for Bryan and his team. He then addressed the staff in the Gorgie Suite explaining the process we were in and highlighting the main targets for everyone associated with the club. He did say that there would be some inevitable redundancies but that he would not keep people waiting and those affected would know during that day. The staff were already down to a skeleton, but everyone was resigned to the fact that the club had to survive and costs had to be pared even further. Bryan explained that he had to do projections on a worst-case scenario because if you can't make the money you just have to shut the doors and that was not what he was intending to achieve.

Bryan was asked if there was anything that the team could do to help with cost cutting including the offer of potential salary cuts. He made it very clear that he knew how much everyone had put in to saving the club up to this point and, as importantly, the work that would have to be done in the coming weeks and months, so he could not ask for any more sacrifice from anyone. He did say, though, that if things got so tough that he needed to ask for that then he would come back and look at taking up the offer. He also stated to the assembled staff, as well as later that day in the press conference, that there was very little left to cut as the work had been done in the months and seasons prior to this point. The administration process had essentially commenced some years beforehand, albeit in an informal way.

Everyone left the Gorgie Suite and went into the car park that separated the function suite from the old administration block. By this time, the media had gathered outside the large metal gates which had been closed for security reasons. The media were desperate for comment and Bryan confirmed he would be speaking to them that afternoon. It didn't stop a rather unsympathetic journalist shouting, 'How does it feel to lose your jobs?' through the security gates. There was a momentary hush from the assembled media which I was later told by one of my friends in there was to allow some of his media colleagues to explain to him in no uncertain terms the finer points of reporting such sensitive events.

That incident aside, my experience of the media's management of the events as they unfolded was that it was done in a professional way that once again showed that Heart of Midlothian was viewed as something to be saved. While the national media could and should never be cheerleaders for any particular group, as their impartiality is paramount, they did reflect the wider belief that this was not a crisis of the making of anyone working at Tynecastle and least of all its supporters. The importance of the club to football, the local community, Edinburgh, Scotland, and much farther afield was not lost.

I did use the media a lot over the coming months. Bryan, FOH, other parties and I tried to ensure that we left no stone unturned in the saving of Hearts and that sometimes manifested itself in using the media for our own purposes. An unsung hero of this time was Lawrence. He kept the thirst of the media for stories quenched by keeping them well briefed and on-side.

I knew the administration was imminent and had been advised over the previous weekend to expect an announcement. If I was being honest, I knew it would happen but it was something I didn't want to admit. I felt numb knowing that the proverbial fat lady was warming up her voice. The FOH had to make a move and soon. I didn't want the singing to start. Collectively, we had to rise to the call to arms.

That afternoon was difficult for everyone. It was toughest for the people that did lose their jobs and also, to a lesser extent, those who remained and who were losing colleagues that many had worked with for years.

All the redundancies happened on the first day. That's just the way it had to be. It was brutal. Fourteen non-playing employees and four players were made redundant. On top of this, employees who had gone unpaid the previous month had to be asked to work for free until cash was raised, with Bryan admitting he had no idea when that would be. There was no money in the pot to pay anyone. It was as simple as that. Just 21 full-time staff remained and cuts would have to be made to an already small 26-player squad, despite vows to remain competitive for a new owner into the new footballing season. Most of the high-earning players had left the club over the previous years. Four senior players were asked to take wage reductions. In instances like this, they can either accept the contract change or be released from their contract. Three of the senior players accepted and one left the club as a result.

The administration was as sad as it was sore, but it had begun and now the fight for the future of Heart of Midlothian Football Club was on. The referee had blown the starting whistle, and this would be the club's most important match to win. Winning would not just be about saving the club but making sure it was saved by the right people. We couldn't afford to go through another period of instability.

Bryan was one of the most passionate, knowledgeable and dedicated football administrators in the country, but his assessment was bleak. He said to me that all football administrators would always be 51 per cent confident of getting a deal over the line. Football clubs are always saveable but that doesn't necessary mean that it will be. For the first time in his career, he put Hearts chances at just 49 per cent. Bryan may not have admitted this to his wife, but the fight of his professional life was on...

CHAPTER 12

Hearts and the Hobbit

OUR BELOVED HEARTS was now in administration. The Romanov era had come to an end. The future ownership of the club was uncertain. For now, the captain of the maroon ship would be Bryan Jackson and his team at BDO. Bryan was going to do everything he could to save the club. I was sure of that. I was also sure that I was going to strain every sinew to make the supporters the next owners of Heart of Midlothian FC. A dark chapter in Hearts' history had closed. What would the next chapter look like?

If going into administration was a disaster, the major positive was what it did to FOH pledges. Within days, we rocketed to 5,600 after a media release from FOH to encourage a final push before conversion. This was an extraordinary response from the supporters and just what Bryan anticipated. It demonstrated to Bryan that when the supporters were called upon, they would deliver.

The administration coincided with the launch of the GoCardless system to convert these pledges to cash and pledgers to full FOH members. Alastair and his tech team at Shaw Marketing had been liaising with Tim Rogers at GoCardless to try and get everything ready. Calum, as the project lead, was working very closely with them on the logistics whilst Andy was looking at the reconciliation of management data that the system would give us in order to keep track of individual pledgers. If I was being honest, we should have taken a few more weeks for us to be totally confident that the system was everything we wanted. I only wish we had that luxury.

Two dynamics were at play. The first was the need to use the crisis of administration to hit home the serious message that this was the time for the supporters to come together and act. The second was the completely dysfunctional FOH Board. Almost everyone was working their fingers to the bone to make things happen but Alex could not let things go. He never wanted to use the GoCardless system. He made that clear at every opportunity despite it having Board approval. That turned molehills into mountains.

To my utter astonishment, a series of emails were exchanged on the days after our Thursday meeting in which Alex said he was 'taking control' of the system from Calum. He was unconvinced it was going to work. I was keeping a very close strategic overview on the project through Calum and Andy. Alastair had assured us that everything was in place. Andy did have some reservations on management data but kept restating his position: 'We are 95 per cent there. I just need to clarify the five per cent, but I am sure it is all going to be fine.' I only got wind of this when the head of GoCardless copied me in on an email trail between him and Alex.

I was absolutely furious. As a result, I decided to make a unilateral decision. It was the first and one of the only times I did this. A few days previously, we had been putting together the final touches to the system. I had been given heavy hints that the club was on the edge but, frustratingly, I couldn't share this with the FOH Board. I concluded that we had to set a deadline for launching the system. We had tested the system. All Directors went through the FOH pledgers page to the GoCardless portal and set up a direct debit. It worked. Any small problems could be ironed out later. What we didn't need was more chiefs confusing the process. Ann and Robert were hugely important at this time. Their experience and wise counsel gave me the motivation to try and inspire the rest of the team. It was now or never. We would start the drawdown of pledges on Tuesday 18 June 2013 at 9.00am. We would just have to be ready.

It demanded a lot from Alastair's technical team and Calum in his dealings with GoCardless, but I was confident that they would be able to deliver. I cemented this in by getting Lawrence to tweet about it. All the journalists were following his every word on social media:

> @The_FOH will begin converting pledges to cash imminently. An announcement will follow – likely next 24 hours.

My criticism of Alex in this instance was that he had too much of a safety-first approach. His career as a professional and experienced auditor had taught him that. I'm glad we had someone on the team that took this approach but the issue in this case was that we would have to take risks as the clock ran down. '95 per cent' from Andy and confidence from both Calum and Alastair was enough for me.

One of the complicating factors was the messaging to the supporters. Bryan couldn't have been more honest about the situation. The club had to sell at least 3,000 season tickets in a couple of weeks or there would be no way of keeping the club alive as a going concern. At the same time, we were asking the very same supporters to commit to a monthly contribution so we could purchase the club. These were not necessarily mutually exclusive, but we couldn't cut across each other. We were both fishing in the same pond.

I did a considerable amount of media over this time. Bryan and I kept our respective messages separate but we co-ordinated what we had to do. We would have to use the relative power of FOH to encourage supporters to listen to what was required to keep the club afloat. That was, after all, the most important hurdle to get over. Our strategy was to repeat the same message over and over again. I had done a lot of political media over the previous years as a Member of Parliament, but this was intense. Bryan and I were traversing the TV cameras, radio studios, newspapers and bloggers as a tag team. The fact that FOH was about to ask the supporters to show us the colour of their money and Bryan was pleading for them to do the same would be a big ask. It was coincidence that it was happening at the same time but perhaps that was a benefit.

I remember getting a text from a good friend, Shaun Milne, who was at STV at that time. He was and is a hugely skilled and respected journalist. He certainly knew his stuff, so I was immensely grateful when he said, 'You looked utterly shagged last night but you came across well. I suppose it's tiring, but the message is loud and clear.' I suppose that was a compliment in a way. I had been burning the candle at both ends and, if I was being completely straight, I wasn't getting much sleep. I was worried sick about the club. I was worried sick about it all working. I was worried sick about what I had taken on. The reality of Hearts now being in administration hit me harder than I thought it would. It was an inevitability, but I didn't quite anticipate how I would feel when it occurred. I had a back and forth text conversation with Shaun. It made me feel a bit better until his last text that evening. He simply said, 'You ready to make history?' I knew he was meaning it positively but making history isn't always necessarily a good thing.

To make matters worse, the risk I had taken to get the pledgers conversion system up and running on Tuesday 18 June wasn't going to happen. The fly in the ointment was simple. If we set an initial drawdown date of 4 July, could we move it to a future date? We promised that we would only initiate the first direct debits when we knew we could make a bid for the club. Richard assured us that the date could be moved easily. The problem was that his 10,000 Hours project didn't ever get to the stage of requesting the funds, so it was never tested.

Aaaargh! Not only had this thrown up a huge problem but it re-opened the arguments about the GoCardless system. If I had a pound for every email that was sent by the ten Directors of FOH over those days I could have bought the club myself. It was hugely frustrating. Alex went too far by claiming Calum wasn't taking responsibility for the 'mess'. That set the cat amongst the pigeons and Calum rode to the rescue. He often did. Calum has a warm character that means everyone likes him. That endearing nature was recognised by the team at GoCardless. Tim and others had got on well with Calum when they came to Tynecastle to see Hearts. Out of frustration, Calum called Tim and demanded an answer to the simple question of whether the drawdown date could be altered if necessary. Did the system and direct debit guarantee allow for such a circumstance? Yes. Everything was in place. We couldn't go forward without this assurance. Tim, to his credit, understood what we were trying to achieve and the pressing need to get the system operational. He clearly didn't know but said he would make it happen. It wasn't a showstopper despite it being exploited as such by some.

Calum confirmed it was positive from Tim, so I hit the button. The only alteration was to set the initial drawdown date of 2 August 2013 rather than 4 July. Even if the timescales were as quick as we were being led to believe by the Lithuanian authorities, it would not be done before July. I wasn't going to let all the progress we had made be lost. The extraordinary efforts of Alastair and his team were also not going to be in vain. Wednesday 19 June at 09.00am was the time and I would not be altering it for a second time.

That was until the final GoCardless bombshell. We had to sign a £100,000 indemnity with them. This was not usual practice. It arose because we had committed to returning all the money to pledgers if the purchase of the club was not successful. The utilisation of a direct debit system meant that a pledger could call on the direct debit guarantee and have their funds returned if the service that was being provided was not supplied. That would leave GoCardless on the hook for all the money that had been collected. That was not something they would be willing to carry. The direct debit guarantee was a legal mechanism. FOH had no money. We had no way of ensuring we would be successful. We had promised the return of funds minus any minor banking costs. It would not be fair or appropriate to ask the Directors of FOH to sign an indemnity that would have them responsible for such vast amounts of money. We just wanted to save our football club. We didn't want to lose our homes in the process. After much deliberation, Alex stepped in and said he would sign it. I don't know if he ever discussed it with anyone else, but he was convinced that he would be able to persuade GoCardless to drop it in time. In fact, the likelihood was that it would be unnecessary. The indemnity wasn't signed by the time we went live. It would become a bone of contention with GoCardless. They were perfectly appropriately asking for an indemnity but surely it would only be required when we actioned the inaugural direct debit.

Henry and Richard had been working around the clock to finalise the members agreement that would determine the rules for each pledger. By converting their pledge to a direct debit, they would become a member of FOH. They had also drafted a FOH Board election policy paper and a voting system paper alongside a draft Directors policy. These were posted as PDFs on the revamped website. We were ready to go.

The website was live the night before. It was wonderful to see the fruits of our labour in real time. The conversion buttons were in place – £10, £20, £30, £40, £51, £100, and £200. We had debated, discussed, changed our minds and back again before we had settled on these amounts. We wanted to ensure it was both affordable and ambitious. 'For the cost of a pint a week' remember. The £51 button was a homage to the 2012 Scottish Cup Final score. A bit of fun perhaps. A significant money earner certainly.

On the morning that Hearts officially went into administration, we launched. Lawrence had set up the media. We also issued a statement to all those who had already pledged. 5,601 people would be asked to convert their initial pledges into a direct debit and all new entries would go straight to the direct debit system.

Dear Pledger,

The Foundation of Hearts is delighted to announce that the system for converting your pledge to a monthly direct debit is now live.

We all know how critical the next few weeks will be for the club and the Foundation is moving quickly to try to formulate a credible bid by the end of this month. The level of bid will be determined by the number of pledges and the number that are converted.

On the conversion page (www.foundationofhearts.org/now-is-the-time-to-make-history/), you will see a range of buttons, each corresponding to a level of contribution. Click the button that you wish to choose as your monthly direct debit and it will take you through to the simple automated system run by GoCardless. Also, on the page is a pledgers' marketing document, a draft membership agreement, a draft Board and Election Policy document and a draft Directors Policy document. These are all drafts. They will be adopted at the first AGM of the Foundation and can be altered and developed by the members.

If you are an overseas pledger, you will not be able to use this system. However, an overseas system will be available very soon.

We had set the direct debit drawdown date as 4 July but we have altered this to 2 August following advice about likely bid timescales. However, we will come back to you if we wish to push this date back or bring it forward. We will collect no money until we are sure a deal can be concluded.

The instructions on setting up your own account are contained in the conversion system.

The process of fan ownership is not an easy task but with your help we have a once in a lifetime opportunity to make it happen.

On behalf of the Foundation of Hearts and every Hearts supporter – thank you.

The irony was that the purchase of a majority shareholding in Hearts would be much easier now the club was in administration. That may have been a bitter pill to swallow, but it was a reality. The bid team was continuing to develop the proposals. The new landscape of dealing with Hearts staff and BDO directly would help. No longer were the Lithuanians in the way. John Reid and his team at Deloitte were on board to assist and Ann was pushing it forward.

We were all very nervous at FOH. It was all good and well having pledgers, but we were now asking them to put their money where their pledge was. Would they do it? It was very easy to pledge but, when push comes to shove, they don't necessarily materialise. It would not be helped by Bryan asking for every penny the fans could muster. We didn't have to worry. In just 24 hours, we had converted 2,366 pledgers and added a further 326 new people. We had also identified around 200 bogus pledgers. These would become known as 'suspected Hibbies'. The average amount converted was over £21 per person. This equated to nearly £45,000 per month. Critically, there were fewer than 300 people who converted less than their initial pledge. It was utterly phenomenal.

The fact we had even managed to get this far in such a short space of time was extraordinary. The total devastation of the club we loved being in administration was tempered a by the sheer elations we all felt at the numbers converting their pledge. I am not sure though that Calum's employers were too enamoured. We were all flying a bit by the seat of our pants. Calum had set up the system and connected it to his work email system. This was for no other reason than to be able to keep an eye on what was happening with the progress of getting the system ready for release.

What Calum hadn't factored in was the small matter of the receipt of an email with every pledge converted to a new direct debit. The system sent an email for everyone who set up a direct debit, alongside an email when it was authenticated. 2,366 emails in 24 hours would have been quite a challenge for his employer's email server to deal with. However, that was just the tip of the iceberg. His email completely collapsed. Calum laughs now but I don't think he knew what had hit him when he got over 5,500 emails to his work email account on the first day. Two emails per pledger arrived. Calum was made redundant about a year later. I am sure that had nothing to do with this 'incident' but he was 'pulled up' about it.

Alongside this the supporters were buying season tickets in their thousands. People who had already bought theirs were buying others and giving them away. The various fundraising bodies like the 1874FF and Jambos Kickback were doing their bit and buying as many as they could afford. Celebrities were being encouraged to purchase theirs and do media events around it. I recall getting a call from Rt Hon Alastair Darling MP who was going to buy one. He wanted to ensure maximum exposure to help the cause. I did find it highly amusing though when he posed the question, 'If I buy some, I don't need to go, do I?'

The purchases went to kids from local primary schools via the Big Hearts charity as did many hundreds of others. A lot of people like Alastair cared for the club but they knew that buying a season ticket was essentially a charitable donation to a worthy cause. His eagerness to know if he had to attend was probably because there are not too many worthy causes where you make a donation then sit in the cold and rain to shout at men playing sport. A host of former players and managers including John Robertson, Scott Crabbe, Peter Houston and Craig Levein and the former First Minister Alex Salmond were digging deep to donate season tickets to the charitable initiative – Big Hearts, Big Tickets. David also tells the story of taking time to thank supporters at the ticket office. On one occasion, he came across a group of 17 men who all golfed together. They were using their annual golfing green fees to buy season tickets rather than golf that year. That was what it meant to people. Even those golfers went maroon before greens.

The rallying of support was crucial. It was pretty much the only income. People and corporates don't want to buy sponsorship and hospitality when a club is in a distressed situation. It's viewed as toxic and their money is not secure, especially if you are buying something that may not be able to be fulfilled. There weren't other income streams readily available.

There was so much going on that our feet never really touched the ground. Every waking hour that was spare of work was being devoted to the project. It didn't help that everything seemed to happen at the same time. Just two days after Hearts officially went into administration and we launched the conversion system, I got a ping on my email account. BDO's lawyer, Peter Duff at Morisons LLP, contacted me for confirmation that we wanted to follow through our initial expression of interest in purchasing Heart of Midlothian Football Club or its assets, either to the Joint Administrators of the Heart of Midlothian PLC or to the Lithuanian representatives of ūkio Bankas.

Peter had been instructed by the Joint Administrators to seek confirmation that we maintained our interest and were serious. It was likely that BDO would issue a formal invitation to interested parties for offers to acquire the assets in the coming days. They would seek a bid from FOH that set out a price, a deal structure, a timescale, any conditions and proof of funding. It was the proof of funding aspect that would be fundamental to the success of FOH. After consulting with the FOH Board and the bid team, I replied to Peter to confirm our interest and asked to be kept abreast of what the process would be and how we could submit our bid.

What BDO had to do was achieve a bid that would be acceptable to the secured creditor. That would be achieved via the consent of ūkio Bankas through a successful CVA process. It would have to involve them obtaining the 50 per cent shareholding from UBIG, otherwise we would be buying something that UBIG continued to control. This complicated process, in a different jurisdiction with unusual regulations, would be a long haul. Bryan would have to juggle that process alongside having to generate enough money to ensure there was sufficient cash in the club to fulfil their fixtures.

Given it was going to be a long process, we were slightly taken aback when BDO responded to our initial formal expression of interest with a deadline of Friday 12 July for bids. I guess this short timescale was both a reflection of the seriousness of the financial situation at Hearts and the need to flush out the tyre kickers. This was about serious bidders now.

We had set a target of submitting a bid by the end of June, but we had been consumed by the events of administration that led to the premature launch of FOH systems. Ann was pleased that a deadline had been set. She had already met with Bryan and Trevor at BDO with Kevin and Robert to bottom out the financial projections. All I could respond to Ann with was, 'What a week we have had and what a week we are about to have.'

The email on 26 June informing us of the deadline coincided with an announcement that we had converted half of the 5,601 pledgers and had another 400 new ones on top. We were up to our magical number of 6,000. A non-disclosure agreement was signed with BDO to obtain their sales memorandum.

The following day, I was flying out to Berlin to speak at the European Trades Union Conference on the Governments proposed changes to workers' rights. There was a legislative proposal to completely liberalise the UK labour market to make it easier to hire and fire people. One of my long list of shadow ministerial responsibilities was workers' rights. I was pleased to go. I arrived at the conference venue in Berlin a little before my slot. I was invited in to have coffee and lunch. As I was about to take up the offer, my phone rang. This was not unusual. In fact, if my phone hadn't rung for an hour or so, I would check to see if it was still working. Anyway, I answered the call. It was a representative from Wonga. Wonga had been Hearts shirt sponsor for the previous few years. It wasn't a comfortable relationship given the nature of the company and the sector they operate in but, to be fair, they stepped in to help Hearts when they needed it by bringing forward some of the sponsorship money they were due. That helped the club with cash flow when Bryan needed it. He didn't have the luxury of having morals. It was about saving the club and that required cash. Keeping it going preserved the value.

The call was an offer of help. Wonga had been in close contact with David and BDO throughout this process. They wanted to explore if they could help beyond their shirt sponsorship arrangement. As I paced the floor of the conference lunch venue in Berlin, Wonga outlined that they could perhaps advance FOH the capital sum to purchase the club. It would then be repaid over a fixed term on the revenues from pledges. It would be purely a commercial arrangement but on favourable terms broadly in line with current business mortgage rates and be secured on the assets.

I was quite taken aback. I had been pushed into a moral maze. The details of any such deal was not really forthcoming but the figures FOH had been working towards was in the region of £5 million. I didn't want to close down any possibilities but surely it wouldn't be a comfortable proposition to the supporters to enter into an arrangement with a company such as Wonga. We would be benefitting from a competitive interest rate paid for by the extortionate pay day lending rates offered to their customers. I knew that I should discuss this with the FOH Board, but I was convinced we would not be able to entertain such a proposition. I sincerely thanked them and said it would be considered. It was a genuine offer of help and I acknowledge that, but I knew in my heart of hearts it couldn't be done.

We wanted to be the most serious bidder. A major component of that seriousness would be how the stadium would be dealt with. Actually, it was about the crumbling old Archibald Leitch main stand more than anything. Safety certificates were costing more and more to obtain every year. Maintenance costs were going through the roof, almost literally, and it would be a huge capital expenditure item for any new owner. The value of the stadium was dictated by the investment required to replace the old main stand. The stadium had been three quarters redeveloped over the past 20 years. Architect and Hearts supporter James Clydesdale had designed the three new stands and had proposals for the main stand. Fortuitously, James had got in touch with me when Hearts went into administration to offer help. He was as good as anyone at being able to help us with what would be needed to bring the stadium up to full modernisation and also perhaps a framework for the value of the stadium for the purposes of our bid. The FOH Board agreed that Director Brian Cormack should use his vast professional experience in the property and development sector to produce a proposition document on the value of Tynecastle and the options for replacing the main stand. He had already done some of this work back in early 2012 with James Clydesdale, Bernard Johnson and Brian Souness. These were the architect, surveyor and quantity surveyor of the three existing new stands.

We didn't give Brian a remit to look at anything other than staying at our spiritual home. We did have a constructive and lively debate about this and whether we should leave our options open. It came down to a judgement about being custodians of the club and should the membership of FOH wish to take these fundamental decisions in the future they would be allowed to as owners. It was not for us as an FOH Board to make these decisions, so we simply said that we would commit to staying at Tynecastle and our plans would be underpinned by that commitment. It was a practical decision. We were portraying to the Lithuanians that they would not want a dead duck stadium property on their hands as it would be difficult to develop and be practically worthless for any other purpose. We couldn't therefore have a proposal to sell it and move elsewhere. Fundamentally, though, this was what the supporters wanted. We were all supporters and it was what we wanted too. That made our minds up. After all the machinations in the previous decade about the position of where Hearts would call home, it was absolutely the right decision to take this issue off the table. Brian was commissioned to produce a report on the stadium. He would work with his contacts in the property world and James Clydesdale.

The media was absolutely full of stories about the plight of Hearts. Most were overwhelmingly positive about FOH plans and the efforts of the fans in supporting the club by buying season tickets. It was a frenzy. Lawrence came up with a programme of media stories that could feed this frenzy. The key strategy for Lawrence was to utilise those with which the supporters had an affection. We needed maroon voices to get the message across.

We recognised the importance of the media and vowed to work collaboratively providing them with the information they required and opportunities that will be of use, both at that point, and should we be successful in becoming the new majority shareholder in Hearts. The relationship between the media and Hearts had not been positive for a long period of time. Romanov had a very uneasy and often hostile relationship with them, even throwing bananas and nuts at them when he referred to them collectively as 'monkeys'. This was our chance to repair that relationship. It was also an opportunity for the media.

The first major press event was to do a full media day at Tynecastle. We would invite a Hearts favourite along to speak about what the club meant to them. I would do as much TV and media around this as possible. We would even include all the Sunday sports reporters. Getting access to use the stadium and the club resources was much easier now that BDO were running it.

We wanted to use this media set piece to make one final push as the race to buy Hearts entered a crucial phase being just one week prior to the BDO bids deadline. We would use that deadline to start a final countdown, calling upon supporters to convert their pledge and for others to sign up. Given the rate of conversions and new pledgers, we projected we would be at about 4,000 by the time the media event took place. That provided a great story for the press and we would announce it on the day. That figure would give us huge credibility with the media that we could make our bid a reality.

We would also make it clear that we had two options to fund a takeover of the club. The details of these would have to remain confidential until after the bid deadline. We didn't want to allow others to get wind of how our bid was shaping up. However, whatever form the FOH bid took, it was based on securing the best possible number of supporter monthly direct debits and then working in partnership with major business partners to deliver a controlling stake and long-term security for Hearts.

We knew we were in touching distance. All we had to do – I say 'all' as if this was easy – was to hit our own target for pledges. That would leave us in a position of being able to draw down substantial monies to confirm a viable bid. Lawrence insisted that the best way to communicate with the supporters was to pull on the heartstrings. Those heartstrings were most easily pulled by Hearts stars making the case that, if we were successful, the club would be owned by the people that matter most – the supporters.

I had been pushing these messages out for some time, but Lawrence was a master of feeding the media beast just the right amount. He choreographed these events like a performance from the Royal Ballet. This media event was no different. I would continue to deliver the lines about FOH and what we were trying to do. Garry would present the view from the terraces as a fan. This was Garry's great strength. He not only spoke from the heart but he meant every syllable. He had always seen himself as a supporter, nothing more, although he was much more than that to the cause of FOH, that's for sure. He had fought for the previous few years to bring this dream into a reality. His message was clear and simple:

> I'm genuinely a punter, a guy who loves the Hearts and I can see a dream come true here where we finally take control of our own destiny and create a future we can all be a part of.

As if that wasn't enough, Lawrence had arranged for club legend and former Scotland internationalist, Dave McPherson to appear. 'Big Slim' was certainly a hero of mine having made over 300 appearances for Hearts and helped lift the Scottish Cup in 1998. It had the added advantage of me spending the morning with a constituent. Dave McPherson was everything off the park that he was on it – articulate, respected, skillful and sheer class. I had watched Dave play for Hearts hundreds of times. He was a consummate professional. I had to keep reminding myself not to get too star-struck.

We got all the media together for pictures of Garry, Dave and me at Tynecastle with foam boards emblazoned with the FOH logo and the message, 'Our Future. Let's Own It.' This was surely a dream? The media lapped it up. Dave may have been an idol of mine on the pitch. That day he went even further up in my estimations. He delivered his part perfectly:

Now is the time. I want to offer my complete support to the Foundation of Hearts. I hope the Foundation can secure the very final pledges required to make the sort of bid to the administrators that they consider most appropriate to the future of this club.

What a morning that was. What an impact it had. We would use this generally for media purposes but also to communicate directly with those who had pledged but not yet set up their direct debit. Calum, Andy and Alex worked to get everything up and running. We now had our direct debit system. Furthermore, our international supporters could now access monthly contributions via PayPal, and we had produced physical standing order forms for those not online. More importantly, to coincide with the Dave McPherson media call, we were given permission to use the Hearts database. This meant a message to support the FOH and what we were trying to do could go out to over 48,000 email addresses:

Dear Supporter,

On Friday 12 July 2013, the Foundation of Hearts will submit its bid to potentially acquire a controlling stake in Heart of Midlothian Football Club.

The Foundation is committed to a transparent, fan-owned, supporter-governed model of ownership which puts our community at the heart of everything we do.

Your role in the battle for survival has been remarkable. However, the part you play in the future is equally critical.

For that reason and to help us secure preferred bidder status we ask you today to set up a monthly direct debit to the Foundation of Hearts, and in doing so join nearly 4,000 supporters.

From just £10 a month you can ensure Hearts has a future as special as its past.

We intend to take a first payment on or around 4 August. Your transaction is 100 per cent safe and secure, and in the event that any purchase is not completed, all money will be returned (minus very small costs).

Time is of the essence however, and with a matter of days to go before the deadline this email is a final rallying call to the wider Hearts support to play a part in owning the club you love.

Alongside this, Trevor announced that the 3,000 season tickets they required to sell to keep the club afloat had almost been met. What a day. What support. What an opportunity.

That same week I got a call from an unknown number. I normally pop these calls to answering machine and catch them later. This time, for some reason, I answered it. I was glad I did. A recognisable voice was on the line said, 'Is that Ian Murray?' I couldn't work out who it was. 'Jim Jefferies here.' I was in heaven. Our Scottish Cup-winning, Hearts fanatic, two-time manager and all-round football idol of mine. Jim wanted to help. He was manager at Dunfermline FC at the time so was a little restricted on what he could do but called to see if he could be useful.

I met him in the Braid Hills Hotel in my constituency after a local event. He was as superb as I always thought he was. We spoke for over three hours. Admittedly, two-thirds of that was about his time as a player and manager of Hearts. We also talked at length about the obvious – winning the Scottish Cup. His experience of managing Hearts under the Romanov regime was as manic as you would have expected. He wanted FOH to be successful and offered his services for anything we needed from him. He came into the room at the hotel a champion of mine and left an even bigger hero. I felt under tremendous pressure but these meetings reminded me what I was doing this for.

And talking of famous Hearts faces, we also had something else up our marketing sleeve – a Hobbit! Iain and Lord Foulkes are long term friends of *Rebus* actor Ken Stott. Iain had got to know him when he helped in the Save Our Hearts campaign in 2004. It was suggested that he would be a great figure to have helping with our marketing. Iain had contacted Ken and he wanted to do anything he could to help. The only problem was he was in New Zealand filming *The Lord of the Rings*. What a coup it would be to have him on board. It would not be possible to have him holding a Hearts scarf above his head at Tynecastle or delivering a media message like Dave McPherson from 12,000 miles away, though. Ken suggested he could simply record a message or get some photos taken in New Zealand and pop them over to us. What a star. Little did we know what would arrive. Not only did we get Ken Stott the actor with one of our 'Own the history. Shape the Future' FOH boards but we got him holding it in character as Balin as well. Buy one get one free. It was a headline writer's dream. *The Scotsman* went with, 'Stott the Hobbit puts his Hearts on his sleeve to appeal to fans'. His interview was just the tonic.

How many other club takeovers were backed by a Hobbit?

CHAPTER 13

Bids and Bobs

THE ADMINISTRATORS HAD given a deadline of 12 July for interested parties to submit their bids for Hearts. There were six interested parties that I knew of up to that point. The key would be who would actually manage to get a formal bid to Bryan and his team by the deadline.

The FOH bid was progressing well. The pledges were being converted to monthly direct debits and the numbers were growing all the time. The issue was how we would obtain a capital sum to deliver the CVA. Cash flow was not going to be a problem. The monthly contributions from FOH members would adequately cover the day-to-day funding gap and the servicing of the capital sum required to make the initial purchase.

There were other bidders mooted in the media. We had no idea if any were serious or what they were offering. I was adamant that we had to find a solution to Hearts' plight; however, a bidding war would not only be counterproductive but potentially destructive. We were all on the same side – or so I thought. If we ended up battling each other, we would increase the bargaining power of the Lithuanian authorities. Conversely, though, this was not all about the FOH, this was about the saving of Hearts.

I was inviting any serious bidders to come and talk to FOH because, if they genuinely had the long-term interests of the club at heart, then there was no better thing to do than speak to us as we had the fans and fan groups behind us. One group who we did spend a lot of time with was a consortium led by Gordon McKie. The bid led by Gordon was particularly attractive as he wanted to work with FOH to provide a supporters' ownership model. They wanted to fund the purchase and development of the club but were concerned about how they could plug the revenue gap. Gordon was a conduit for investors and kept in constant touch with me. They had absolutely no issue with fan ownership. There was a complicating factor in selling this proposition to their investors. They would be asked to invest several million pounds upfront to buy the club and FOH would be putting up a couple of hundred thousand a month in pledges, but FOH would get the majority shareholding from day one.

We discussed ways at getting around this because the opposite was also true. The supporters would be nervous at putting their collective resources into the club again without a clear route to ownership and decision making. There would have been an unequivocal undertaking by the investors that if a certain level of revenue was raised in pledges and invested then they would get 50 per cent plus one shareholding in the football club. The principle would be that a gradual transition would be made to majority shareholding by transferring a proportion of shares based on money advanced. The principle of having full ownership remained in place once the capital loan was repaid. They would also work with other potential investors if the capital loan could be repaid quicker. I wasn't sure we would be able to sell that to the supporters or how it would work in terms of governance of the club. It was certainly an attractive proposition though.

The problem with this proposal was that they didn't have the cash as yet and were preparing a deal sheet for investors. Haines Watts would have provided a letter to the FOH about the identity of the investors and comfort that they would pass any fit and proper persons test. They were also Hearts fans as well as accountants so would have no issue in taking over the club.

The McKie team was fantastic. The people around him were undoubtedly reputable, credible and individually wealthy and had Hearts' best interests at heart. Most of them were Hearts supporters – genuine Hearts and sports fans who just wanted to save Hearts and ensure it did well in the future. I met them at various times and the FOH Board also asked Richard to meet with them independently for a second opinion on their proposal. The proposition fell apart as the group became concerned when BDO confirmed that any new purchaser of the club would need to find £2.7 million of additional cash, net of any cost savings, to get through season 2013/14. The decision had already been made, rightly in my view, that the 7,000 season tickets that were sold in advance of administration were to be honoured by BDO. Furthermore, the proceeds from the additional 3,000 season tickets that were sold to keep the club afloat would have been used up by BDO before transfer to a new owner.

That had a material effect on their overall investment proposal. They would need to include a further sum to secure the CVA. Those circumstances meant that the group would be unwilling to provide the additional, unforeseen financing for what they described as the 'black hole'. They did remain interested in trying to provide investment to secure the CVA and the stadium. This would reduce the McKie bid to something of a property deal with them purchasing the stadium as an asset and FOH buying the club.

FOH mulled over this for some time. There was a balance to be struck between being able to save Hearts and not getting into the same difficulties as before. We just couldn't get our bid to stack up without being able to obtain the main asset – the stadium.

Gordon, Stephen, and Fraser magnanimously decided not to pursue their bid. They did leave the door open to FOH should it be needed. I appreciated that. They are good guys.

Whilst they were obviously disappointed and had invested a lot of time and effort into putting forward a credible bid for Hearts, they were genuinely delighted at all the hard work FOH had been doing. They were also aghast, but not surprised, at how loyal Hearts fans were digging deep into their own pockets again. Gordon always said the supporters were 'the greatest credit to their club'. Stephen offered to continue to help FOH with due diligence and tax matters if we required it. He had done a lot of due diligence with Gordon and was keen to share that.

We also wanted to maintain good relations with other potential bidders. The way forward was still very uncertain. Anyone who could save the club would be supported by FOH and, if they wanted to do it in partnership with us, that would be a bonus. It was becoming clearer by the day that FOH were the right people at the right time but with not enough time. The same day that Gordon intimated that he would not be taking his bid forward, Trevor at BDO admitted that Hearts could be forced to pursue the 'newco' route similar to that of Rangers. It was becoming increasingly complicated in Lithuania and he was concerned Hearts could not get out of their financial crisis through exiting administration via a CVA if it was obstructed in Lithuania. The difficultly was obtaining the 50 per cent shareholding owned by UBIG, who had still not formally started their own insolvency process.

We had to set this warning aside. Trevor and Bryan were right to paint this doomsday scenario in the run-up to bids. There were undoubted complications dealing with another jurisdiction in Lithuania and the process was cumbersome, but I had a hunch that Trevor placed this in the media to encourage the genuine bidders to come forward prior to the deadline. I got this hunch because there were a host of other bidders demonstrating their proposals through the pages of the newspapers, rather than on the desks of the BDO team.

One of the most recognised was a Scandinavian consortium led by a Kai Isaksen from Crest Sports. For some time, the fans were aware of the 'Norwegians', as they became affectionately known. It all originated from a press article late in 2012 entitled, 'Viking Raid on Hearts'. The fans were always mentioning this as the white knight bid. There were a large number of threads on Jambos Kickback forums saying that this was the only way forward. I do recall saying in the press that the speculation (about other bids) was such that if I had a pound for every time someone mentioned Scandinavians or Norwegians to me, I would be paying to have Lionel Messi hold a Hearts scarf above his head as Hearts new signing.

Kai had been in touch with Alex over a number of months. He was representing a number of Scandinavian business investors. I had reached out to Kai before Hearts went into administration to try and get a handle on where they were and what they wanted. It was not an easy task as Kai couldn't meet with me until he had a formal mandate from his group to conduct talks with me and FOH. This seemed strange as he had been talking to Alex for some time. Eventually, he was able to commence discussion and it was cordial, but I left not quite sure what they were planning or who was behind it. I asked if there was any way to communicate directly with the lead investor to try and better understand their motivations. I was concerned that the Norwegians had been spoken about in the media and by the fans for many months, but nothing had materialised, nor did it look as though anything was going to come forward. They all wanted the best for Hearts – of that there was no doubt in my mind – but I just couldn't fathom if it was real and credible.

As the deadline for submitting bids approached, Kai and his group decided not to bid. I didn't really think they would. I had no evidence to back this up but I had a feeling that they just didn't seem to have either the resources or a detailed plan. Although the Norwegians decided not to submit a bid to BDO as a single entity, they did try and partner with one of the other bidders a little later in the process.

The frustration for me was that I, and others, was spending far too much time with potential consortia when they didn't really have any serious intention of bidding. I was also angry that Alex had been speaking to them for a considerable time outside FOH. I only discovered this after being accidentally copied into an exchange of correspondence between Kai and Alex. I put a stop to that. It was not viable for discussions to be happening with others in tandem with our own bid. We all had the sole aim of saving Hearts. That was all that mattered.

To their credit, they did believe in supporter ownership and what FOH was trying to do. I always appreciated that. We left our relationship open after a lengthy process of trying to persuade them not to issue a press release about their future intentions. As a politician I know all too well that the media as an outlet for information is critical but against all our instincts, and a great deal of advice from Lawrence, we all had to have a degree of discipline in not talking to the media. Kai reluctantly appreciated this. He wasn't bidding so what was the point? Nobody wanted to do anything that could potentially make it more difficult to save Hearts. If there was an opportunity in the future to cooperate we would talk, especially given the experience Kai and his team had in sponsorship and marketing.

I also had very productive discussions with a contact given to us by Ewan Murray from *The Guardian* sport section. He introduced us to a commercial property expert who was a Hearts season ticket holder. David Drew had a wealth of contacts in the sports industry and, in particular, with a sports investment bank that specialised in turning distressed sports businesses around. They were very productive discussions. It ultimately didn't materialise as there was no certainty in future revenues and the group wanted exclusivity. Exclusivity was not something I had in my power to deliver. It was not something that even BDO could deliver. Drew left the door open in case we required his advice in the future. On signing off his last email, he said he was still hopeful a solution would be found and asked after the status of the 'Norwegians'. His email showed that all the media talk by the Norwegians had penetrated through to the fans.

One other interesting approach came from the grandson of Barney Battles Jr, who played for Hearts and Scotland between 1929 and 1936, scoring 133 goals in just 140 appearances. He was also called Barney Battles and had a background in London corporate finance. He approached me to offer his assistance in helping raise the capital for the FOH bid. It was good to chat to him. He would certainly be someone to bear in mind should we require the funds.

That left two other potential bidders: an American sports company called Club9 Sports and an Italian bid from Five Star Football Limited led by Angelo Massone. Club9 Sports was a serious bid. It was being funded by a consortium of US businesspeople fronted by Jon Pritchett. Jon was the Chief Executive Officer of Club9 Sports, a subsidiary of Prometheus Capital Partners from Chicago. They specialised in advising in the US sports and media industry. Lord Foulkes and I had been in touch with Jon Pritchett a few months previously after a tip off that he was interested in Hearts. Discussions were cordial but didn't really come to anything. However, they had come back on to the scene in a big way. Jon was co-ordinating a group of US and Scottish partners on a deal. He was also one of the key players in American businessman Bill Miller's attempt to take control of Rangers. They had also had a failed attempt to buy Sheffield Wednesday that went so badly wrong that they were dubbed 'Cloud9 Sports' by the Wednesday supporters.

The interesting thing was that Jon's Edinburgh partner was the now infamous Bob Jamieson from Kex Sports Shoes Ltd. Bob had been trying to purchase Hearts for a number of years from both Chris Robinson and Vladimir Romanov. These bids failed because he simply wasn't able to show anyone proof of funding. Bob had set up HMFC Ltd in June 2013 for the purposes of making a bid for the club with the support of Jon and his consortium. He was being advised by former Director of City Development at the City of Edinburgh Council, Dave Anderson, who left the Council following the property conservation shared repairs scandal in his department. Dave was cleared of any wrongdoing and later praised for his honesty and integrity. As a council employee, Dave had been approached by Hearts in 2011 when Romanov was looking to redevelop Tynecastle. He was involved in producing a report on the club's future that concluded the refurbishment of Tynecastle was 'not a viable option' and a new home for the club should be found. That may account for his part in the HMFC Ltd proposal which was to move Hearts away from Tynecastle to an unspecified site on the outskirts of Edinburgh. That site eventually transpired to be the back pitches of Murrayfield stadium – on the floodplain.

I knew Dave Anderson from my own days as a City Councillor. I always found him to be an excellent council official who had vast experience in economic development. It helped that Dave and I trusted each other as Bob was almost completely impossible to deal with. I couldn't cope with the conspiracy theories, the thousands of emails he would send and the fact that I didn't believe he had either any money or any intention of trying to buy Hearts. He was convinced that FOH were in cahoots with Romanov and Sergejus to steal the club from the fans. That theory would have had a tiny amount of credence had the Lithuanians not been disposed of by way of the administration.

Bob and Lord Foulkes also didn't get on well at all. It may have a lot to do with the Bob being a 'Walter Mitty' character in his previous bids for Hearts when Lord Foulkes was Chair. Bob always referred to Lord Foulkes as the 'auld codger'. That was particularly funny as I think Bob is older than him. I was surprised Dave would want to work with him and I was even more surprised at Jon but, as I always maintained, we would not close any doors if it meant the saving of Hearts.

Jon had been watching the club for some time. He had developed some ideas for how to do something strategic and significant that went well beyond a mere acquisition. Bob was the person who first reached out to Jon after he didn't take forward a bid for Rangers. Jon made it very clear that, whilst Bob had been helpful and energetic as a Hearts supporter, he was not the lead on this bid. I don't think he told Bob that though. He also didn't like fan ownership. He knew partners, strategic allies and advisers were critically important, but he believed firmly that someone needs to be in charge of a football club to make it work. He may have had a point of view that would be shared by some, but that resulted in them not wanting to work with FOH. The result being that Bob became hostile to FOH and deliberately destructive.

Jon and Dave were wilier operators than Bob. They knew the value of consensus and appreciated the potential of unified supporter groups that could put their shoulders behind their plan. They also knew the value of having the political skills, knowledge and relationships that FOH and I had built up in the city, footballing fraternity and beyond in Lithuania. However, Bob didn't think that FOH or, more specifically, I was working in the best interest of Hearts. I didn't know where he got that from but that was his firm view and he was going to do all he could to undermine us.

Their acquisition plan, as far as I could ascertain from discussions with Dave, was that they had set aside £3 million for working capital in a total bid of around £5 million. That would realise approximately £2 million to deliver the shares from the CVA. It was clear that Dave had done his homework as they had come to the same conclusion that significant working capital would be required and that would, therefore, reduce the value of the assets. Surprisingly, their plan was partially funded by a Chinese investor who wanted to build a stem cell research facility at Tynecastle and bring this to the world of sport in terms of the healing and repair of injured players. Hearts would be their test bed. It sounded to me a little strange, but the Centre for Regenerative Medicine at the University of Edinburgh was doing similar research, so it was plausible.

I had many interactions with Jon and I had no doubt about his sincerity. He had on a number of occasions intimated that a bid would be forthcoming via lawyers in Glasgow. Although it became increasingly clear that he had concerns about the level of subsidy required for the ongoing running costs of the club.

HMFC Ltd released a statement through Bob to the BBC two days before the BDO bids deadline. He gave away a lot of detail – specifically that they were planning, and seemingly already had commitments, to design, finance and build a new stadium for Hearts away from Tynecastle. The new stadium was a pivotal component of their plan. This is where their bid and FOH differed. We had already committed to staying at Tynecastle. This was both important for the fans and critical to saving the club. I was furious with Bob for this press release. He was perfectly entitled to do so but he completely missed how this could change the dynamics with the Lithuanian administrators. If the new owners of Hearts didn't require the stadium then they could sell the club to HMFC Ltd for a specified sum and rent the stadium to them until such time as it was no longer required. I fully understand that the value of the current stadium would have been required to fund a new stadium, but Bob was bandying around figures in the region of £20–25 million. If I was Deimantė in Lithuania I would be considering the current stadium asset as being worth a lot more than was being intimated at the time of sale. If any of these two options was to come to pass, Hearts would merely be a tenant of the owner. This hasn't worked well for other clubs like Coventry City. The stadium becomes merely a property transaction that the landlords could sell at any time. Bob had created a huge problem that wasn't going to be easy to manage. Bob saw the FOH as a rival rather than a partner, so he didn't really mind if he was causing difficulties in this way.

I was so furious with the BBC story that I immediately contacted Jon. He had to stop Bob from making it more difficult for us all. If he cared about the future of Hearts, he would have to prevent Bob from going to the press on a speculative basis. Jon agreed. He said he was making it abundantly clear to all parties on his side that he wanted no comments, statement or leaks to media while they were in the middle of the bid process. Jon was less than happy about Bob making comments like this to the BBC. Jon assured me that it wouldn't happen again. He didn't want to undermine FOH and wasn't sure why Bob did. He assured me that Dave and others involved were perfectly attuned to everything that was happening and the sensitive nature of any dialogue in public.

Despite Jon's assurances and his advice to 'ignore Bob's emotional rants and communicate directly with me', problems with Bob continued. Bob was a proud third-generation Hearts fan and attended his first Hearts game in 1955, aged eight, with his grandad. He kept emphasising that he wanted the best for Hearts. I had to take that at face value. I had no choice, but I was hugely concerned that Jon didn't appreciate how the press worked in Scotland and they would continue to seek out information from Bob if he was willing to feed the press beast. Bryan Jackson pleaded with the media to stop providing Bob with an outlet. They were merely fuelling the difficulties that these stories were creating. I also found out that the Norwegians had signed a letter of understanding to help Club9 should their bid be successful. It was all getting very complicated.

The final other potential bidder was Five Stars Football Ltd. It was a company run by Tommaso Angelini with former Livingston and Dundee Football Club's owner, Italian businessman and lawyer Angelo Massone as a Director. The deal was being put together by John Kerr from Glasgow and Edinburgh law firm, Anderson Strathern. I had met with John back in early May when he said he may have a client who would be interested in buying Hearts. We didn't know much about the Five Star bid but it had been indicated that it was around the £4 million mark. We weren't sure if this was including working capital to keep Hearts running or was simply the amount to deliver the CVA. He had already had a bid for £4.5 million turned down by the Romanov regime the previous November.

The issue for FOH was whether the Five Star bid was right for Hearts and whether Mr Massone himself was a 'fit and proper' person to be running a football club. It was well documented what happened at both Dundee and Livingston when he was involved. It is not for me to analyse those situations but to say that both ended in the clubs nearly going out of business. He was only in charge of Livingston for just over a year. They were plunged into administration after he led a consortium that bought them for just one pound. What we did know was that they had access to resources and were keen to get back into football.

Richard knew a little about Tommaso Angelini so we asked if he would be willing to meet with them to determine if they were serious and if it would be even slightly possible for FOH to work with them. Five Star had been a competing bid when Richard was attempting fan ownership at St Mirren through the 10,000 Hours campaign.

I have to be honest and say that Five Star's involvement gave me most concern. It would be impossible for FOH to ask the supporters to partner with someone who had a sketchy football ownership reputation at best and would be a real danger to Hearts' survival at worst. I could only go on what people were telling me and the advice I was receiving from people who had been involved with the footballing authorities when he was in charge of Dundee and Livingston. I'm sure BDO were getting the same advice. This nervousness was underpinned by their bid being for £4 million when it didn't appear that they had done any due diligence or examined what would be required to keep the club operating. A successful purchase was one thing, but we could end up back at the same place in short order if there was no additional funding for operating costs and for rebuilding the club.

I also had it on good authority that Mr Massone would not pass the SFA section 10 'fit and proper persons' test given that he had been a:

Director of a club in membership of any National Association within the five-year period preceding such club having undergone an insolvency event.

This would include the insolvency event at Livingston. The problem was whether that would be a consideration for the Lithuanian administrators or if any Five Star bid would be discounted by BDO as it could not be achieved if the new owners couldn't pass the conditions of the SFA. We would just have to see what happened next.

The positive was our own bid. Kevin Windram had been given full access to all club finances by Bryan and Trevor. This allowed Ann and the bid team to start to shape the bid. Kevin had put in a Herculean effort to provide three years of financial projections. This was not an easy task at all. He took a very conservative approach by discounting anything that we would not be in control of, including player sales and cup runs. It also included the assumption that we would be relegated to the lower division at the end of the season and stay there for two years. It was this work that identified that the club would require over £3 million in additional working capital over the three-year period from 2014 to 2016 to break even. This was critical to our bid as it would fundamentally affect the amount we would be willing and able to pay for the club and what we would need to keep it solvent.

Kevin had provided all his workings and assumptions to Kris Keane and John Reid at Deloitte as they would be handling the preparation and submission of the bid on behalf of FOH. Our bid would involve the creation of two vehicles. BIDCO would be set up to make the initial purchase and it would be the intention that BIDCO would transfer to fan control and owner-ship of the club via FANCO (this would in essence be FOH). The bid envisaged that BIDCO would take control of Hearts by the club exiting administration through a CVA with a minimum of 79.9 per cent of the issued shares of the Company being transferred to BIDCO for £1. The funding for the CVA would be provided by way of a loan from BIDCO which would be used to pay the creditors, meet the costs of the administration and the CVA. That loan would be repaid over time from FOH. The offer would comprise £2 million less the

£500,000 or so payable as football debts and would not include any cash shortfall anticipated for the season 2013/14.

Our bid had to have some stringent conditions attached. These were to ensure that BIDCO got full control of the club and also all of the assets of the club. We needed a belt and braces approach given the experience that Bryan had already encountered with the Lithuanian authorities. We had to ensure that any deal delivered a minimum of 79.9 per cent of the shares. It was no good just being able to get the 29.9 per cent of shares from ūkio Bankas as this would leave UBIG with continuing majority control. Bryan would have to deliver all the shares for this to work.

The bid was also conditional on a CVA being agreed with the creditors. This was to clean up the Hearts balance sheet and to rid it of the crippling debt. There could be no outstanding liabilities other those backed by a matching cash balance at the club. We had to be satisfied that BIDCO would have security over the stadium and other assets. All this would have to be done to allow a successful takeover to occur.

It may have been obvious, but the bid had to be conditional on confirmation of Hearts preserved membership of the SFA, SPFL and position in the Premier League for the start of the football season 2013/14. The value of any football club is in the assets it holds. One of the key assets is the membership of the league structure. That is what gives the club its ultimate value. There was an existing 15-point penalty deduction on Hearts for the season ahead; however, we added a condition that there should be no further penalties on the playing status of Hearts if there was a successful purchase. Given the discussions that had happened about the separation of the club from the stadium, we were adamant that no assets should be disposed of prior to the CVA process concluding. We didn't want the Lithuanians to sell the stadium and then conclude the CVA without all the current assets. Lastly, we were aware that the relationship with HMRC had been strained for some considerable time. The bid insisted that BDO provide us with confirmation from HMRC that there was no tax liability arising from the forgiveness of debt from the CVA, and no liabilities due beyond that, as stated in the financial projections.

The bid also included the route to full supporter ownership. On completion of the transaction with Hearts, BIDCO would enter into a legally binding agreement with FANCO whereby it would acquire BIDCO's interests, both debt and shares, over a period of time. The principal elements of this deal structure would be that FOH would fund FANCO (or be FANCO) and over a three-year period FANCO would repay BIDCO. At the completion of this process BIDCO would transfer all shares to FANCO. BIDCO would solely run Hearts but FANCO would get a representative on the Board prior to full supporter ownership. The interesting line in the bid proposal was that BIDCO would be funded by an individual investor.

At lunchtime on 11 July, Ann, as Chair of the FOH bid team, submitted our agreed proposal to BDO. The FOH Board had agreed to let the bid team produce and submit the proposal our behalf. We delegated that responsibility and unanimously supported the structure of the deal. Ann signed off her submission email by saying the bid was fully funded. Having proof of funds would ultimately determine the direction the club would go next.

I subsequently provided an informal addendum to BDO that FOH would fund the club for three years from its revenue to the tune of £1.25 million per year. This wasn't included in the formal bid as it has no impact on the actual bid itself. However, BDO wanted to see the figures and understand both the purchase of the club and how it would be maintained as a going concern post-purchase. That made the total package with the initial purchase and working capital worth £5.75 million.

Our bid submission was a reaffirmation of our commitment to seeing a supporter-led takeover. Given we were the only bid that included the supporters, I had no hesitation as labelling it 'the only real game in town'. At the point of formally submitting the bid, FOH had more than 5,000 Direct Debit mandates from supporters. We had broken the £1 million per year mark. We were still heading towards our 6,000 pledgers target. For the moment, we had enough to give comfort to both BIDCO and BDO that we could cover the financial shortfall at Hearts. What a supporter base we had. Their generosity was saving their club.

The bid team and I were utterly confident that ours was a well-researched, credible, affordable and sensible bid that would offer financial stability to Hearts, give the creditors a fair price through the CVA, and provide the foundations for a bright future. It was a low risk bid for BDO compared to what we were hearing from the other potential bidders and that would give us a huge advantage.

Lawrence had planned to do a big media event with FOH handing over the bid. If the event had gone ahead, it would be myself and Donald Ford. However, the deal with BIDCO was that it would be submitted on our behalf and the least publicity the better. It was a BIDCO deal supported by FOH.

We decided that we would not issue any further comment or give interviews in the days prior or after to show respect and give BDO due time to consider any proposals they received. We knew that others would want to showcase their bids in public and that would have been unfair to BDO. We didn't want them to come under external pressure and we certainly didn't want to give the Lithuanian administrators any additional leverage. The biggest challenge for me was going to be resisting the obvious question – who was BIDCO and who was the sole individual funding the bid?

Ann had been involved in FOH since its inception back in 2010. Her advice had proven to be immeasurable and the people she brought in to help FOH were of the highest calibre. She had taken on the role of leading the bid team and the proposals around the creation of BIDCO. The construction of the bid allowed FOH to clear the hurdle that always hampered progress, that of having considerable revenue resources but no capital. It was always the case that any deal would require FOH to borrow the money required to complete any CVA and buy the shares. That was why we kept productive discussion with other interested parties such as Gordon McKie. Even Wonga offered their lending services for the purpose.

It was the unspoken truth during FOH discussions. Would Ann be willing to fund FOH to purchase Hearts? We had discussed it informally when we retreated to our second office after meetings – The Westroom bar on Melville Place. We often discussed if Ann was interested or if she was merely giving her experience and time.

I spent a lot of time with Ann since I got involved with FOH. She was a tremendous support and confidante. Yes, she was chairing the bid team and working very closely with Robert, Kevin and John but she was also regularly attending our FOH meetings. I would seek her advice on numerous issues from the politics of the FOH boardroom to the people involved, her thoughts on the way forward and my own performance as Chair. We were never off the phone to each other.

We were witnessing huge progress but we still hadn't got over the hurdle of needing the money to finance buying the club. I was providing detailed feedback at every FOH meeting on who I had been talking to with regards to capital funding and where it could come from. In essence, this was the aspect that was taking up most time. I can't fully recall who it was – I think it may have been Jane Lewis – who suggested at a Board meeting that I should just be straight with Ann and ask if she was willing to finance the capital for the purchase. It was an obvious suggestion, but us Brits don't really like talking about money and I was no exception. I also recall Calum saying to me, 'Throughout every discussion I would never play poker with Ann Budge.' I just bit the bullet.

Primarily I used to meet Ann at her home on a Sunday evening. It was the only evening that I had relatively free from work. Normally these Sunday meetings would be to keep each other updated about the general FOH thinking because, even then, Ann was totally immersed in how to sort out the club. These meetings were useful in aiding communication and understanding. I wanted to ensure that Ann felt confident that FOH was moving to a more professional footing and in the right direction. This Sunday would be different.

I was as nervous as I have ever been the Sunday I approached the issue of whether Ann would put in the money. I was like a child at a school prom asking a female classmate if they'd like to dance. Anyway, I broached the subject and Ann said, 'Of course.' On reflection, I didn't really think I would need to persuade her, but I did, out of courtesy, have to ask her. Latterly she told me that she decided herself to look at financing the bid when it became clear that administration was not only inevitable but also presented a real opportunity to achieve the FOH objectives.

That made the BIDCO proposal a no brainer for us. We had someone whose involvement with FOH stretched back to the beginning, who was a committed and passionate Hearts supporter, who believed in supporter ownership and was one of the most successful and prominent businesswomen in the country. When I reported in confidence back to the FOH Board they couldn't have all been more delighted. I would bet money on this being the only thing that was ever unanimously agreed!

Although Ann had committed the money, she wanted to remain anonymous. I could see why. There were many aspects to this. I just guess but I think the main one was that Ann is a very private and unassuming person. She didn't want the glare of publicity or the pressure that went with being in the public eye. There was also the fact that the project may not be successful and that would be a hard thing to swallow. It could also have been to protect her family. She was used to going to games with her daughter and she wouldn't want that to be disturbed in any way. It was also a deliberate move. If the Lithuanians knew that the person funding the BIDCO proposal was Ann, then they may have demanded more money. I have little idea and no inclination to know how much individuals are worth, but newspaper reports would have no doubt been read in Lithuania and that could have created additional problems. There was also the added layer of the supporters. They were joining FOH in their droves. We didn't want a narrative to grow that Ann would be financing this and, therefore, their contribution was not as important as before. The reality was that the opposite was true. Ann only made the decision to get involved on the back of the response of the supporters in pledging their cash to the project. Had it not been for them, Ann may not have been interested. The deal, after all, relied on the provision of revenue support for three years to help the club through.

Lawrence was superb on this point. I know he found it agonising and frustrating that he couldn't present Ann to the media. I was confident that it would have helped the FOH pledges considerably and provided credibility to the BIDCO proposals. Following discussion between myself, Ann and Lawrence, we agreed that the best way forward was to say that the bid was not about the people financing it but about the supporters. We would reassure that the individual was not in it for any personal gain. All they wanted was to save their beloved Hearts. The person was a successful Scottish entrepreneur, a Hearts supporter and had the confidence of everyone involved at FOH and BDO. We would continue to say that the identity of the individual funder was not relevant at this stage. The only relevance was the supporters and encouraging them to continue to set up their direct debits. Without that revenue, the club could not survive in new ownership and there would be no money to repay BIDCO as per the agreement.

I have to say the media were superb on this point. They all could have guessed who it was. A combination of their willingness to see the FOH bid succeed and the relationship Lawrence had with them kept Ann's name out of the public eye, even after John Robertson accidentally announced it at a press conference! He mentioned it once, but I think he got away with it!

Lawrence also arranged for me to go on the BBC Scotland's 'most ill-informed and petty' football chat show, *Off the Ball*, with Tam Cowan and Stuart Cosgrove. Disappointingly, Stuart was replaced by former Scotland striker, Pat Nevin, for the day. I was only disappointed because I'm a huge fan of the show. Nevertheless, I would get an easier time of it without the terrible twosome presenting. I was joined by Scottish Olympic runner, Eilidh Doyle (née Child). I knew she was a massive Jambo so I would have someone on my side.

It went really well. Tam had been a great supporter of Hearts during their financial crisis and supported FOH whenever he could. He gave me a load of time to explain what we were trying to do. Eilidh and her husband to be, Brian, were fantastically supportive. Eilidh is a great ambassador for Scottish sport and a lovely person.

I did get into a little bit of trouble though. For a reason that I can't recall, Tam started a conversation about bad sunburn and asked if we had ever suffered from it. I told them the story of a holiday to Greece back in 2004 when the sunburn on my ankles, and subsequent sunstroke, was so bad I genuinely believed the waiter in a restaurant I was eating in was former Democratic US Presidential candidate, John Kerry. I even asked him why he was in Greece. That got Tam talking about other people that he had seen with bad sunburn. One such person he claimed was Dolly Parton. Without thinking, I proclaimed live on national radio that I bet Dolly never had sunburnt ankles given the shade she naturally throws on them. I thought it was a fairly innocuous and innocent comment. My social media feed and some constituents thought otherwise.

It was easy to do media but the biggest issue was how we explained such a complicated structure and process to the fans. Lawrence was set the task of moving the narrative away from Ann to explaining the vehicle for buying the club and then selling that to the fans.

Oh, and there was a new football season being prepared for...

CHAPTER 14

Three, Two, One... Preferred Bidder

THE BDO DEADLINE of 5.00pm on Friday 12 July passed and, after the months of discussions, negotiations and tyre kicking, we were down to just three bids: from BIDCO, Club9 Sports and Five Star Football Ltd.

The next milestone was to achieve preferred bidder status. This part of the process was where BDO took all the bids that had been received and narrowed them down to just one. That bid would then be used to prepare the CVA. We were still much closer to the start of the process than the end. However, it was a boost to everyone that we could now concentrate on the task in hand with two rival bids. I was confident that we would be the only viable option.

BDO were now in discussions with the legal representatives of the administrators of ūkio Bankas, Valnetas. They had hoped to be in a position to name a preferred bidder as soon as possible. At that stage, there was no information as to how long that process would take.

Bryan was continuing to run the club and support the manager in his preparations for the forthcoming season. He wanted the club to exit administration as quickly as possible, but he emphasised how important it was not to get carried away. The day after the deadline, Hearts played their first friendly match of the season in Scotland. Dunfermline Football Club was also in administration and it looked likely that they would end up supporter-owned. Their fan group, Pars United, was just a few weeks away from successfully completing their CVA. SDS had been working with Pars United and thought it may be a good showcase for the fans to put on a pre-season friendly between Dunfermline and Hearts for the SDS Fans Cup. It would generate a bit of interest and all monies raised would be split between FOH and Pars United. The added spice was that Dunfermline was managed by Hearts hero and 1998 Cup-winning manager, Jim Jefferies.

I was invited to the Directors Box with my fellow FOH Directors to meet with Ian Hunter and Bob Garmory from Pars United. We wanted to share experiences on the administration process and supporter ownership.

It was a good initiative and a fun afternoon for FOH and the 4,500 supporters who turned out. It swelled our coffers by a couple of thousand pounds and allowed us the first glimpse of the team for the new season. Every player in the team was a Scot apart from our Australian defender, Dylan McGowan. We won the game 2-1 and took the first and only SDS Fans trophy back to Tynecastle. I have to admit I don't think I've seen it in the trophy cabinet!

The only downside to the day was that Bob Jamieson was also in attendance at the match as a guest, invited by someone indeterminate. He spent the entire game telling me how FOH would not work and we were pulling the wool over the eyes of the supporters. The only way to save Hearts was for FOH to throw their weight behind his bid. I really just wanted to enjoy the match.

Bryan had asked the fans for their continued support and patience. There was still a great deal of fundraising going on. The fans had come good by exceeding the 3,000 extra season ticket sales target that Bryan had set. Money was tight but it was coming in at least. Cash flow would be eased a little with the start of the season just around the corner. Shirt sponsors Wonga brought forward a £100,000 payment for the entire seasons to try and help. Jambos Kickback had raised in excess of £35,000 in donations and a supporters' family fun day rally, organised by Graeme Kay, the husband of Hearts long-term employee, Shelley, that I attended the weekend before raised an astonishing £30,000.

It was a fantastic afternoon. Tam Cowan and Donald Findlay spoke. Tam was on top form. He had always been supportive and, again, waived his fee. He started his contribution by holding up cards with the numbers five and one on them. That got the audience on side immediately. We all thought he was rubbing in the famous 2012 Scottish Cup Final score against Hibs. Not Tam. Whilst everyone was trying to grab a mobile phone photo, he held up as '1-5' instead and proclaimed it was the number of points Hearts had been deducted for being 'cheating bastards'. Tam is a self-confessed Motherwell fan. He knew exactly how we were feeling. They had gone into administration in 2002 and only survived with the intervention of supporters and local businesspeople. Tam also had a real go at Donald Findlay QC's expense. He was the other speaker and was terrific. A lifelong Rangers fan, Donald is now chairman of Cowdenbeath. A role that confirmed to Tam that he was a 'true glory hunter'. Donald spoke warmly about the need for all Scottish football fans to pull together and why the country would be a poorer place without Hearts. It was great stuff, although Tam did point out that some of the audience were surprised that Donald had the microphone for 40 minutes 'without singing a song'. Tam ripped everyone in the room. I got my fair share from him. He finished by paying tribute to our tremendous supporters. His seriousness was only punctuated by saying that even former Hearts defender, the classy Davie Weir, was helping by 'donating his Winter Fuel Allowance'. No wonder the amount of money that was raised. Tam was an absolute star who will always be thanked for his contribution to Hearts' plight.

The Gorgie Noise Facebook page run by a Prestonpans fan, Paul Harthill, had raised over £6,500 to purchase season tickets. It was just phenomenal. The fans had raised over £750,000 in little over a month. This was all happening to assist BDO in running the club and prevent the sale of players from the threadbare squad. Jason Holt was the prized asset and had been subject to two offers from Nottingham Forest. It was the fans' fundraising efforts that meant Bryan could decline derisory offers for our players.

The three bids to buy Hearts were rejected by Valnetas. They wanted more money. Bryan tried to quell the disappointment by saying that this is normal practice ahead of further negotiations and warned that it was 'unrealistic' for Hearts to be out of administration, and have their transfer embargo lifted, before the end of the transfer window. We were in this for the long haul.

There had been indications for some time that the administrators would want £5 million to agree a CVA – the only means by which Hearts could exit administration. It was the figure that Robert had worked with some months before. However, that was before the numbers were released that showed how much it would cost to keep the club operating as a going concern. The reality was that Hearts was a distressed sale and it was only worth what someone was willing to pay for it. We had put a lot of effort into determining what it was actually worth. Bryan had left us in no doubt, though, that we would have to raise the value of our bid.

The Lithuanians would never have approved any of the deals that were on the table. They didn't like them. They thought the ground was worth close to £20 million given what Cala Homes was willing to pay just a decade before. The Lithuanians tempered it down to £5–10 million but would not accept anything below £5 million. The valuation that was put on the club by BDO was a much more realistic £3–3.5 million. The Lithuanians had to bear in mind the huge difficulties if they sold the stadium as a development opportunity. Any purchaser would be faced with the wrath of the fans and political communities. It would not be an easy purchase for a housing developer. It would just be too toxic an issue to touch. Then, if they were able to get a buyer, they would have obstacles to planning. The ethanol tanks at the distillery have always been the impediment to development. It was this that allegedly scuppered the £51 million development plans of Romanov. As a construction project it would be expensive. Clearing the site of a century-old stadium would not be cheap. Consequently, the costs involved with insurance and security would be astronomical between purchase and development. All in all, it would be a reputational and development nightmare for any new owner with significant potential hostility. This was all written into the valuation for Valnetas.

As FOH, we tried to make the case for a lower valuation. We weren't trying to influence the value but ensure that it was realistic and fair. The market had moved considerably since the Cala approach in 2004 and we didn't see it as being a parcel of land that anyone would be interested in. The reputational damage of purchasing the stadium for any purpose other than being the home of Heart of Midlothian Football Club could be extreme. I also wasn't allowing the chants of 'flats, flats, glorious flats' from our friends in green to come to pass.

Portsmouth FC had the same problems prior to their emergence from a two-year financial hell as the largest fan-owned football club in English football history. One of the complexities of the Portsmouth administration was trying to agree a deal on the value of the ground. The parties who owned it sat outside of the security of the club. They were hoping the ground owner would accept a reduced value, but they were threatened with an application to go to court to establish what the true value of the ground was. We couldn't afford the time or expense for that to happen. That would have been a real added complication for Hearts as we had a secured creditor looking to achieve maximum value. We were in a worse position than Portsmouth because of the secured nature of the stadium to ūkio Bankas. That meant they had quite a few of the aces up their sleeve. It was not an equal relationship. We also had differing objectives. We wanted to own the club so we could see Hearts survive. Valnetas wanted to maximise the asset value for their creditors.

The City of Edinburgh Council as the planning authority and the Health and Safety Executive (HSE) would be key to ensuring this message was made loud and clear. We asked some of our friends in the media to make overtures to the Council and HSE. The *Daily Record* ran a story: 'Toxic Alert at Tyne-castle after Hearts' stadium is branded a 'hazard zone' by safety inspectors because of whisky vats'. The article said there would be 'huge problems' and any developer would 'face huge clean-up costs' that would make the stadium 'far less attractive to buyers'. Several other media outlets picked up on the story. They would often talk about the sale of the stadium as a separate transaction but add, 'but that would likely bring problems with planning permission for any prospective buyer'. The Council planners said they wouldn't comment on any proposals unless there was a formal planning application and they would then consult HSE at that point, but they had examined this issue for previous applications and concurred with the HSE analysis.

I knew that this could have a potential knock-on effect in the future if Hearts wanted to modernise the main stand, but if we got that far it would be a positive problem to deal with. In fact, it did become a problem. An emergency meeting was hastily arranged with the BIDCO team to examine how we could improve our bid. John Reid at Deloitte had produced some options for us to look at after discussions with Bryan. A very lengthy meeting concluded that the initial bid would be revised. The capital sum would be increased from £2 million to £2.5 million and we would take on the football debt. That debt was confirmed as £532,000 and BDO were given the task of re-profiling the amounts to see if they could be negotiated down and payment terms lengthened. The total package would be just over £3 million plus the £3,750,000 for three years revenue support. It was a substantial improvement and matched the BDO valuation, although it may not have matched the aspirations of the sellers. The obstacle for FOH was that Ann was only committed to £2 million. We would have to look at ways of finding the additional half million. The revised proposal stated that this would be paid in ten monthly instalments of £50,000 per month as a deferred consideration. That could be met by FOH through pledge monies.

The new proposal was presented to BDO as a full and final offer. We felt it was a fair price at the end of the day and it wouldn't be in anyone's interests to get into an unaffordable bidding war. I understand the Massone bid was also improved. Given that they were rumoured to have offered close to £4 million in their original bid, I guessed that they were perhaps closer to the £4.5 million they offered back in 2012. If truth be told, we had no idea how much it was worth. We did know that it didn't include any revenue support for the club to survive on a day-to-day basis. A similar story to how Livingston got into trouble so quickly perhaps.

It also appeared that Bob Jamieson's HMFC Ltd had 'ceased to negotiate' with BDO so were effectively out of the process. It would not be the
end of the communications though. Despite all the meetings and discussion
with dozens of potential purchasers and investors, it had come down to just
two. There was space for others to come forward, but our experience so
far showed that this was not likely. In the end, we were confident our bid
matched the valuation that had been produced. BDO were getting the valuation for the club that they calculated. Whether the valuation was high or
low doesn't matter. It was the valuation. Nobody could argue anything else.

The revised bids inevitably ended up in the press. This was fine by us
as it created more of a narrative for the supporters and they responded. It
also generated an email from the father of former player, Andrew Driver.
David Driver was acting on behalf of Andrew. He was owed a considerable
sum from Hearts in unpaid salary and other fees. There were lots of former
players helping the club and David wanted to offer help from Andrew. He
was happy to negotiate other options for the debt to help Hearts. It was
obviously not something I was able to do but I passed him to Trevor. The
football debt would have to be honoured by any new owners to satisfy the
football rules, so it was an overture that was very welcomed.

The question for FOH at this stage was when to draw down pledges. We
were running at over 5,000 direct debits and it was growing by the day. We
had committed to taking the first payments on 2 August 2013. Ann was cautious about this date. The way the proposal stood was that we didn't need to
start collecting until we knew we would have a deal. As we had always said,
we wanted to minimise the possibility that we would have to return money
to supporters. That process could be costly and cumbersome. Not taking the
first payments until we needed them was the best way forward.

Delaying collection of pledges would give FOH time to bottom out any
outstanding issues with the GoCardless system such as refunds and management information. It would also allow time for a simple message to the
fans about the shape of the deal they were signing up to and what would be
expected of them.

The delay in drawdown did open up old wounds within FOH as to the
system we should use. We had these arguments months before. The same
day that we decided to delay the drawdown of direct debits to 2 September, Alex contacted Calum to say we should shut down the GoCardless
system completely and go back to his original idea of physical standing
order forms. He was convinced that was the only way to control drawdown

dates. The irony was that we had changed the date twice already, so we proved it could easily be altered to a date in the future. I didn't understand why this was even being suggested. We had over 5,000 pledgers converted to a monthly direct debit on the system at that point and ready to go. All I needed was to activate their direct debits and the money would come in. To start that process again with physical forms was incomprehensible to me.

It transpired that Alex had promised to sign the indemnity form but hadn't done so. Until that was signed and lodged with GoCardless, they wouldn't let us activate the direct debits in any case. It was infuriating. It was absolutely correct for GoCardless to indemnify themselves against the direct debit guarantee system in the event that we had to return the money and the individual pledger invoked the refund guarantee. That was how the direct debit regulations worked. However, we knew it would never need to be called upon as we had agreed that we would refund the money minus any small bank charges. We had even written that into the members agreement and our constitution. The indemnity was a peace of mind for GoCardless, but nothing else.

Several posters on the Jambos Kickback site called Gasman and Football First were raising the direct debit guarantee as an issue and what the consequences would be if funds had to be returned. The chat meant it had to be dealt with. The irony was that even a standing order system would require some form of refund if we couldn't fulfil the purchase. I just didn't see how we could cart around over 5,000 sensitive pieces of paper with private details of each individual on them. We all appreciated that Alex was going to sign the indemnity. It was good of him to do so, but if we had received funds from the supporters and we wouldn't spend a penny unless we did a deal, the indemnity would never have been required as the money would have been in the FOH bank account to return to pledgers. It was merely a formality that gave GoCardless the comfort they required. Alex signed the indemnity in the end. Shortly afterwards, I had to remove him from the GoCardless project and let Calum and Andy take it forward on their own.

Ann was keen for us to move our approach to publicity from the inevitable 'who is it' to what will happen next. The FOH bid team would now carry out detailed due diligence to ensure the robustness of the figures. We would simply say that FOH had secured a loan facility to enable an upfront capital amount to be put forward to allow the CVA to be negotiated. We would explain that we had secured agreement that, assuming the loan is repaid in full over an anticipated three-year period, the fans would at that point

have majority control of the club. The job of FOH would be to maximise the
money from supporters. The job of BIDCO would be to work with the administrators to get the deal through. At this point, we envisaged this may take at
least three months. We couldn't have been more wrong on timescales.

The whole project now depended on the pledges continuing to come in.
Drawdown would commence as soon as were confident the CVA was likely
to be agreed. It was important to stress that we still had a long way to go.
The challenge was to explain that this bid would result in Hearts being supporter-owned, not supporter-run. We were within touching distance. It was
as tense as it was exciting.

The Massone- and Jamieson-led bids were explained to me as being very
aggressive. They caused all sorts of trouble to FOH and Bryan. Bryan would
easily diffuse it all by consistently asking for proof of funding. BIDCO could
prove funding as Ann was standing behind the capital sum and the proof
of direct debits was standing behind both the running costs and repayment
plan. We could show clearly where the money was coming from, how much
it was, and what the repayment terms were. Our bid corresponded to those
figures. We provided all that information to BDO. The other bidders never
provided any. Bryan just kept saying to them, 'Thanks for your letter and
bid but can I have proof of funding?' The twenty plus page emails from Bob
were simply answered by Bryan with 'Show me proof of funding'. HMFC
Ltd had dropped out of the race because they decided not to engage with
BDO. Their strategy was to go above the heads of Bryan and his team and go
straight to the administrators in Lithuania. It was a false choice. Lithuania
would merely send him back. Bryan was clear, he wouldn't get into a slan-
derous situation with Bob that would waste even more time. Time was not
a luxury Bryan had.

Then a major bombshell dropped. The Lithuanian administrators, Valnetas UAB, instructed BDO to re-negotiate with FOH and Five Stars Football
Limited. My reservations that this was not going to be an easy process was
proving to be true. Lawrence had been informed of this and found the story
on the Lithuanian equivalent of the *Financial Times*. It was a stark warning.
Both remaining bidders would have to increase their bids 'substantially' otherwise the club would be liquidated. They said:

> ūkio Bankas – the main creditor of Scotland's football club Hearts – obligated
> the club's administrator BDO to continue negotiations with two potential
> investors with the aim to improve financial offers. If the negotiations fail,
> ūkio Bankas will initiate the process of liquidation of the football club.

Gintaras Adamonis, General Director of Valnetas, added:

> I can repeat that we are doing everything we can to save the club function-
> ing. However, I am obliged to protect solely the interests of ūkio Bankas
> and its creditors. If no feasible offer with terms and conditions acceptable
> to ūkio Bankas creditors is achieved, ūkio Bankas will remain with the only
> solution – liquidation of Heart of Midlothian PLC and enforcement of the
> standard security over Tynecastle Stadium. I sincerely hope this is the way
> of things we still can avoid.

Bryan was forthright in his response to Gintaras. He knew that keeping the
club as a going concern would deliver the best return to Valnetas.

This was a shot across the bows from Lithuania. In hindsight, it was
superb for FOH. We maintained a 'business as usual' approach and used this
to drive more pledges to stave off both Massone and the liquidation threat.
The bid team, working on behalf of FOH, would continue to negotiate on
the points of the bid submitted to BDO. We remained hopeful that we would
be able to demonstrate to the club's creditors that our proposal provided the
strongest return and carried the lowest risk, in short by far the best solution.

We immediately set up a meeting with Bryan and Trevor at BDO. We
wanted to understand where this public pronouncement had come from
and what options were available to us to satisfy the administrators. BDO had
hinted that the FOH bid was the only real bid on the table. The administrators had insisted on giving the Massone bid a bit more time to prove funding
as it was worth 'substantially' more. Bryan and Trevor stated the case that
they believed that we had the only deliverable bid. Valnetas stood by their
decision that it was insufficient for them not to consider the stadium be sold
as a property play. A revised deadline of 9 August was provided, and all bids
were asked to be full and final at that date.

We had considered whether Valnetas would entertain a continued equity
participation in Hearts. That would give them something of value that they
could realise at a later date. The equity stake would make up for the cash
shortfall value of our bid. BDO discounted this as they wanted a clean break
from any element of control.

That left us with few options. We could alter the bid to around the
£4 million mark as that was seen as what may convince the Lithuanians
to deliver the CVA. But given Valnetas could only deliver 29 per cent of the
shares, we would have to ensure we got all the shares at the time of transfer.
That was not in the gift of Valnetas. To get the bid to £4 million, we would

have to extend the deferred consideration over a much longer period. This would make a higher cost more manageable, but a longer period of time may require a residual security over the assets by the administrators.

We could alter our bid to remove the deferred consideration and make the £2.5 million available in its entirety. This would give a clear target for the FOH to raise that may attract a few marquee investors. The downside was that if the money wasn't raised there would be no deal.

There could be a hybrid alteration where a funder would effectively buy the stadium and the majority of the shares in the club and the fans would buy a slice. It would be clean, and the full control would be out of the hands of the Lithuanians. The negatives were that the football debts were still to be taken care of and there would be a lot less money for the club's ongoing revenue needs. It would also not be supporter ownership which had been promised to FOH members.

Finally, we could have looked at a 'club now, property later' model. We could purchase the majority shareholding in the club to get full control with very limited residual influence from the Lithuanians. It would also give time to raise the funds to buy the assets. The downside would be the additional rental charges for the stadium with the threat of eviction if the funds were not found. This would take a much longer time which would increase the cost and risk. Of course, we could also take the decision to leave our bid unaltered.

We decided to roll the dice a little. The goalposts were moving all the time and we were hearing that Valnetas were continuing to court other parties. That made it difficult for us to further amend our bid at that time.

This was a bold move from Ann. The bid team had come to the conclusion that other parties would not be able to deliver. Additionally, there were no property buyers in the market for the stadium. If there were, they would have come forward by now. The longer this process dragged on the less Hearts would be worth. It was the best financial bid for Hearts and the cash was ready to complete it. It had a credible working capital solution and combined the best businesspeople alongside strong supporter involvement. It was professional. We knew we could work with BDO to deliver the CVA and the survival of Hearts. We decided to say that we would consider progressing our bid if they swept all of the imponderables away and gave us preferred bidder. That way we could be confident that the games would stop.

Those games were not a surprise. I was getting messages from all over the place saying that bids were now going in. Kai from the Scandinavians had been bombarded by emails from HMFC Ltd offering – or 'begging' as he put it – for the Scandinavians to put up £5 million for the CVA, as Club9 Sports had apparently not managed to secure this. The latest offer from Bob came on the same day the Lithuanians warned of liquidation. It offered them 52 per cent ownership of HMFC Limited. In return, HMFC Ltd would own Hearts.

Kai was sending me this information as he didn't want any bid to be harmed by speculation. He also had no idea who else Bob was sending these proposals to. That was why it was important that we got preferred bidder. That way all this would stop. I had lost track of how many times Bob had threatened me personally with legal action. To be fair, he wasn't keeping in the best of health and that is partly why we gave him such latitude.

The way we would demonstrate to Valnetas that we had the only credible bid would be to insist the Massone bid demonstrated funding. It was also the case that their deal may not be able to be concluded due to the nature of the footballing rules on 'fit and proper' person. I had no shortage of information or people willing to impart stories and information. The media essentially did the job for us. It was the right thing to do, otherwise BDO would have been instructed to liquidate the club. A number of stories appeared in national newspapers highlighting the problem with the Massone bid. BDO had given a number of extensions to Five Star Football to provide funding for their bid and it was never forthcoming.

BDO wanted to try and declare a preferred bidder by the end of August 2013. At the beginning of August, I received an email from a representative of Massone to ask if I would be willing to enter discussions with him. I didn't think it was wise and declined. I would have done so had they provided proof of funds, but they still hadn't. A day or so later, Massone broke his silence in the press to urge the FOH to pool our resources with him to stave off liquidation.

The press article said that the Five Star Football bid alone was very complicated, and they wanted to provide money to help FOH create a stable future for the club. He appealed for everyone to work together as he didn't believe we had the resources. He wanted to prove to us that the newspapers were incorrect and that his interest in Hearts was genuine. He concluded by stating:

I want to sit and speak with Ian Murray in private and explain my thoughts and assure him that we have the same goals.

We decided not to take him up on the offer. A day or so later, the *Edinburgh Evening News* ran a front-page splash, 'Step aside, Angelo and let the fans take over', which pleaded with Massone and Five Star Football to stand aside and allow the FOH bid a clear run at preferred bidder. If the FOH bid collapsed, he could come back in.

The *Evening News* were utterly supportive over this time. They donated a full-page advert to FOH in return for a donation to their Sick Kids Friends Foundation charity appeal. It asked supporters to join them in playing a part in 'Scottish Football's Biggest Ever Supporter Movement' to 'Create History'. It was more than just an advert. It was a statement of credibility, momentum and intent.

The football season had commenced in earnest. A narrow defeat away to St Johnstone on the first day of the season was followed by an Edinburgh Derby against Hibs at Tynecastle. The club had arranged for the perimeter advertising boards to carry the FOH message. Kenny Wittmann, a former Hearts Sales and Marketing Manager, through his The Football Company, afforded us the space for free.

Hearts went into that game 15 points behind Hibs courtesy of the points deduction. We ended the game just 12 points behind. A wonderful headed goal by Callum Paterson halfway through the second half gave Hearts a famous win. The old ground was absolutely rocking. Hearts was off the mark. The dream of staying in the Premier League was alive and well. The togetherness was palpable. This is why we were all pulling together to save the club – for games and wins like these.

I missed the game as I was on holiday in Sardinia. I say I was on holiday, but I spent most of my time either on the phone doing constituency work or talking to FOH Directors. Ann was also on annual leave. Our bid that had been submitted would not be altered. We just had to sit tight and let Bryan and Trevor do their jobs.

They gave yet another extension to allow the Five Star Football bid to show proof of funding. Again, it never materialised. It left Bryan with no choice. He had to recommend to Valnetas that they give the FOH-backed bid preferred bidder status. Bryan is the court-appointed official and has to operate in the interests of the client with the secured lending.

THE FOH BID was the only bid that had proof of funding. It was the only bid that was remotely deliverable. Massone had put in a better offer than FOH, but it wasn't massively more and, without proof of any funds, it was undeliverable. Ann and I understood that this process was never going to happen overnight but the fact that it took as long as it did was hard to handle.

It was the one of the most joyous phone calls I ever received, Bryan informing me that we had been granted preferred bidder status. Admittedly, I was receiving the call by the swimming pool and I had perhaps had a small libation, but it was tremendous to hear. I immediately emailed the other FOH Directors. Alastair summed it up in his response: 'Amazing. Just amazing.' Another hurdle crossed. I just wished I could see the finishing line over the remaining hurdles. Valnetas had reluctantly agreed to FOH being made preferred bidder. They were still very disappointed in the price.

It set in motion a frantic couple of hours and days. I was absolutely over the moon for the supporters. It was an important day on the pathway towards putting Heart of Midlothian back on its feet. I was so proud that the bid backed by FOH had been named preferred bidder. Whilst the supporters would likely be ecstatic, the journey was in effect only beginning. Our bid had not yet been accepted, albeit we were hopeful an agreement could be reached. Valnetas still wanted more money but those negotiations would now be solely with us. Bryan cemented this view:

> We all still have a lot of work to do to demonstrate to the major creditors that the bid can offer them the best possible outcome. Let's not get carried away – now is the time for everyone to get behind FOH to make this bid work.
>
> This is a positive development but does not guarantee that a CVA will be successful. That will require a considerable combined effort from FOH and BDO to ensure that all interested parties are satisfied.

It did give us an opportunity to remind everyone that in order to make this happen, we needed as many supporters as possible to sign up to make a monthly contribution via direct debit. I had an extra holiday beer that evening to celebrate. After all the hard work from everyone connected to FOH, we deserved a little breather to take stock and enjoy the moment.

I also received a rather magnanimous email from Angelo Massone. I appreciated it. He said:

> Mr Murray congratulations. I wish you and FOH can close a CVA and save the club! My organisation never was against you and the fans. My model is a Board with investors and fans at the same table. Congratulations again and believe me I'm writing with my heart.
>
> Best wishes,
>
> Angelo Massone

Now, for the first time, the fate of Heart of Midlothian Football Club was really in the hands of the supporters of this remarkable football club.

CHAPTER 15

A Chorus of Drawdowns and Putdowns

BILL SHANKLY FAMOUSLY said that football was much more important than life or death. As I got more and more immersed in the saving of Hearts it certainly felt like that. What kept me going were the supporters. They were absolutely superb. I couldn't buy a pint of milk at the local shop, take a bus journey or go to the pub with my friends without fans asking me about the latest news from Tynecastle and the chances of saving the club.

The media calls were frenzied. Lawrence continued to impress how important message discipline was at this stage. We organised a media conference at Tynecastle with Trevor from BDO to explain how preferred bidder status would work. I stepped into Tynecastle's Executive Suite that morning trying to look confident and undaunted at the task ahead. I was in my usual uniform of a suit and red tie. The assembled press knew me from politics and I knew I was going to have to mix the world of football with the inevitable political wrangling ahead of us.

I sat down ready to chat about the FOH bid to take Heart of Midlothian out of administration and deliver a supporter-owned club. I was amused by the *Edinburgh Evening News* commenting:

> It would be entirely fitting if Ian produced a deck of cards and a suitcase full of £100 notes, for he is now embroiled in a critical game of poker. And make no mistake, the stakes are high.

The stakes were high. Whether Hearts survived was now purely down to us – The FOH and BIDCO. It was no longer a theoretical question. No pressure at all when the *Daily Record* commented:

> The club's future now rests in the hands of the fans' umbrella group chaired by Murray.

Trevor and I both spoke about what should happen next. We had to explain the formulation of the bid. Lawrence came up with a line that worked very well. It was essentially a combination of having the capital and business

expertise from BIDCO and the revenue and supporters input from FOH as
FANCO. It was a recipe that I was convinced would work very well. After all,
we couldn't buy a football club with direct debits. We would always have
had to capitalise them in some form and this was the best way to do it. The
bid meant that the stadium stayed with the football club and the football
club stayed with the supporters. I also had to keep emphasising that there
was no personal gain in any of this for the Edinburgh businessperson that
has contributed the capital sum. I used to hear Lawrence tell the journalists
that they could ask anything as long as they didn't ask me who the mystery
businessperson was. To be fair, they never did. Ann wanted anonymity for
the moment and we had to respect that. I agreed but it did leave me to do
all the media.

We were now, without argument, the biggest supporter-led bid in the
history of Scottish football. For me, this was no longer just a bid for the
club, it was a movement. We decided that we would draw down our first
direct debits on 2 September 2013 and make the case that every single
pound mattered. The parameters were limitless and the more we had the
more we could do.

There was a long road still to travel in the process. The number of
pledges rocketed as a consequence of being granted preferred bidder status.
We hit 6,000 within days of the official announcement. An email to the
Hearts database from manager Gary Locke gave us another boost. The marketing was cranking up. Shortly after the press conference, the direct debits
hit 6,700, equating to £1.3 million a year. Utterly phenomenal.

Garry Halliday was in charge of the marketing team. He never let up on
his ideas for marketing. The marketing group threw everything on the table.
Some ideas were wacky, others were inappropriate, many were inspired.
Emotional videos were produced on Hearts European adventures, Scottish
Cup exploits and with legends impressing the importance of saving their
memories of the club. They certainly pulled the heartstrings. There was
everything from pin badges and ties, to pieces of the pitch and donation
tins. Everything that would sell, we sold. Every opportunity where we could
collect money, we did.

The marketing team worked on the assumption that if we were successful in securing a deal, then it would be historic. A once in a lifetime event.
Something tangible and real to celebrate that in terms of a 'reward' would
be fantastic. Garry worried, and he was not alone, that being a member
of FOH might not be enough to keep fans contributing. We all know that

us football fans are fickle. The team wanted to put together a marketing campaign that maximised pledgers at the same time as looking at longer term opportunities.

One of the recurring themes was pitch ownership. Each supporter who set up a direct debit would be a member of FOH with defined rights. Every member who reached a minimum contribution would access a certain level of intangible benefits. One of the benefits of membership would be to receive the ownership of a virtual plot of pitch. There were huge legal complications around this type of idea. We didn't want to end up in a situation where a supporter laid claim to a piece of land. We also didn't own the club as yet. Promising something we couldn't deliver would not be advisable. Garry laid out the process to allow for a fan rewards scheme. A fan becomes a member of FOH by pledging a set amount of money per month. The member will receive a membership card with unique membership number and voting rights within the FOH structure. There would be a direct route from member to FOH Board and ultimately the Hearts Board. Other intangible benefits can be added such as family fun day invites, meet the players, pin badges and such like. All of these intangible benefits would be delivered when the member reached a certain cumulative level of contribution. The top threshold would entitle the member to their own ceremonial plot of the hallowed turf. This would be accompanied by a certificate of authenticity with the co-ordinates of the plot and a famous Hearts moment from roughly the same place. It was an inspired idea. Time for the lawyers to look at it.

Preferred bidder status made it 'squeaky bum time', as Garry would often put it, and fans needed to dig deep or watch Hearts face liquidation. He played on that. Any benefits would mean nothing at this moment in time as it was only about saving the club. However, that would not always be the case. The marketing team worked on the assumption that membership of FOH may have a shelf life, but they wanted it to be a lifetime contribution. How could FOH respond to that?

One of the complicated issues we had to deal with was balancing the wish to 'reward' FOH members with taxation legislation. FOH income was treated by the tax authorities as donations. They fell into that category. That meant that they would not be subject to 20 per cent VAT. We were advised that this tax treatment could change if we gave away anything that wasn't deemed as intangible. As an example, a discount on future season tickets would subject the FOH contributions to VAT and present us with a bill totalling tens of thousands of pounds. That would reduce our income by a substantial amount. We sought the advice from an expert who would, many years later, become the Chair of FOH, Stuart Wallace. Stuart was a partner at accountancy firm PwC and kindly offered to give advice on a pro bono basis. The only cost would be a nice tour of the Houses of Parliament. Stuart and his colleague, Aidan, sought to get this VAT exemption in writing from HMRC and kept the marketing team advised on what 'rewards' could be given to stay within the exemption. Another dyed-in-the-wool Jambo who was only too willing to help whenever it was required.

Now that we were working in tandem with the club, we had access to their marketing channels. David Southern was keen for us to remind supporters that they should be spending their money in the normal way with Hearts as well as supporting FOH. David raised the idea of FOH taking match sponsorship for the second home match of the season against Aberdeen. People employed in the football industry tell me that match sponsorship is one of the hardest things to sell. It is even harder when you are in administration. It seemed like a fairly innocuous request. We had already agreed as FOH to take a table of hospitality for the match and pay for that personally. David had suggested that for an additional £600+VAT we could sponsor the match. That would give us match sponsorship, a page in the programme and announcements before, during and after the match. We could even be on the pitch at half-time to say a few words and award the man of the match.

It was a Board decision but SDS had just sent us the £2,000 cheque for the SDS Cup for our marketing budget. It was a great time to speak directly to 15,000 supporters. It set in motion a course of events that nearly brought FOH to its knees. We had seen off every problem presented to us and achieved preferred bidder status with over 6,700 pledgers, but it was a debate about match sponsorship at Tynecastle that created ruptures in the FOH Board. It wasn't about the sponsorship. It was about how we did it. Would fans perceive that we were spending their money? We hadn't collected any to that date, so I wasn't convinced that was even an argument. Should we just pay for it personally? I didn't want Board members paying out for this kind of stuff. It wasn't fair. I didn't know their individual personal finances. I knew that some around the table were better off than others but should any of us be paying directly to sponsor the match. We were already committed to the hospitality costs and we did want to help the club if we could.

One hundred and twenty emails were exchanged. Every FOH Board member had at least one view. The upshot was that those that could afford it would pay for it personally. I lost the argument. I subscribed fully to the idea that integrity is hard earned and very easily lost. When it is it can never be regained. It again turned into a battle between the 'founding' Directors and the supporter groups. What it demonstrated was the underlying issues with FOH. I was so focused on saving Hearts that I didn't spend enough time making sure the FOH Board worked properly. The resentment the founding Directors had for the supporter groups was palpable at times. If it wasn't for Hearts, I am sure many would have walked away. That dynamic was exploited by some to make things more difficult. I regretted that. We were all in this project together, we were all passionate fans and we all wanted it to work.

We sponsored the Aberdeen match. We got an enormous amount of publicity from it and the hospitality we paid for personally went a little way towards mending some of the relationships that were becoming more and more strained. We used the time in the Gorgie suite to talk to other fans and businesses. It also allowed us to put an FOH leaflet on every seat in the ground. That was a mammoth task but one of the best marketing things we did. Lawrence accosted me just before the match to say that he had agreed with stadium announcer, Scott Wilson, that I could go on the pitch at half-time and announce to the fans directly that we had reached 7,000 members. I'm used to talking in public and rarely get nervous, but this petrified me. The half-time interval was when stars of the past came on to the pitch to give their assessment of the first half entertainment. I felt a little better when I heard that Eilidh Doyle was also a special guest, as I'd got on well with her on *Off the Ball*. I made my way on to the pitch with Eilidh and gave the message of thanks to the supporters:

> We've got over 7,000 now supporting the Foundation of Hearts. This is the largest supporter movement in Scottish football history. The deal is not done yet but what we are saying to other fans is that this is your club, this is our club and we should own it. We are here today watching Hearts play Aberdeen because of what you have done for the club. We have got preferred bidder status because of what you have done for this club. I have to say quite clearly there are no words to say other than 'Thank you' to every fan in this stadium.

The Aberdeen fans started to sing towards the end of my contribution, but the message had been delivered. Thank you and keep going. The reception from the Hearts fans in the ground left a lump in my throat. Their warmth, encouragement, delight and determination were there for all to see. They even sang 'There's only one Ian Murray'. Given a certain Ian Murray was a Hibs player who used to be a hate figure for Hearts fans, that was a big moment. I bet it's the one and only time they would be pleased to see an Ian Murray grace the Tynecastle turf.

Lawrence came up with the great idea of using the FOH Twitter feed to get the supporters to choose the man of the match. It spoiled the occasion of watching the game for me. In the last 20 minutes, Lawrence read out the names as I tallied them. 'Walker, Walker, McGhee, Wilson, Walker, Paterson, Holt, Holt...' 657 times. It frustrated those around us. The man of the match was chosen as midfielder Jason Holt.

Then it happened. Something I wasn't expecting. The game was finely balanced at one each going into the final minutes. Hearts was hanging on, after being reduced to ten men when Kevin McHattie was sent off, giving away the penalty that gave Aberdeen their equaliser. Then a floated free kick from Callum Tapping was met at the back post by Jordan McGhee for his first senior goal wearing the maroon and white. Tynecastle went absolutely ballistic. We were right behind the goal and we celebrated as if we had won the Premier League. My relationship with Alex was not good at all. In fact, it was pretty low at that stage. However, as football does, we found ourselves embracing and peppering each other with the kind of kisses you reserve for your other halves. That is what football does to you. The elation was incredible. You could just feel the anxiety and pressure of the previous few weeks ooze out. It was a memorable result that put us within touching distance of second-bottom St Mirren in the league. The decision to sponsor the match was fully justified. It couldn't have gone any better – until Alex leaked the entire Aberdeen match sponsorship saga to *The Scotsman*. Our friend, Stuart Bathgate, didn't run the story. It felt like two steps forward and one back. It wasn't pleasant.

Lawrence was looking to do a weekly drumbeat of marketing and press conferences. It was an intense period for everyone. Lawrence was doing a full-time job for FOH at that point on a completely voluntary basis. In the space of a few weeks. He devised a programme of events at Tynecastle that would be used to drive up direct debit sign ups. In the space of a couple of weeks we had Dylan McGowan pictured with the FOH branding. The players had been through a great deal both financially and with uncertainty about their jobs, but they couldn't have been more helpful. John Murray, the Youth Academy Director, who was credited with bringing through Craig Gordon, Christophe Berra, Lee Wallace, David Templeton, Andrew Driver and many more emphasised in a press event that he was fully backing FOH. The supporters were needed to build the Hearts of the future. It was undisputed that without the work of John and his team the club couldn't have fielded any kind of competitive side for this season. The spine of the team were the players that he had brought through. The academy was pivotal to much of the work done at the club over the previous few years. Without them Hearts wouldn't have a team on the park. I am sure of that. We were also lucky to get a full session with Rudi Skácel. He got pictured with all FOH branding and messaging at Tynecastle. He was unarguably the best message carrier for anything Hearts related. It was brilliant.

The plan was being executed superbly and was working a treat. On the day we were to draw down our first direct debits, Lawrence had arranged to do a media call with manager Gary Locke. Gary was popular with the fans as they could see he was one of them. We all desperately wanted Hearts to stave off relegation for him. His message was powerful:

> Today is the first step with much still to be done. To get to this point I must offer a heartfelt thanks to the supporters from everyone at Tynecastle. The club exists because of the supporters and the club has a chance of a future because of the supporters. As you know, we're all right behind the Foundation of Hearts. They are, to a man and woman, Hearts people. More importantly, they've got the skills necessary to support the club through what will be an ongoing transition. Today's first direct debit drawdown is the start of a very long process. It's going to take several years to get the club back up on its feet, but with the dedication, commitment, and unity shown in the last few months I've no doubt we'll get there.

The first drawdown of direct debits was a momentous day. It was just the start, but after all the sweat – and a few tears – we were collecting money from supporters. The supporters were playing their own, massively significant part in creating the first step towards the survival and rebuilding of the club. I was in awe of the supporters. I couldn't find the words. All I could say was a simple but heartfelt 'thank you'.

I did have a small concern that many of the direct debits would not be able to be collected. Some would have inputted incorrect details or their direct debit would bounce due to lack of funds. My concern couldn't have been further from what happened. We had a 99 per cent success rate. £113,265.90 hit our bank account from 7,296 direct debits. Only 11 payments failed. It was an extraordinary success rate. GoCardless could not quite believe it. I had to remind them that these were Hearts fans and their commitment to the cause would be unprecedented. They were so impressed by the efforts of the support that they became a sponsor at Tynecastle with pitch-side advertising boards. Our international subscribers added another £3,500 from PayPal. Wow. Just wow. The announcement of the success saw numbers rocket over that weekend to 7,500.

Garry and the marketing team wanted to try and reward the new 7,500 members of FOH. To celebrate and recognise the first of many years of monthly commitments, they launched a celebratory 'SuperDraw' for supporters to win a series of unique prizes. The usual types of prizes were on offer, including a dream day at Tynecastle, the opportunity to present a player with the FOH man of the match champagne from the recent game against Aberdeen and various pieces of signed merchandise like strips and footballs. They also came up with some wacky ideas. The best of all was 12 pairs of tickets to participate in a re-recording of the famous Hector Nicol Hearts song with singer/songwriter Colin Chisholm, who sang the much loved 1986 version, and more recently appeared on BBC's *The Voice*. I thought it was a mad idea. I've never known a prize draw to be so eagerly awaited. I had this picture of a cross section of Hearts fans with their 'cans' on singing the Hearts song in dozens of different tones.

Colin Chisholm was superb. They got 24 Hearts supporters with manager Gary Locke and assistant manager, Billy Brown, in a recording studio and recorded a new version of the Hearts song. Never has 'This is my story, this is my song. Follow the Hearts and you can't go wrong' sounded so, well, professional. It gave FOH huge publicity and the winning members had brilliant fun. I don't think I have seen Gary and Billy smile so much. Tone deaf, I hear! They even played the new version at Tynecastle before a match. It's not played anymore. Disappointing but not unsurprising.

Back in early July, Lawrence had reached out to Craig Levein to see if he could give his support to FOH. Craig is Hearts through and through, a player of total class for both Hearts and Scotland. His career was cut short due to a devastating knee injury after 326 appearances for the club and 16 for Scotland. He went on to manage Hearts for four seasons, taking the club into European competition in successive seasons for the first time since the 1960s. Those excursions brought us wonderful victories that I was lucky to witness in Bordeaux and, weeks after his departure, Basel. He left in 2004 to manage Leicester City. He hadn't done much since leaving the Scotland managerial job, so it would have been a real coup to get him on our side.

Unfortunately, he couldn't find a time to meet with Lawrence in early July but was impressed with what FOH were doing. 'Tell the guys to keep up the good work' was the message he sent back. He was very supportive of any outcome that stabilised his club and put Hearts-minded people in possession of it. He offered to assist when he was available. Lawrence didn't let that pass. At the end of August 2013, he made contact with Craig again. Things had obviously moved on considerably since they first spoke. An hour and a half later, after Craig had interrogated Lawrence with his own brand of due diligence, he agreed to help FOH with a photo opportunity and press conference. Craig wanted to be sure that Hearts was going to be in safe hands before committing. He commented that he had never known a support of any club that had been asked so regularly to save their club, especially from those fans that don't have that much spare cash. He knew Ann Budge was behind the BIDCO team. That convinced him that this was going to ensure everyone pulled together to work for the cause. The press that we got from the Craig Levein event gave us our single largest uplift in direct debits, such was the penetration of the message and his popularity with the supporters.

At the end of that press conference Lawrence suggested that it may be useful for Craig to have a conversation with Ann. Ann knew there were many people who wanted to speak with her, including other managers involved in football. At that time, Craig said to Lawrence that he had no interest in getting back into Scottish football. Lawrence guessed that Craig perhaps thought he had unfinished business in England after the Leicester City job. Despite being ultra-cautious he came around to the idea of doing FOH stuff and was happy to help Ann in any way she felt he could. This set up a chat with Ann about her very early plans for the club and FOH should it be successful in taking over. Lawrence arranged for them to meet for tea at Channings Hotel in Edinburgh after the Tynecastle press conference. Lawrence reported that Ann was delighted with the meeting as they shared ideas from the perspective of Hearts supporters.

I know better than most that it is difficult to keep stories and gossip out of the public domain. This is especially true in politics and sport. Lawrence kept a tight leash on all FOH publicity. He had a plan and it was working well. That was why we were all shocked to read a back page exclusive story by Derek McGregor at *The Scottish Sun* saying that Craig Levein would be the new manager of Hearts. Ann hadn't even been announced as the mystery backer at that point. Lawrence was hugely concerned so went to see Ann at her house to find out what was going on. He knew he had to control the media process and had to make sure both FOH and Ann herself were protected. Ann was absolutely clear that she hadn't met with Craig since their Channings meeting. Nobody knew where Derek McGregor got the story. Perhaps we are all too close to events. Sometimes journalists add two and two and get a speculative five but, because we know the issues inside out, we assume they also know. Occasionally journalists have an educated guess and they get it right. In this case he got it wrong, but it set hares running.

Ann was soaking up as much knowledge and information as possible. Lawrence had set up a meeting with Leeann Dempster. Leeann is now the Chief Executive at Hibs but, at that time, was the hugely well-respected and influential Chief Executive of Motherwell FC. She was well known to be doing a terrific job. Motherwell was slightly further ahead in terms of supporter ownership and the model they had adopted was similar to that of the BIDCO and FOH relationship proposed for Hearts.

I didn't really enjoy watching Hearts play at this time. Every throw-in, corner, penalty or goal I viewed as another direct debit or a pound note. I really enjoyed talking to supporters at games. We played Celtic at Tynecastle in mid-September 2013 and I was asked to appear pitch-side live on BT Sport at the end of the game. It was difficult to be enthusiastic after another unlucky defeat to our Glasgow rivals. I joined presenter Darrell Currie and commentator Michael Stewart at the end of the match. I was taken aback when I was asked by Darrell for my thoughts on the game and my view of certain incidents from the stand. Maybe I was entering a new career as a football pundit. We spoke about FOH – where we were, the latest news and what was next. It was great to do BT Sport and get the message out to a wider UK audience. It generated a lot of interest from supporters of other clubs that were in distressed situations. We also seen a spike in UK and European pledgers. I'm not sure if there was a direct correlation but the wider exposure was beneficial.

Lawrence was troubled that the incident with Derek McGregor was a seminal point in the FOH story. He was concerned about leaks and people talking out of turn to the press. He started to wonder how much was going on that FOH, myself and others didn't know about. We never found out where *The Scottish Sun* did get this story. I was doing wall-to-wall media and the thirst for more and more was unquenchable. Even Hugh Keevins at the *Daily Record*, who had never been seen as a fan of Hearts, wrote some very helpful pieces. He described the 7,500 direct debits as 'eye-opening'. He allowed me to do a colour piece in the paper to explain the importance of the Hearts family to the cause. There is no larger community institution than a football club and I wanted to get that point across to dispel a growing myth that it was morally wrong to ask ordinary supporters to part with their hard-earned cash to save a club from reckless former owners. It was a voluntary scheme, fans gave what they could afford and supporters viewed their football club as a key part of their lives.

That integral part football plays in the lives of supporters is underpinned by Hearts' history. The story of McCrae's Battalion is one of the most emotive of World War I. Historian Jack Alexander's book, *McCrae's Battalion: The Story of the 16th Royal Scots*, tells the story of how 11 Hearts players exchanged their position at the top of the then Premier League to go and help the war effort on the Somme in 1914. Seven didn't come home – Wattie, Currie, Ellis, Speedy, Boyd, Gracie and Allan. Another two – Crossan and Mercer – would die much later but from war-related diseases. Briggs got crippled and never played again. Hearts lost the league to Celtic that season despite being well ahead until they left for France. At the end of September 2013, the club held their first of a series of events to mark the centenary of the 1914 war effort. I was humbled to take part in the ceremony. It reminded us all how critical it was to preserve this story and those memories. That is what FOH meant by 'owning the history'. This was our proud heritage. It had nothing to do with silverware and winning games. It was about who we were, what we were about and how proud we were of our own history.

This is a story that was regularly relayed to the Lithuanian administrators. This wasn't an ordinary business transaction. This was about the soul of a community and the memory of those that gave the ultimate sacrifice for their country, magnified through the lens of our football club. That is what it meant to me. That is what it meant to my fellow supporters. That is what drove everyone on at FOH.

CHAPTER 16

Scrooge Jackson Cancels Christmas

HEARTS SUPPORTERS WERE becoming experts in administration processes. Bryan Jackson and Trevor Birch were trying desperately to get the BIDCO deal over the line with Valnetas. The normal process for this kind of administration is that the assets go up for sale and BDO gets hold of the shares. A CVA is delivered and you give the shares to the new owner in return for the price of the bid. That money is then distributed to the creditors of the company. The shares go across to the new owner with a completely clean balance sheet free of debt and any security on assets although, in the case of a football club, you have to take on the football debt. Getting the shares is never normally a problem as they come with the business from the previous owner. In most instances, it is the Chairperson from the company in administration, who owns the shares, that gives them over knowing that a deal can't be done without them. Normally when the CVA meeting is approved, the job tends to be finished as you already have the shares in your hand.

Bryan realised early on that he couldn't do that in Lithuania. Valnetas hadn't given him the 29 per cent of shares that they owned and the other 50 per cent were effectively unavailable as UBIG hadn't officially been placed in any administration proceedings as yet. A court date in Lithuania to appoint an administration for UBIG was postponed on a number of occasions. We had expected the process to be concluded in September but, by 24 October 2013, it was still being delayed. It was very frustrating but nothing could be done about it.

Whilst the situation with UBIG was being resolved, BDO were determined to push Valnetas to give an answer on the BIDCO offer. It was going to be a long haul for BDO to get the Hearts shares, so Bryan decided to try and do the CVA first. This was unusual. He would try to get the whole CVA approved subject to getting the shares, otherwise he feared they would run out of time. Bryan decided to have the CVA as soon as he could and then chase the shares. To this end, Trevor and Bryan were in constant touch with Deimantė and were providing her with all the information she requested in order to push for an early decision. If this was positive, they would start the CVA process. That would leave the matter of the 50 per cent shares held by UBIG as the only outstanding obstacle. Also, they felt that if the eventual UBIG administrator was not prepared to do a reasonable deal on the shares, they would be well placed to exert some political pressure if the CVA was agreed. However, the CVA would still need the support of the other major creditor and shareholders, and there would have been a delay in securing that support while administrators were appointed to UBIG. Therefore, the sale process would take some time before a deal could be concluded and the club exited administration.

Patience was certainly something we all needed. The process of administration is always very complicated, not least when you are dealing with issues almost entirely out of our own country's judicial system. The FOH were working on the legal, governance and long-term member retention strategy whilst BIDCO were diligently examining all aspects of club business with David and the Hearts team. The lack of a firm route map to exiting administration was infuriating as we were going from strength to strength. Our second monthly drawdown had a 99 per cent success rate from over 7,700 members. Our numbers and success rate were up on our first month. It was astonishing.

Although I was constantly emphasising patience, some Hearts fans were fearful of what was happening. Deimantė sent an email demanding to know if FOH were behind a *Daily Record* story claiming that there were moves to try and get the stadium listed. The email ordered BDO to let them know what should be done to stop such actions and processes, as they considered it fraud and a wilful action to reduce the value of ūkio Bankas assets. They deemed such actions as an impediment to entering into a CVA. They felt that it ruined confidence and trust between potential parties to the CVA. They threatened 'all the initiators, FOH, etc. to reimburse the loss' if it was proven to be the case. It was an Archibald Leitch stand and the newspaper report quoted the Cockburn Association saying that Tynecastle certainly falls into the historic category. The listing authority, Historic Scotland, added that it would not be unusual to have football grounds listed. We didn't need this. It came just two days prior to the expected court approval for the administration of UBIG. It was undoubtedly well-meaning from some supporters, but it caused all sorts of problems and additional delays. I had to sign the equivalent of an affidavit with Deimantė to confirm that FOH had nothing to do with this and that it was purely speculative. Lord Foulkes tried to get things moving through the UK Ambassador to Lithuania, David Hunt, but we just couldn't get things going. The UBIG court date got delayed again.

The reason seemed to be an appeal over the suggested candidate to be UBIG's administrator. It would now take place on 7 November. It was one hurdle after another. The new delay put back our plan to announce Ann Budge as the backer of the FOH bid.

Despite this, BDO issued a statement on the CVA. Bryan said the CVA process should commence immediately by initiating meetings of the creditors and shareholders. They wanted to be able to begin the formal acceptance of the FOH bid and legally agree terms. The efforts of the supporters in setting up direct debits in such large numbers had an effect on the Lithuanians. Gintaras Adamonis, specialist bankruptcy administrator of AB ūkio Bankas said in response to Bryan that:

> the zeal and tenacity of the fans have persuaded us that the process of CVA should be launched as soon as possible by the administrators of Heart of Midlothian FC. We are still far away from the end of the legal process which we all shall endure, but this is a step forward nevertheless.

Bryan was taking an unorthodox approach by doing the CVA first but it was working. His stuck record routine was also getting another airing as he again stressed how important it was that the fans to continue their extraordinary support:

> The fans, the staff, the players, the management and the FOH have all been outstanding over the last few months in keeping the club going but it needs to carry on. We still need to keep fans coming to matches, and money flowing through the club to ensure that we have sufficient funds to push the CVA process forward.

Bryan couldn't run out of money now. That would be the worst scenario. The team was also starting to struggle on the pitch. The victories we witnessed at the start of the season became the exception, not the rule. The performances on the park made Bryan even more nervous for revenues, although there was a famous 1-0 victory at Easter Road in the quarter final of the League Cup and a tremendous 3-1 victory away to Aberdeen at Pittodrie.

The CVA date was set for 22 November 2013 in the Gorgie Suite at Tynecastle. We would keep our fingers crossed that the legal position of UBIG would actually be resolved by then and the Lithuanians would accept the BIDCO deal.

We were working on getting control of the 79.9 per cent of shares held by ūkio and UBIG but there was also a 15 per cent share held by a Swiss registered company called Quantum Holdings. It appeared that the sole Director of the company was Romanov's niece, Julija Goncaruk. She served on the Hearts Board for a period of time. The Scandinavian consortium led by Kai Isaksen had been negotiating with *Quantum* to purchase this 15 per cent stake. I wasn't sure what was in it for Kai, but he had indicated that both the Massone group and Bob Jamieson were asking about purchasing them to get a foothold at the club. They had secured a 'more or less exclusive' agreement with the Swiss Company to purchase the shares and in fact had made an offer. After speaking to Trevor at BDO, they agreed to stand back. The Swiss company, as a consequence of them backing out, started talking about administration for Quantum Holdings and going to Bankruptcy Court in order to recover their costs. They were estimating them at approximately £15,000. The lead Scandinavian investor offered to buy the shares (to avoid unnecessary complications) and then gift them to FOH for a coupon value of £1. They claimed they had no desire to own football shares in Hearts.

The lawyers acting for Quantum accepted the offer. BDO and Ann were concerned that this could have an impact on the main bid. Ann had asked her lawyers to investigate the issues around FOH or BIDCO trying to buy these shares in advance of any deal and they outlined concerns that it could impact the main deal. Kai was very magnanimous about this. They agreed to put any purchase on behalf of FOH on hold until it was clear that the main deal had been approved. We would have to try and get hold of these shares in order to dispense with having to deal with another major shareholder at Hearts but, as we understood the situation, no other party could buy them for the moment as it would require approval from the main shareholders. For the record, the other small proportion of shares were held by individuals who had participated in the many share issues over the years. Most were members of the Hearts Shareholders Association.

It was over the period in the run up to the CVA that FOH resolved some of the long-standing problems it had. The overwhelming feeling after every FOH Board meeting was one of frustration. It was like wading through treacle. Everyone had the best interests of Hearts but I just couldn't get it to operate properly. Outwardly we were a collegiate, effective and driven group of volunteers on the verge of saving our club. Inwardly, the only thing that held us together was Hearts. Often organisations and businesses struggle to progress with the originator at the helm. I was convinced that was also the case with FOH. Alex was one of the originators. His passions for the club and reasons for FOH was something we all shared. I just got the impression that he resented the supporter organisations being involved. He certainly resented me chairing FOH. It all came to a head when Ann and

Robert recommended that FOH appointed a full-time project manager to see the deal through and get it into a shape to satisfy the BIDCO legal relationship. We were now collecting over £120,000 per month and the governance arrangements were still not properly in place. The individual strands were being progressed by the working groups, but a project manager would be able to bring it all together quicker and work much closer with the bid team. Professional project managers are not cheap or readily available.

It was suggested that we should consider appointing a project manager from the FOH Board. Henry Snedden had been a project manager in a host of fields for a large part of his career both in the Ministry of Defence and Scottish Justice Department. He took early retirement and supplemented his income with a part-time driving job. He had the time to do it and the skills to succeed. He was already immersed in FOH so was already up to speed. Ann and Robert were very keen for this to happen. Henry had met with Ann to discuss the specifications for the role and also his experience. The FOH Board wouldn't need to change. The key difference would be that a project manager would have the authority to drive the specific working groups with the remit to report back to the Board on progress and to discuss 'critical' decisions. They would also work closely with the bid team. A Board paper was produced by Ann and Robert that strongly recommended FOH appoint formal legal and financial advisors to be co-ordinated by the new project manager. It was a pragmatic and sensible way forward.

I just couldn't make it happen. Henry was willing to take on the role. Ann and Robert were keen for Henry to do it. I couldn't get it through some of the FOH Board. The supporters group Directors were on side but I didn't have any support beyond them. It was seen as another diminishing of the former Chair and founding Directors' hold on the organisation. Their argument was the agreement to pay the project manager for loss of earnings. Henry wasn't earning much, but it would not have been right to ask him to give up his job and not recompense him for it. After all, he was going to cost a tiny fraction of employing a professional project manager and we were going to have to pay significant sums to lawyers and financial advisers to conclude the deal. The governance of FOH stated that no member of FOH could 'profit' from the organisation. We had discussed ad nauseam the need to revise the FOH Articles of Association, but it hadn't been concluded. That meant that Alex and others resisted Henry becoming project manager.

Henry wasn't going to 'profit' from anything. He couldn't take on the role unless his loss of earnings were replaced so we lost this avenue. Ann was furious. I have only ever seen Ann lose her temper once and this was it. I think what angered her more was that the discussion around this was cordial and constructive while both her and Robert were in the room at the FOH Board meeting. It went downhill fast after they left. It was also apparent that there were pre-Board meetings taking place before the formal meeting for groups to discuss how they would vote. Henry removed his offer to do the project manager's role. We were left back at square one. Ann sent an email to me to circulate to the rest of the FOH Board that was signed off 'a hugely frustrated and rapidly running out of patience Ann Budge.' My primary concern was that the main resistance on the Board was in danger of undoing all the good work that had been done in recent months and that, in doing so, it was placing the very existence of FOH and our club at risk. There was a still a great deal of work that remained to be done on the FOH governance arrangements and getting the deal over the line. What would happen if Ann decided that it couldn't work and she walked away? Where would that leave us?

To make matters worse, I had been trying for some time to get access to the Clydesdale Bank account. The only Board members who had access to it were Alex and Bill Alves. Bill had been setting up all the necessary online access alongside Andy Grant on the finance working group. The problem was that Andy had full control and wasn't a Director of FOH. It was infuriating. Andy had only been brought on by Alex to provide some knowledge on how a technical system could be devised to set up a payment system. He was the son of someone who worked with Alex's wife and had impressed the FOH Board with his involvement with HMSA. He helped them build their website. We spent hours going around in circles arguing whether the Chair of FOH should have access. I eventually gave up. In all the time I was Chair of FOH, I didn't have the ability to access the bank account, nor authorise any payments. We did have others added to ensure signatories would be available. There was never a problem with propriety as there were strict financial controls on the movement of money and it required at least two authorising signatories (in some cases for large amounts three) but it was just another frustration that we couldn't resolve. We were like swans, calm and assured on the public surface but paddling for our lives underneath the waterline.

I would be lying if I said that I wasn't close to leaving as Chair of FOH. I didn't have the time or inclination to spend in endless circular discussions.

We had to focus. I did consider it a lot after the bust up about the project manager. What in earth were we doing? The FOH had gone from nothing to preferred bidder status in just over three months. We had a backer who was willing to fund the purchase and we had more direct debits than we could ever have imagined. The decisions that we made had proven to the be the correct ones. Everything in the process was going well. The only issue was that FOH wasn't working. Meetings at Melville Street were horrible. Absolutely everything was a battle and a fight. If it wasn't for Hearts, we wouldn't have made it all the way through. I could have walked away at that point, having taken it to a point of success. I was too busy in my job as a Member of Parliament for any questions to be raised about why I was leaving. Every waking hour of my spare time was being consumed by FOH. Being involved in FOH and this story was hugely rewarding but the FOH structure was certainly unrewarding.

I had a heart to heart with Ann and Robert. Ann did what she always did – came up with a plan. She would take on the project manager's role with FOH and bang heads together. She also rightly advised that it would not be good timing for anyone to leave the FOH Board. It was an unwieldly size but that was the way it was designed to ensure all voices were involved. We would find more focused roles for everyone and make sure they stuck to them. Ann had the respect of everyone on the Board, especially Alex, so this could be a solution. Anyhow, who was going to object to Ann managing the project? I am convinced that Robert and Ann saved FOH with this intervention. I couldn't see how it could progress otherwise. There was a lot still to do. Ann was a long-standing advisor to FOH, and leader of the bid team, which had developed much of the relevant detailed work to date. She was perfect for the job.

Ann always saw herself as part of FOH although she shared the same view as me when she said, 'I don't have many fond memories of FOH Board meetings.' Her role as provider of the upfront capital was largely irrelevant, as our goals were the same. Her role with FOH wasn't ever a decision-making one. It was about coordinating the FOH Board with professional advisors to ensure the work required to complete the deal was done and preparations were in place for the future.

The main purpose of appointing professional advisors was to ensure that all legal documentation was up-to-date and complete in relation to how FOH will operate and function in the future. They would help us to review and amend the Articles of Association, Members Agreement and any other legal documentation. We had to get things like 'company blazers' out of the governance. I kid you not. In fact, the notion of the blazer was the prism of which everything seemed to be viewed by some. This was one of the stumbling blocks for pretty much every decision and perspective. The FOH Board arrangements and the voting mechanism for Directors had to be reviewed and updated to reflect the varying and deepening roles and responsibilities of FOH. This would involve a number of staging posts.

There was a lot to be done in the pre-CVA agreement phase. The only role of the FOH Board was to ensure fans were kept fully appraised of progress towards achieving a successful CVA agreement. That would mean all legal, financial management and control processes had to be in place.

Then there was what needed to be done if the CVA was successful. There would be a period of approximately three years where the main responsibility of FOH would be to build and maintain pledges to the level necessary to allow the fulfilment of the BIDCO legal agreement. During this period, funds would have to be diverted, by mutual agreement of the club and FOH, to meet working capital needs while the club strived to regain a position of stability.

The final stage was well into the future. What would need to be done when fan ownership was achieved? The relationship between the FOH Board and the Hearts Board would have to be clearly defined. The responsibility of the FOH Board would be to continue to provide financial support to the club by maintaining pledge levels from the fans; and to provide suitably qualified Board representation on the HMFC Board. It was crucial to understand and agree the long-term role that FOH will play in the running of the club and to document this accordingly. We would need a degree of flexibility as the relationship crystallised, but this project was always about a fan-owned club and not a fan-run club. That distinction is critical and would have to be written into the FOH constitution.

The other main pillar of work was to ensure that the FOH Board could demonstrate to fans that appropriate due diligence had been carried out in terms of the legal agreements being entered into that would commit monies collected from them. Lastly, to underpin these other activities, we would need to agree the marketing plan. Garry and his team had done an excellent job in coming up with a range of initiatives designed to maintain and grow pledge levels.

My strong recommendation to the FOH Board was that we accepted the offer from Ann to become the project manager and we agreed the steps that needed to be taken. It wasn't easy even getting that through. Ann had given an ultimatum and I couldn't be clearer with them that we should listen to it. I also decided that I had to give a similarly harsh ultimatum. I contacted Henry, Bill, Jane, Calum, Brian and Garry prior to the crucial Board meeting. I knew they were on my side and would agree to the way forward with Ann and the programme of work. I made it clear that if this wasn't agreed, there was a real danger that Ann would remove her involvement and, if that happened, I would also resign as Chair. It was the biggest roll of the dice I had ever taken. The meeting was on a freezing Saturday afternoon in Brian Cormack's offices in Melville Street. I presented the plan that Ann would become the project manager, we would seek the appointment of specialist advisors and I laid out the suggested programme.

The meeting didn't start well. We had to endure an hour of crawling over the old debates: Romanov and Sergejus; why we chose GoCardless; how SDS were involved; how this all came about. I just laid down the black and white of it. We either go forward with my recommendation or Ann pulls out and I go with her. I got up from my seat and put my coat on. Henry, Jane, Bill and Calum did likewise. All I could think about was how this would affect my beloved Hearts. I walked towards the door and said I would report back to Ann that the Board didn't make a decision on her proposals. I wished them luck.

It's amazing how sometimes little things happen that change the course of events. We were in Brian's office on a Saturday afternoon so there was no one else around. It just so happened that entry to the building was controlled by an intercom system via the reception area. There wasn't a receptionist to answer the bell on a Saturday. It just so happened that Calum got to the front door first, opened it and left. Just as the rest of us were about to go, we were shouted back. Thank goodness. Sense had prevailed. It was like the 11th and a half hour. We all went back into the room and took our seats. A sensible and measured discussion ensued and we got unanimous agreement for the proposal. Well, it was unanimous without Calum. We had forgotten that he had gone outside with the front door closing behind him. He had spent the last half hour standing in the street trying to get our attention through the window. It was only when Garry went out to feed the parking meter that Calum came back in. It was the uncontrollable laughter at Calum's misfortune that changed the atmosphere on the Board.

The following week, Alex resigned from the Board of FOH. Without the vision of Alex in the early years we wouldn't be in the position we were in.

That was indisputable. I don't know if Ann had any hand in his decision. I organised a lunch 'summit' with Alex at her home a few weeks before to try and get his issues resolved. If she had a heart to heart with him after I left the lunch, then that may have helped. I still don't know exactly what happened and Ann has never said, but it was the correct conclusion to allow FOH to move on. Donald Ford resigned at the same time. His own business interests meant he couldn't attend any meetings and wasn't involved in FOH on an ongoing basis. He felt that this was the correct time for him to bow out.

On the same day as Donald's resignation, Bryan from BDO told us that, at last, the Lithuanian Court of Appeals had announced the decision in the UBIG insolvency case to change their administrator and appoint UAB Bankroto Administravimo Paslaugos. The decision about both the institution of insolvency and appointment of administrator was final and in force as of that day. It was a poignant milestone week following the annual armistice service at Haymarket the Sunday before and a reminder about one of the main reasons we were doing this. We were all gearing up for the CVA meeting to take place. Just a day before the CVA was supposed to take place, Bryan informed us that it had to be postponed at the request of the administrators of ūkio Bankas and UBIG. It was so frustrating. The delay was to allow the Lithuanian-based major shareholders and creditors time to consider the BIDCO proposal. Every week that went by made the survival of Hearts more difficult. Bryan rescheduled it for the following week on 29 November.

We all crammed into the Gorgie Suite at Tynecastle for the CVA meeting. Bryan addressed the media and the creditors in the room. All he needed was a vote of 75 per cent of those that participate in the CVA process for it to pass. He only got the approval from ūkio Bankas half an hour before the start of the meeting. He had been expecting it for a number of days, but it never arrived. The administrators of UBIG sent in their abstention just minutes before the meeting was to start. That gave Bryan a vote in favour of over 87 per cent of votes cast and gave him their 50 per cent voting rights. One hundred per cent of the shareholders who participated also approved. HMRC, as expected, voted against. The CVA was through. What a hurdle to cross.

The CVA meeting finished and everyone was saying 'well done' and 'job done' but Bryan told me after the meeting that he had a terrible feeling about it, saying he had a feeling in his gut that he was only about halfway to being 'job done'. He still had to get the shares even although the CVA was approved. At least that part was done.

Everything from that point was fraught with difficulties. It went from one problem and issue to another. There was no point where the Lithuanian administrators of both ūkio Bankas and UBIG just said 'OK, let's do this'. The CVA was a watershed but it got very messy and difficult after that. They simply kept demanded more money.

We put out a press release praising the administrators and again reminding everyone that they had to continue to be patient, sign up to more direct debits and keep supporting the club. This was not over. Far from it. I allowed myself to say that they could pop a bottle of something sparkling in the fridge, but it was not yet time to pop the cork. My message was in sharp contrast to Bryan's. He decided it would be a good idea to tell Hearts supporters to 'cancel Christmas'.

Following the CVA, social media messages and emails were flooding in to Bryan saying 'well done'. Colin Wright, the BDO PR guru, said that before Bryan could go home after the CVA, he had to do the Sunday newspapers. Moira Gordon, a hugely supportive Hearts fan from the *Scotland on Sunday*, was there and she repeated the congratulations to Bryan as soon as he walked into the press room. Bryan's heart sank. He explained that it was part of the process. He knew that he would have to keep the club going for a long time yet, probably several months. Moira asked Bryan what he was planning to do next. Bryan responded, 'Cancel Christmas and whatever you were going to spend on presents give it to me to keep the club going.' Colin Wright was holding his head in his hands. All he could envisage was the headline, 'Scrooge Jackson'.

The reaction to 'Scrooge Jackson' was good as it dampened expectation levels amongst both the fans and the media that the job was done. It kept the money coming in to Hearts to keep it going. It was very tight money wise and the club was doing dreadfully on the pitch. There were cries from the fans to get rid of Gary Locke to see if fortunes could be improved. It was never fully recognised that the culprits for the problems at Hearts were long gone but Gary and his team would have to take the brunt of the blame. Even if his sacking was a desirable outcome – and nobody really thought it was given the circumstances – he was in a contract and the club simply couldn't have dismissed him. Gary had a contract just like other employees, he would have to have been in breach for there to be a legal case to dismiss him and the normal statutory steps would have to be taken – verbal warning, written warning, etc. Bryan never felt there was a legal case and, of course, there was the potential time and costs of going through the process. Bryan fully backed him in the media. Bryan and Gary had a superb relationship and that helped. Bryan appreciated the support Gary gave. He felt a legal and moral obligation to Gary, although accountants are not really supposed to consider such things as morality.

Gary was also doing an absolutely brilliant job off the field. He was always on message to help both Bryan and FOH. He was a great ambassador with dignity and diplomacy. Hearts had gone on a run of ten league games without a win, including a 7-0 thrashing at home to Celtic in the Scottish Cup. The fans were running out of patience with the team and Bryan was running out of patience with the Lithuanians. Bryan would sanguine about the fortunes of the team. He always said to supporters and staff at Hearts that this process was about saving the club, not the current season.

Bryan went to Lithuania to open up talks to try and persuade them to get things through. Every time there was a meeting to get issues resolved, the court appointments would be cancelled. It wasn't a deliberate attempt to derail the CVA. It was just that their processes were overly bureaucratic. Court dates were cancelled time after time after time. Every time, the funds at the club reduced.

Despite the club being fully marketed, the preferred bidder price, although accepted, never really met the aspirations of the Lithuanians. They kept demanding more money but, to be fair, that was their job. They had to maximise the resources for their own creditors. The difficulty for Bryan was that he simply didn't have any more money. What money he did have was being used to run the club and was diminishing by the day.

Bryan kept emphasising to Deimantė that if Hearts was worth £5–10 million, where were the bidders? If they had processed the shares earlier, they could maybe have been given a little more. The Lithuanians kept saying they had a better handle of UK legislation than Bryan. One of the main frustrations was that they would send Bryan very lengthy emails and when they 'lost' a point or argument they would just ignore that part and move on to the next issue. Bryan had to regularly point out they were bound by the same EU-wide rules. They then kept asking for more and more information. Every time more information was submitted (which was essentially the same information that had already been provided), they had to go through the administrative courts system all over again. They probably knew there was no real merit in what they were asking. Bryan didn't know why and couldn't work out the reasons for the delays unless it was just about more fees. During this period, Ann started to feel that the deal wouldn't happen. She also found it difficult at times to understand the various positions of the different Lithuanian Administrators. We all did.

Part of the problem was the muddying of the waters by others. Bob Jamieson sent regular letters to the Lithuanian authorities offering £10 million for the shares or £50 million for the stadium. He was a nuisance and really obstructive. One such letter landed on the day Bryan arrived in Lithuania. Bob was offering all sorts of money to get control of the shares and saying that the Lithuanians could just 'dispose of the old stadium' if they wished to recoup the £5 million he claimed it was worth. It took Bryan hours to demonstrate that these were not credible approaches from Bob. I supplied a copy of hundreds of emails he had sent to me and Ann. Lord Foulkes and I wrote to the Lithuanian Ambassador to try and get her to intervene with the administrators. We impressed on her that everything Bob was doing was wholly false and that he did not have the funds to conclude any offer.

To be fair, even the Lithuanians got fed up with him. They ended up responding to his approaches by saying he had to revert to Bryan with proof of funding if he had an offer to make. Those approaches wasted an inordinate amount of time that Bryan didn't have. He would contact the media and plead with them to stop giving Bob the oxygen of publicity as everyone knew it was nonsense. They too were finding him a real pest now, so the stories of Bob dried up.

Then there was another complication: supporters of Hibs writing to the Lithuanian President claiming that a fraud was being committed at their expense. A random letter to the President made it to the administrators:

> I write to you as a concerned and ashamed Scotsman to inform you of an attempt by fellow Scottish people to defraud the Republic of Lithuania of many millions of pounds.

It went on:

> Since 2006, Romanov has ploughed many millions of pounds, estimates believed to be as much as £85 million, which has now turned out to be money he nor his banking groups could afford to invest, and these concerns raised many times over by the financial and football authorities here in Scotland. These concerns were continually ignored by officials at Hearts and also by their support who were happy to accept the success that has turned out to be the people of your country's money.

It concluded:

> I would like to make you aware of several areas of prime development land in Edinburgh that have sold recently for many millions of pounds over the £2.5 million currently being offered to your people.

Bryan was presented with a copy of the letter from the lawyers of ūkio Bankas and asked what he was going to do about it. Bryan had no knowledge of such a letter. Deimantė believed the content of the letter and demanded to get an explanation from Bryan. Bryan explained that it had probably come from a rival fan. This was a complete anathema to the Lithuanians who couldn't believe such a thing would happen. Bryan insisted that it was a Hibs fan and asked his office to try and find out who it was, so they could prove it. Bryan's office got on to it and quickly confirmed it was indeed a Hibs fan.

Bryan wanted to go public on the Hibs fan in order to prove it was a hoax. He had a decision to make as it may have encouraged copycat people. Hibs themselves couldn't do anything about it so there was no point in a public spat. It was a bitter pill to swallow for Bryan not to engage with it. This letter, and many others, caused a huge delay and, by virtue of the Lithuanians holding the shares, the CVA could have collapsed as a result. I always found it difficult to comprehend why some Hibs supporters wanted to see Hearts die. Both clubs would be much diminished without each other. No more derbies, no more sheer joy at winning and utter dejection at losing. The vast majority of Hibs fans that I knew or came across were hugely supportive. They understood this dynamic. We got a large number of supportive messages from their supporters. Hearts and Hibs gain strength from the rivalry with each other.

Without the shares, you can't deliver the entity so they can fall. That is what happened to Rangers. They couldn't get the shares, so they couldn't get a CVA done. That could have been the consequence of these letters.

Bryan kept saying to the Lithuanians that the CVA was done and this had to be moved on. It kept falling on deaf ears. He was running out of time and money. I bet he let out a huge sigh of relief when the club received a five-figure sum for 18-year-old Adam King in the January transfer window. He transferred to Swansea City. That gave a little breathing space.

Ann had commenced working inside Tynecastle with David Southern and his team. She wanted to have every piece of knowledge at her disposal should the deal be successful. To BDO's credit, they consulted Ann on major decisions that had to be taken for the year ahead. The 2014/15 season would be an important year of commemorations, being the centenary of the McCrae's Battalion. The club had already suggested producing a commemorative kit for the team. The issue was the shirt sponsor. Wonga was currently the shirt sponsor but their support ran out at the end of the 2013/14 campaign. They put a proposal forward to continue to sponsor the kit with a number of options depending on the level of branding the club thought was appropriate on a commemorative strip. It was not suitable for any sponsor, let alone Wonga, to be emblazoned across the chest of the players on such an anniversary. Ann made that point very clear to the club, but the money that was on offer from Wonga for a more suitable and subtle shirt sponsorship was not really enough. It would also be halved if we were relegated from the top division. That now looked likely. Ann asked the club to go and see if a renegotiation with Wonga was possible and to look for additional shirt sponsors.

Ann, as project manager, was also driving the FOH working groups. I had agreed with her that each group should have a defined purpose and be advised by one of the bid group members. That meant Kevin looked after the finance group, Robert would give support to the legal and governance group and Alastair would direct the marketing group. We also went in search of financial and legal advisors. We had been using informal advice from Stuart Murray from Shoosmiths, but he was giving this in a personal capacity. He made that clear on a number of occasions so his advice was heavily caveated. We would need to contract specialist legal support from a Scottish legal firm that could look closely at the kind of contract FOH would be presented with by BIDCO and the future structure of FOH.

Henry drew up a draft scope of legal work and payment terms, assisted by Richard Atkinson of SDS. The plan was to ask at least three leading legal firms to bid after the draft specification had been approved by the FOH Board. Robert fully supported the proposal. We needed to be able to demonstrate to the Hearts fans that full due diligence had been carried out and that their donations had been spent properly and wisely. It was important, though, to keep the costs down and, if possible, to convince any potential bidders that it would be in their interests to provide us with support on a pro bono basis until a deal was done. Scottish legal experts Dundas & Wilson produced a proposal that was head and shoulders above any other. They also agreed to our deferred payment terms. One of their senior partners, Donald Cummings, was a Hearts season ticket holder. We had engaged one of Scotland's top law firms on our terms. It was a massive coup and again demonstrated the depth and breadth of individuals and organisations that wanted to assist.

We also engaged Kay Thomson from Scott-Moncrieff as our corporate finance and accountant advisors after a competitive bid process. Lastly, we brought in JS Accounting to provide day-to-day book keeping and management reports. I felt much better after the experts were in place. For me it wasn't just because of their experience and that they were the best in the business, but it defused all the tensions with discussion at the FOH Board. Who was going to argue with Donald Cummings about governance? It also allowed me to focus on what mattered rather than the minutiae. We were now more focused on getting FOH fit for purpose.

One huge piece of good news. We were all worried that, as the deal hadn't been concluded at Christmas, that the January drawdown of direct debits would take a huge hit. Family and personal budgets would be stretched after the festive season. Guess what? That Hearts fans didn't disappoint again. Why did we ever doubt it? The January direct debits had a success rate of over 99 per cent from over 7,600 FOH members. Utterly astonishing. FOH was sitting on over £500,000 in five months from supporters' contributions. It was a true maroon miracle.

As the New Year approached, we sent Henry, Calum, Dougie, Garry and Iain around the supporters' clubs on an FOH roadshow. Bonnyrigg, Merchiston, Orwell, Longstone, Borders and Manchester Hearts were all visited. The response was magnificent. We were running out of superlatives to describe the supporters of this great club.

Now to get the deal over the line...

CHAPTER 17

Deal Done

THE NEXT FEW months would make or break our Hearts. The FOH had been preferred bidder for nearly five months and the CVA had been agreed for a couple of months. The football season was two-thirds through and it looked as though the club would not be able to prevent relegation. Hearts was 16 points behind Partick Thistle, who were second from bottom at the end of January 2014. Our arch-rivals and neighbours, Hibs, were a further seven points to the good. I had said that after the successful CVA meeting, Hearts fans could put a bottle of something sparkling in the fridge but couldn't as yet open it. I was starting to think the champagne could be vintage before it met the lips of any happy Jambo.

The one bright spot was a League Cup semi-final against Inverness Caledonian Thistle at Easter Road. The Football Company had again donated some free perimeter advertising to FOH. We could continue our #createhistory campaign that Garry and the marketing team had devised with Lawrence. It had been the FOH social media campaign slogan for the last year generating about 16,000 tweets with a reach of over 3,000,000 users. You may recall the importance to the survival of Hearts of the 2012 Scottish Cup Final success and getting to the final of the League Cup in 2013. The income from those games kept the club going. This was also the case for this semi-final. If we could get to the final, we may get a few more hours' sleep at night. It would certainly have given Bryan fewer sleepless nights. It was also a great opportunity to remind the fans what supporting Hearts was all about. It certainly did that. You don't need to go too far back in the history of every Hearts supporter to hear an experience of witnessing the club snatching defeat from the jaws of victory. This was no different. With 95 minutes on the clock and the referee poised to end the match to signal a 2-1 victory for Hearts, Inverness equalised.

We couldn't believe it. Callum Paterson had been one of our star young players that season and he had the ball in the Inverness corner of the pitch as the clock ran down. It all went wrong. Inverness quickly broke up field and scored. What a disaster. It was made worse by the fact that Inverness were down to just nine men. Despite the disappointment of the late equaliser, surely we would win the tie in extra time with the two-player advantage. Well, we didn't. Hearts totally dominated extra time but lost 4-2 on penalties. I was so annoyed. Yes, we had lost a semi-final when we should have won, but it was the financial consequences that hurt the most. It would have been a great recognition for Gary Locke and his young team for everything they had done and been through in the previous months to reach the final. I also wanted the fans to be rewarded by taking them back to Hampden Park. That was disappointing. If any supporters in the world deserved a final trip it was us. That's football I suppose. That's why we love it and hate it in equal measure.

This wasn't the fight though. The fight was the survival of the club, so we could experience the feeling of bitter disappointment at cup semi-finals and finals for generations to come.

Trevor and Bryan headed to Lithuania for a second time to try and get the CVA concluded. They had a huge number of meetings set up. The most important of these was their attendance at the UBIG creditors committee meeting. The UBIG committee would make a recommendation to the court as to what they would do with their shareholding in Hearts. This differed from the ūkio Bankas process who had an open all creditors meeting before recommending actions to the court.

It is important to remember that UBIG held 50 per cent of Hearts shares but had no security over them. There was absolutely nothing in the Hearts CVA for them. The £2.5 million in the BIDCO offer would be sucked up in its entirety by ūkio Bankas as they had the standard security over the stadium. Bryan had agreed with Ann to offer £100,000 for the shares which was really just to pay the professional fees for administering UBIG. Bryan had to go to the UBIG meeting and persuade the creditors committee that they should pass over the shares for nothing.

Bryan was told that the creditors he was about to speak to were a real mix of people. Some of the committee would even be friends and family of Romanov. There would be businesspeople and creditors from all walks of life. The young lawyer that was advising and translating for Bryan said, 'Do you know our biggest national sport is basketball? Can you name me the top Vilnius team?' Of course, he answered no. For the record, it is arguably BC Rytas Vilnius. 'Well,' the lawyer said, 'if you don't know the top basketball team, they will have no idea who Hearts are. The club will mean nothing to them.' The advice was to speak to them in short, slow sentences and he would translate. Bryan went into the meeting. It took hours and hours. Bryan was the only one presenting to the creditors committee. He was invited into the room to address them. Trevor accompanied him but allowed Bryan to do the presentation. He thanked them for giving them their time and then spoke at great length. Then he took the advice he had been given. He wanted to provide a little colour around the issue:

> I need to tell you what Hearts means to local people in Edinburgh. It is like you losing your local basketball club. Although I am not offering you anything, if you don't vote for this you don't get anything anyway, so I am asking for your sympathy.

Bryan said that they were straight-faced the whole way through his contribution. He had no way of knowing what they were thinking. It was not a particular convincing message. He was asking them to give away their shares for nothing and they wouldn't be losing anything as, if they didn't approve it, they would also get nothing. The process allowed the committee to pose questions to Bryan. There were one or two about the club and the procedure. They seemed more driven by curiosity. One poignant question was who would get money if they were getting nothing. Bryan just responded by telling them the way it was. Bryan left the room and had to wait for the conclusion. When that would happen was not easy to determine. UBIG did eventually approve it in early February 2014. When they did confirm that they would transfer their shareholding in Hearts to BIDCO for £100,000 to enable the CVA to conclude, it was superb news. Bryan almost had his hands on the illusive shares. We just had to get ūkio over the line now.

Bryan also met with the Lithuanian Ambassador. He agreed that she was a very impressive diplomat with a strong presence. Bryan and I had a very positive relationship with her but in a call set up by Bryan, in the desperate stages of the process, she ended up telling him that a good deal needed to be done and was in his hands. She was quite agitated and almost aggressive, blaming Bryan for a deal not being done. That seemed strange to us all. Bryan explained that a deal had already been agreed in the terms of the CVA and it just had to be actioned at the Lithuanian end. At the end of the call, she did say that she thought the deal would happen although it was mainly down to Bryan to deliver. In the end, she promised to make a few calls to try and make things happen. I don't actually know if the Ambassador helped or not but she gave the impression that she would. Bryan was convinced she made calls to help. In the end, Bryan and I were very grateful of her help.

An explanation for the slow progress, and the Lithuanian Ambassador's approach to Bryan, was given by the UK Ambassador, David Hunt, in Vilnius. He explained that there was a culture where they didn't really appreciate the consequences of decisions they were making. They don't quite make the connection between decisions and consequential loss. The culture was that they didn't want to be seen to lose. Negotiations on the issue of money were always difficult partly because of the cultural differences in the way these talks would go. This culture could enlighten us about the Romanov regime in many ways. Decisions he made were often looked upon as peculiar, often crazy, but it was about not losing the battle rather than doing what was in the best interests of Hearts.

This can be demonstrated through the prism of player transfers. If Romanov wanted a player, he just had to win that battle, regardless of the financial and other consequences. If a club wanted to offer for a Hearts player, he would keep going back and asking for more until the deal would be called off. The consequences could be into the millions of pounds but that didn't matter. Saying to Romanov, 'If you ask for another £100,000, you risk losing the £2 million deal', he wouldn't care. The Andrew Driver transfer saga to Burnley was a prime example.

It wasn't just confined to the Lithuanian Ambassador or Romanov though. At one stage, Deimantė at the ūkio Bankas administrators said to Bryan that they would not accept anything less than what was being paid by Ann and, on top of this, whatever money was in the Hearts bank account at the date of completion. Bryan kept having to explain that the money the club had was being used to keep it alive and was being used up trading. The quicker they did a deal the more likelihood some money may be available. I was worried that if Deimantė didn't get additional money, the deal would be off. She didn't want to understand the consequences of pulling out of the CVA deal. They didn't seem to care that they would not get the CVA monies but also have the huge costs of being back to square one with no viable offers. If anyone was going to be paying £5 million for Hearts, where were they? They would have come forward by now. It was a merry-go-round that Bryan couldn't get off.

Lawrence had kept a lid on Ann's identity for a long time. Ann didn't want to come out to the media until the deal was almost over the line. We had cancelled the big reveal on a number of occasions. The time had to be right for Ann. That was the only factor in determining this and rightly so. I was a tiny bit irritated as it meant I was still carrying all the burden of the press and media. I didn't mind doing it. In fact, I loved it. However, I was getting an increasing number of emails, letters and social media posts from angry constituents demanding to know how much time I was spending on FOH business and why I hadn't passed it on to someone else. *The Scotsman* sports reporter, Stuart Bathgate, contacted me one morning to say he had received a letter signed by 75 people claiming to be constituents trying to get me to resign from FOH. He didn't take it any further, worried about its authenticity. I suspect they were not voters of mine in any case or they were from rival clubs, but it did rankle. I was annoyed as I was doing all of this in my spare time. I had no spare time left.

It was remarkable that the media didn't divulge Ann's identity. They all knew but they respected Lawrence and me. It came to a head when Brian McLaughlin at the BBC knew other media outlets were about to blow her cover. He had known since the start and had toed the line by saying nothing. It would have been unfair for others to expose Ann when Brian had been so good at staying quiet. Brian was left with no choice in breaking the news. Lawrence and Ann worked very closely together on a well-choreographed plan.

It was complete coincidence that the reveal would be on 13 February with Brian Mclaughlin, just a day before Valentine's Day when all the headlines would be about Ann and Hearts. The headline writers had a field day with their different versions of the unimaginative 'Queen of Hearts'. It went perfectly though. It was announced alongside the finer details of the bid and the rescue package for Hearts. The biggest surprise for me in the reporting of this was that most media called the announcement of Ann a 'surprise'. It wasn't to most of them. I was thankful for what they did in respecting Ann's privacy. The emphasis would be on the future plans for Hearts and the critical point that Ann would not be profiting from this venture. She would take up the role of Chief Executive and Chair of Hearts on a no fee basis. This was very attractive to FOH. We were getting the experience and knowledge of Ann as a hugely successful and respected businesswoman at no cost to Hearts. That was worth more than the £2.5 million to deliver the CVA. Ann would make the case for supporter ownership and BIDCO would run the club for at least three years, via a newly appointed Board with representation from FOH.

It was, in my view, a match made in heaven. She publicly stated that she was conducting a detailed review of the club in anticipation of the takeover. If Ann's biggest dread was 'waking up one morning with nothing to do', then she was just about to embark on a project that would consume every waking hour. All those games with her daughter Carol at Tynecastle, across Scotland and into Europe would be eclipsed by taking her seat as Chair in the Directors' Box. She was a fan, first and foremost. As the Hearts European song goes, she had travelled by 'bus and car and then by railway' and 'tied her scarf around the funnel'. In fact, we shared a favourite Hearts memory in European adventures – Robbie Neilson's goal in Basel. The press lapped it up. I think now others could see why FOH chose to partner with Ann and not other bids. It was too good to be true – strong leadership combined with tight fiscal control. My role as FOH Chair would change now, and quite rightly. The focus would be on Ann and the club. She would be leading the club in preparation for supporter ownership.

It was a bit of a weight of my shoulders although I did one of the most unusual interviews shortly afterwards. Hearts played a home match against Dundee United on a Friday evening and it was shown live on BT *Sport*. They wanted a one-to-one interview with me for their coverage. The problem was I was on parliamentary business in Southampton and didn't get back to Edinburgh until very late on the Thursday evening. The game was the following day, so BT *Sport* had to film the interview that evening. We asked if it could be done at the airport but they refused. They said they would find a venue close to the airport. That venue was an Italian restaurant on Corstorphine Road owned by a Hearts supporter. I jumped off the airport bus just before 11.00pm and went into the restaurant to find they had turned the entire restaurant into a TV set. It was surreal but the first interview I had done in months where I didn't have to be careful not to let the identity of Ann slip.

Another piece of the jigsaw had been completed. Ann was in the public domain and now able to communicate her vision for Hearts to the supporters. Every newspaper and broadcaster got an interview with Ann. The newspapers had double page spread after double page spread right up to and including the Sundays that weekend. The next home game was against Celtic. The Hearts programme designers, 442 Sports Marketing, were producing an FOH special with a poster insert to help drive up pledges. They would also make a donation from their sale proceeds. Ann, against the recommendation of Lawrence, took her usual season ticket seat beside her daughter in the Wheatfield stand. The media were told that she wouldn't be available, but Lawrence had to confront match broadcasters Sky in the concourses. They had already managed to get Ann to speak to them privately. This was 2.45pm on match day so was frantic. BBC Reporter Jim Spence was pitch-side and seen Ann coming into the Wheatfield stand. Lawrence again intervened and went to Ann at her seat to tell her Jim Spence was there with a microphone. Everyone got through the game intact. The pictures of Ann in her seat made all the newspapers. It worked wonders.

Ann's reveal propelled the number of pledgers to over 8,000 after she wrote with her vision to the now 55,000 fans on the Hearts database. Lawrence thought this was a golden opportunity to have a supporter deliver the FOH message. The 8,000th subscriber would be a great story. That person was 40-year-old Derek Shade. He appeared at Tynecastle with Dylan McGowan and a Hearts top that read '8,000 #createhistory' across the back. His smiling face was plastered over every newspaper. It was the involvement of Ann that persuaded him to pledge. That was the power of Ann. We were well ahead of our targets. It just had to be sustained. 8,000 members gave us over £1.5 million a year in revenue. The opportunity that gave to Hearts was immeasurable.

Donald Cummings from Dundas & Wilson (D&W) was tasked with reviewing all the FOH governance documents and present recommendations for what needed to happen next. This was getting serious. We were on the cusp of realising the dream of saving Hearts. Donald did this work with his colleague, Grigor Milne. Grigor was partner at D&W and an expert on these matters. I think he was the only one in the team that wasn't a Hearts fan. To his benefit, he could look dispassionately at what needed to be done. Grigor and Donald underpinned their advice with reference to Stuart Murray at Shoosmiths. They came up with a proposal for moving FOH forward. Even after almost a year at the helm of FOH, we were still debating the relative merits of different company structures. Their view was that FOH should keep the structure as simple as possible. If the desire for a particular structure was driven due to concerns about legacy issues within FOH, these should be specifically identified and examined in detail. They could then take a view on whether these concerns were material to the FOH structure. D&W were superb. They provided invaluable support to FOH throughout the period of administration. One of the ironies was that the governance documents that Henry and I wrote in Beanscene on that Saturday afternoon many months previously all but endured. Most are still in place today.

D&W's dispassionate and legalistic approach was just the tonic for the FOH Board. Donald, with a colleague and fellow Hearts supporter, Chris Walters, attended the FOH Board meeting to give their findings. There are few better in the Scottish legal industry than Donald. His attention to detail and forensic approach is unsurpassed. He is hugely friendly but exception-ally unassuming. One of the skills he does lack, though, is enthusiastically presenting an idea. All the pre-meeting emails and discussions I had with him and his team to try and steer the conclusion went out of the window. We did get agreement at the end of the day for the main issues of govern-ance, but it was a bit of a struggle. Some on the Board who were enthusiastic supporters of what Donald was proposing became lukewarm at best. I often chide Donald about this. It was funny. The conclusions finalised the FOH corporate governance for the time being. The more detailed work would be done in the future. FOH wouldn't be taking over for at least three years so we had time to get it right. Donald and Grigor would now turn their attention to the BIDCO/FOH agreement.

It was all coming together nicely. We just had to get the Lithuanian courts to approve the deals and get this over the line before it was too late. Hearts would be relegated. We knew that for some time. A colossal rebuilding job was required. We weren't out of the woods yet. Hearts could still be liqui-dated and go out of business. The positive news was that all the consents from Lithuania were close to being granted, but there were new problems.

The latest problem that created a delay came from more Hibs fans trying to scupper the deal. The administrators at Valnetas were being deluged with emails trying to thwart the deal. Gintaras Adamonis from Valnetas kept saying that he expected the deal to save the club to go through but was con-stantly having to respond to 'a lot' of emails with concerns over the value of the deal. Those emails were also questioning the ability of Ann Budge to pro-vide proof of funds. It was so infuriating for Bryan. He was at the end of his tether. He had no choice but to look at a plan B. That led him to contact the Scottish Football Association (SFA) to make a plea for a special exemption to the rules on the consequences of setting up a new company. The member club of the SFA was Heart of Midlothian FC as they were currently consti-tuted. If they were to disband and New Heart of Midlothian FC was set up, the membership of the SFA would fall and a new application would be required. That would have to be approved by the other SFA member clubs.

The consequence would be to start again either at the bottom of the lowest division or, worse still, in the pyramid system outside the 42-member clubs of the top leagues. This rule was tightened after the Rangers situa-tion. Bryan wanted to test the new rule as it was put in place for clubs that couldn't get a CVA concluded and were, as a result, liquidated. The Hearts CVA was done but Bryan couldn't get hold of the shares. Ours was not like the Rangers situation. It was all done but the authorities in Lithuania were being obstructive and it never looked as though the deal would be concluded. The SFA was steadfast that they would not relent on companies transferring their SFA membership to a new company. They probably had a point, but it was worth a try. Bryan wasn't going to get this far without turning over every stone. He was close to retirement and had never lost a football club. He was damn sure he wasn't going to let Hearts be his last football job and the one that got away.

The football season wasn't going well. The reality of relegation was moving closer with every match, despite there being a real togetherness around the club. The fans, players, staff and management were as collegiate as at any time in Hearts history. It was extraordinary. It was that bond that carried Hearts that season. If we were to be relegated, we would go down both fighting and having a party. Some even looked forward to meeting different teams and going to unusual grounds. The players were truly exceptional. A small band of dedicated older professionals interspersed with youngsters who were given the opportunity to make a real name for themselves. Gary Locke and Billy Brown were Hearts through and through. It showed with the delight on their faces every time their team gave the fans something to sing and shout about. I always thought that a young side playing 30 to 40 games in the SPFL would gain enough experience to grow beyond their years in future seasons. It was a tough season, no doubt, but it gave a real base for the future. The question for fans became when we would be officially relegated.

The worst-case relegation scenario was presented to us – Hibs at Tynecastle. The Hibs fans had billed it as a Tynecastle party. They wanted to relegate us. 3,600 of them filled the Gorgie stand for the match. Many of them had party hats, streamers and beach balls. This had all the hallmarks of a very bad memory for Hearts fans. Not so. The Hearts players were phenomenal. We played Hibs off the park. 20-year-old Dale Carrick struck in the sixth minute to send the vast majority of the 17,000 fans into raptures. Given the difficult season we had encountered, our record against Hibs was rather good. And it got better. As Hibs pushed for an equaliser that would have relegated us, we grabbed a second goal. 93 minutes were on the clock when 19-year-old substitute Billy King pounced. As the ball nestled in the net, we went wild. Gary Locke punched the air and tore down the touchline celebrating like he did when he lifted the Scottish Cup in 1998. The sheer joy on his face was a fitting tribute to what he had done for Hearts over that season. There would be no relegation party for Hibs supporters. The commentator for *Sky Sports*, Ian Crocker, delivered the immortal line that summed up the emotions of the Hearts fans at the final whistle: 'Not on this day, not on this ground.' It didn't matter when we went down now. It wouldn't be against Hibs at home and that was all that mattered.

Just days after the elation of spoiling Hibs relegation party, we were dealt what felt like a hammer blow. Bryan phoned me to say that he was going to go to the media with the threat that Hearts may have to be liquidated. He was fast running out of money and would have to try and force the hand of the Lithuanians to get the deal concluded. It was his 'red button' but he felt, at that stage, that he had no choice but to press it. He was very anxious that he may have to call in the liquidators after all that had been done. Bryan was getting more and more perplexed by the day at the delays from Lithuania. They kept promising to get the deal through but then would stall. The courts had been due to rubber stamp the decisions by the ūkio Bankas and UBIG creditors to accept the CVA offer from BIDCO, but the meetings were put back time and time again. Bryan couldn't determine if it was deliberate or just the weight of bureaucracy in Lithuania. It didn't really matter. He still couldn't get his hands on the shares and he wasn't able to get an explanation as to the reasons. He feared the deal could collapse. He would be left with no option but to wind up Hearts when it ran out of cash. That date was not too far in the distance. A matter of weeks. Bryan and his team at BDO had been pursuing the shares for nearly ten months. He engaged the Lithuanian and UK ambassadors again in a final attempt to plead Hearts' case ahead of the latest 7 April court deadline. Bryan always put the chances of Hearts surviving at 49 per cent. He was telling the media that is was now 50-50 as to whether this deal happened or not. His exact words to me were, 'It's whites of the eyes time and I think, at this stage, 49-51 may be optimistic.'

Hearts would eventually succumb to mathematics and be formally relegated the same week despite a rather impressive 4-2 victory away at Partick Thistle. The inevitable had happened but the Monday court meeting that was scheduled in Lithuania was much more important. I was not willing to allow liquidation to swiftly follow a relegation. We needed this meeting to happen and we desperately required a positive conclusion.

The date of Monday 7 April 2013 may not be etched in the memory of Hearts fans like the date of the 1998 and 2012 Scottish Cup Finals, but it was a date of equal importance. Until it was postponed again. Late in the afternoon of Sunday 6 April, a rogue bid was emailed to Gintaras at Valnetas. It was from Pat Munro. Pat had been in touch with the administrator back in March so had their details. I couldn't believe it. Deimantė immediately contacted Bryan asking for his comments on why this proposal hadn't been taken forward. Pat was offering £1 million a year for 15 years in a total package worth £15 million. The contract would be legally binding and ūkio Bankas would keep a standard security over the stadium until the £15 million was completely paid. I heard speculation from a number of normally reliable sources that the Scandinavian consortium were allegedly behind Mr Munro's intervention. It may have all been random speculation but there were sightings that at least one meeting between them took place in Edinburgh during the previous week. I do have to say that the rumour mill is never too far away in football.

It couldn't have come at a worse time. We were less than 24 hours from the Lithuanian courts approving the CVA and it was scuppered. Late that Sunday evening, Trevor Birch responded to Deimantė to say that this was all new to BDO and they had never been approached by Mr Munro. He assumed it was speculative and designed to wreck the process. I had no idea what it was designed to do. I wasn't even sure if it was a bogus email address that had been set up purporting to be from the sender. Bryan and Trevor asked me to intervene with Deimantė. I emailed pleading for her not to derail the process at this 11th hour. To be fair to Deimantė, she was legally responsible for obtaining the most money for ūkio Bankas assets to satisfy her creditors. That was her only job. If someone is offering a package worth £15 million as opposed to £2.5 million then she is duty-bound to at least consider it. The court hearing the follow day was off. Postponed again.

I was completely shocked. Anyone that knows me will tell you that anger is not really one of the emotions I tend to display. In fact, I can't really remember many times in my life that I have been angry. This was one of them. I was in my flat in Edinburgh and, after coming of the phone to Trevor, I instantly threw a glass off the wall. It shattered everywhere. My frustration just boiled over. We had come so far. We were so close despite all the trials and tribulations. I wanted to save my beloved Hearts. I didn't want to take the ship down. Bryan flew out to Lithuania the following morning to see if being there in person would assist.

He came back without making much progress. He was convinced that things would move in the next week or so but was still sure they would ask for more money. He was also placed under a strict press embargo for a few days. That created even more uncertainty. Money would run out at the end of April. I was sure if we needed a few hundred thousand pounds more, we could raise it with a special appeal. Bryan wasn't sure if it would be needed. He asked the SPFL if some of the monies due from the league position at the end of the season could be brought forward in order to help Hearts fulfil their remaining fixtures. The Premier League had split into top and bottom sections, so some money could have been transferred. The reply was not positive.

It was a nervous period for us all. Bryan seemed to be at the end of the road. He was talking up liquidation. He had been embargoed from talking publicly about Hearts. What was going on? Then it happened.

On 16 April at 10.17am, I got a call from Bryan. The ūkio Bankas Creditors Committee had met and approved the BIDCO deal. It was done. I punched the air as if Hearts had just scored a last-minute winner. Bryan explained that there were some small formalities, but it should just take a few more weeks to get the legal paperwork completed. Bryan had got hold of the all-important shares. I immediately sent a text to the FOH Board to give them the good news:

> Hi all, I may have a little good news for you (Garry you may have to dry your eyes). Bryan Jackson has just been informed me that the ūkio creditors have approved the deal in Lithuania. This is a massive step forward. The sale and purchase agreement needed to be concluded and there will be some issues but not insurmountable. I would guess we are 90 per cent there but we must still encourage a little patience and, of course, more sign ups. BDO and FOH will play this down for now but deal is all but done. Remarkable. Thanks everyone. Ian

We played it down in the press. Until the ink was dry on the sale and purchase agreement, we would be cautious. The last 11 months of nail-biting administration taught us that it was not all over until the fat Robbo sang. Sorry Robbo. The news trickled out slowly online and then in the media. I could almost hear the grins stretching along Gorgie Road as the realisation dawned that we were almost there. But there would be no celebration until it was 100 per cent concluded.

It became imperative that we agreed the contract between BIDCO and FOH. Ann had appointed Graeme Henry from DLA Piper to complete the transaction for BIDCO. Donald and Grigor at D&W would represent FOH in 'Project Westerley'. These discussions were far from easy despite both parties striving for the same outcome. We had to get this right as the agreement would need to endure for some time. The framework was set out in the BIDCO deal but the detail was not. Ann intended her proposal to be 'very prescriptive' and only open to very limited negotiation. It would include her instructions on the composition of the Hearts Board and a requirement that FOH must remain in its present corporate form, the latter qualification putting an end to the perpetual recurring discussions about governance. The main areas of negotiation were around the tightness of agreement. No shares were to transfer to FOH until the last payment to clear Ann's loan was paid.

I was concerned at what would happen if we were, say, £100,000 short at the end of the period. The supporters could have paid the best part of £6 million and ended up with nothing. Even with the entry of a 90-day grace period, it seemed inequitable. We also didn't have any indication of what was to happen with the 15 per cent shareholding that was being bought from Quantum. There had been talk of these being transferred to FOH as a gift but the legal agreement was silent on this. Crucially, FOH had to ensure that BIDCO was tied in for the period. We couldn't have Ann selling her shares in BIDCO. The relationship between BIDCO and FOH was exceptional but we had to ensure it was future-proof. What if Ann was no longer able to be the figurehead or didn't want to be involved anymore? Whilst Ann was essentially BIDCO the deal would be perfect. That wasn't a guarantee though. It was a real struggle to get this recognised in the agreement.

FOH would be contracted to transfer £1 million at the conclusion of the agreement then 95 per cent of all monies totalling a minimum of £1.4 million a year for the subsequent two years. We would then refund BIDCO for the £2.4 million to deliver the CVA, £100,000 for the UBIG shares, the costs of BIDCO raising the funds, the interest on the debt and the £480,000 legal costs of both parties. FOH would be able to retain just £50,000 per year for all marketing, administration and costs.

None of these issues were insurmountable. The only actual problem was that BIDCO were insisting that the FOH Board be reduced to five members. I thought the Board was unwieldy for some time but that is not what we had communicated to the pledgers. Ann was clear this reduction had to happen and, as always, she was right:

> They guys were lovely and it was a real learning experience for me to hear their stories, but FOH meetings were so frustrating. I was on holiday when the changes to the FOH Board happened. I felt from that point that there were far too many people involved... with different agendas. This was why I was insistent that we changed when the FOH/BIDCO agreement was put in place.

I'm sure it wasn't a deal breaker though. It was a vexing process mainly due to the timescales. We had been expecting the draft document for some weeks. When it came, we had to respond rather more quickly than we would have liked. D&W were advising me and the FOH Board that the agreement was unacceptable in early drafts, but I was being forced to agree to it. A fundamental for me was that we were not fully delivering what was promised to supporters and that put ourselves and FOH at risk. What would happen if we accepted a deal that we couldn't pay for and risked thousands of fans demanding their money back? I couldn't do that, and the FOH Board couldn't allow that. During the negotiations, Grigor and Donald described the attitude and approach of DLA Piper as 'similar to dealing with a hostile takeover of a corporate giant', rather than that of two interested parties co-operating in order to achieve mutually agreed aims. I didn't understand why.

The toing and froing concluded and the BIDCO/FOH agreement was all but settled. One of the minor issues that would have to be dealt with was the legal takeover rules. When a person or group acquires interests in shares carrying 30 per cent or more of the voting rights of a company, they must make a cash offer to all other shareholders at the highest price paid in the 12 months before the offer. That meant the 6 per cent or so of ordinary Hearts shareholders would be offered the same price as both UBIG and Quantum for their shares. Ann didn't really want or need their shares. It was another cost with lengthy procedural complications that would delay conclusion of the deal further.

During this period, a fan favourite from the 1980s passed away. Whilst we were all trying to save the club, we would reflect on the role that Sandy Jardine played in restoring the fortunes of our club during the 1980s. He had a quite magnificent footballing career at Rangers and Hearts. A career during which he truly merited being referred to as a Scottish football legend. We could do with more Sandys today.

Bryan continued to press the Lithuanian authorities to get the sale and purchase agreement concluded. He set a date of the end of the first week in May 2014. The FOH Board had approved the BIDCO/FOH agreement on Tuesday 6 May 2014 with the exception of allowing the five-member Board to be enlarged to a six-member Board. That would allow an elected fans representative to be appointed at the first FOH AGM. FOH was due to transfer all the monies we had accumulated to Hearts at the takeover date. My goodness, the club needed the money.

I wrote in previous chapters about the battles at the FOH Board about access to the bank account. This was about to come back and bite us. Bill Alves had for many months been insisting that others be added to the account, including the Chair. It was never actioned. That gave us a bit of a nightmare with getting the cash transferred. The authorisations were still with ex-director, Alex, who was on the mandate for making these large payments. We had to get an FOH Board mandate to allow Alex and Jamie to send the payment. In our experience, the Clydesdale Bank were not very light on their feet. It showed to the FOH Board that these decisions, alongside good and effective financial control, were not just me and others on the Board being difficult. They were essential. Here we had Alex and Jamie standing in a branch of Clydesdale Bank awaiting formal permission from a quorate FOH Board to approve them to send the payments. It was a nonsense but summed up the problems of the last year.

I hoped to sign all the sale and purchase agreements with Ann on the morning of Friday 9 May. Bryan had said they would probably have to work through the night. It would go down to the wire. The final request to Bryan from the Lithuanians was that they wanted to clear the Hearts bank account when the deal was done. It was easy for Bryan to repel that request – there was next to no money in the Hearts bank account.

The final BIDCO/FOH agreement was sent to Grigor late on the Thursday evening. It had incorporated most of our views but was presented as final. It was going to be a long night. My memory of that night is very vivid. I got back to my flat from Parliament quite late. There was an important debate in the House of Commons on the 'bedroom tax'. Grigor and Chris Walters were working on the final documents. Graeme was liaising with Grigor on one side and Bryan on the other. Bryan was in touch with the Lithuanians. Both Ann and I were being kept abreast of developments. Given the timescales, I sent a message to all the FOH Directors seeking their approval to delegate the decisions to me that may be required that evening. I'm glad I did, although we would have to have a conference call at 7.45am on the Friday before the papers were signed. We required formal approval. I was in bed by the time the process started to conclude. I remember it was well after midnight. I had Ann and Graeme on my landline from the DLA Piper offices in Rutland Square and Grigor and his team on my mobile from his Saltire Court offices in Castle Terrace. Grigor was giving me his advice on the agreements whilst negotiations were continuing with Graeme. Grigor was solely taking instruction from FOH. That was his job. Graeme was representing Ann and BIDCO. That was his job.

I was presented with the final documents via email from Chris Walters annotated with Grigor's advice. There were one or two minor points that we went back and forth on in the final agreement. Ann and Graeme were happy to agree to these minor changes. The biggest issue we faced was the Quantum shares. The 15 per cent was a fairly large shareholding. FOH had assumed we would merely take them on and control 94 per cent of the club. The remaining six per cent would be owned by the small individual shareholders who we were delighted to partner with. However, the final contract had the Quantum shares being held by BIDCO as a 'legacy'. It never became an issue and I was always of the view that if we were getting Ann and her experienced team at the helm of Hearts for three years, without payment, then this was a good deal.

The other issue was the working capital requirements from FOH. The contract was written so tightly that any minor infringement of payment would result in default. DLA Piper had refused a wording suggestion from Grigor to soften this for purposes outside the control of FOH or a temporary blip in pledge income. Grigor strongly advised me that I could not agree to these. He was not commenting on the relative merits or otherwise of the proposals, merely that the FOH Board hadn't agreed it and it was not something I had the authority to decide. Here I was, sitting in bed in the early hours of the Friday morning having to make a huge decision. Graeme at DLA Piper could not have been clearer with me after I raised the payment terms for the third time – 'Take it or leave it.' Grigor insisted that I speak directly with Ann in private to get this resolved. We could come back to it later or find a form of words, but he would be advising me that I could not sign these documents later that morning.

I was stuck between and rock and a hard place. After all we had been through, I was left with FOH lawyers advising that I couldn't agree and BIDCO's lawyers saying I had no choice. I was essentially strong-armed into accepting the 'non-satisfaction' clause. It wasn't fair to have to do this at the last minute. I let it lie for an hour or so. I spoke to Grigor again and went through the consequences of all options available to me. The bottom line was that we didn't have any time left. The Lithuanians were ready to deliver the shares and we had to take that opportunity. I called Ann back and agreed. I didn't like being bounced into this decision, but I had no choice at all. At 2.15am, the agreements were all in place. We would reconvene at 7.30am in the DLA Piper offices to officially sign the papers. Grigor later advised that as long as Ann was in charge of BIDCO, there could always be a grown-up discussion should circumstances change. I was happy with that.

I didn't get any sleep at all. I was excited and apprehensive. As long as the Lithuanians came through with their promise, Hearts would have been saved. Even in the last few days and hours there were still problems going on. Both Bryan and Graeme were not confident it would happen as planned. It was a real 'test of faith' for Ann when it became clear that she had to transfer the funds to Lithuania and then trust them to complete the deal.

I went to DLA Piper for 7.30am. I was hoping this would not take too long. I wanted to savour the moment, but I had an advice session at my constituency office at 9.15am and had to be there for that. Ann had sent the money to Valnetas without knowing if the shares would come back. It was tense. We were all walking out of DLA Piper's office, ready to give up, when the call came through to say the papers had been signed and received. We were all hugely elated, including some of Graeme's DLA Piper staff who were Hearts fans.

The fax machine was whirring as the coffee and a glass of champagne or two flowed. I was presented with the BIDCO/FOH agreement that we had haggled over into the early hours of the same morning. Ann signed it and I signed it on behalf of FOH. It was done. Hearts was saved.

I left the offices to grab a taxi to my advice session. In the cab I sent a text to the FOH Board:

> Folks, deal is 99.99 per cent done. Just waiting on Hearts share registrars to sort out the general offer letter to the remaining shareholders for the take-over panel and ensuring that the money arrives safely in the bank account of the Lithuanians. Please keep everything under wraps for now as there are very strict stock market rules that we need to comply with. You've all helped to save our club today. Well done, and no tears. Ian

My advice session was packed that morning. I didn't get a chance to either digest what we had just done or keep up with progress. I got a call from Bryan at lunchtime to say it was almost done and Ann was at Tynecastle with her team. The formal notification of completion was issued by DLA Piper to D&W at 3.30pm. We had sent the £960,000 from FOH with £40,000 to come when we had it. That money was needed for all the professional costs, footballing debt, costs associated with winding up the administration and sorting out the 2012 share issue totalling £1.38 million.

I immediately tweeted out:

> OFFICIAL: Four historic words for all Hearts supporters 'deal done, thank you'.

If any fan had their champagne chilling in the fridge from November, today was the day to pop it open. My thoughts turned to David Southern and the staff at Hearts. They had been in the trenches for years but kept the show on the road. They preserved the club season after season. They all deserved this but none more so than David. I think I could hear his sigh of relief from miles away. We put out a press release thanking everyone involved but re-emphasised the point that this was just the beginning for Hearts. It had survived but the work started that day.

> The Hearts family has come together during its darkest hour to ensure our Hearts are still beating. Everyone should be very proud of themselves tonight in the knowledge that they have played their part in creating history for generations of Hearts supporters to come.

Ann went to Tynecastle with her partner, Eric Hogg, who would become Hearts' Operations Director, and her small team for a celebratory glass of something appropriate. Ann's life was about to change. She recognised that almost instantly:

> It was only really in the taxi on the way home from Tynecastle that Friday afternoon that it truly sunk in and I knew my life was about to change in so many ways.

Bryan congratulated Ann, had his last Tynecastle pie, handed her the keys and left with his hard-won reputation intact. That was him done at Tynecastle a full 51 weeks after he arrived. Bryan went home that evening to his wife. He didn't really sound convincing when he said to her, 'I told you so.' His contribution to the saving of Hearts will go down in the history books. When Mohamed Al-Fayed was owner of Fulham he erected a bronze statue of Michael Jackson outside Craven Cottage. It would not have been out of place to have a bronze statue of Bryan outside Tynecastle. His consumption of Hearts pies may have meant they required a little bit more bronze, but it would have been fitting. Bryan had done so much. His last job in football had certainly aged him. He would retire a couple of years later and go on to write a comedy play about his experiences. *The Pieman Cometh* became a huge Fringe Festival success.

Bryan was right to give some credit to the Lithuanians. Outside the brutal negotiations, Bryan actually managed to build a good rapport and relationship with Deimantė and the other officials. As difficult a process as it was, if the Lithuanians hadn't accepted the offer and given over the shares then it wouldn't have happened. After all was said and done, BIDCO paid the valuation. Whether the valuation was high or low will always be argued but anything is only worth what someone is willing to pay for it.

I was so relieved but I also felt rather flat. I didn't quite know what to expect. Perhaps it hadn't sunk in for me. It certainly did for others. My phone and emails were red hot with messages of congratulations. I don't think I have ever seen so many adults spontaneously burst into tears when they were explaining what it meant to them.

Many people asked me what I did that evening. Truth be told I went to Tynecastle. No better place to be. It was purely coincidental. Garry had organised a fundraising *A Question of Sport* quiz evening. On my way to Tynecastle that evening, I reflected on the day. I sent a message to the FOH Board that summed up how I was feeling:

> I just wanted to thank you all for everything you have done over the last year since I became Chair of FOH. I never thought we would get this far if I was being honest. Each and every one of you have played a key role in rescuing our club. I've had people in tears today unable to speak with the joy that Hearts are saved. You all did that, and I owe you all a great deal of gratitude for your honesty, loyalty, hard work and friendship. Thank you all for saving our wonderful club. Ian.

The quiz was hosted by BBC *Sport* commentator Paul Mitchell. The atmosphere in the room was electric. I didn't buy a drink all night. Nothing new, some would say. I can't remember how I got home. It was fantastic. There was an inordinate amount of work still to be done to ensure Hearts survived, but the supporters were entitled to one night of celebration. The last few days had been bruising. But, as Grigor often pointed out, if parties go to hell and back to do a deal, this often increases their determination to make it work thereafter.

We did it. You did it. I wanted to enjoy the moment. This was a historic day in the history of Heart of Midlothian Football Club.

CHAPTER 18

Relegations, Celebrations and Budgements

THE DAY AFTER the deal was done, Hearts completed one of the most traumatic and turbulent seasons in its history. They said goodbye to the Premier League with a draw against St Mirren at Love Street. It ended a run of just one loss in the final eight games of the campaign. The results were great. Not only did we spoil Hibs' planned relegation party at Tynecastle, but our young team turned them over again on their patch with two goals from Callum Paterson. I would take four wins and a defeat against Hibs in any season. The fact it happened in this season was remarkable. A real tonic for the Hearts fans.

What was to transpire after that famous victory at Easter Road would cheer all us up over the summer. Hibs got relegated as well. They finished joint-bottom and were the first Premiership team to lose a two-legged play off. Hibs won the first leg away from home but lost the home leg. After extra time they were relegated on penalties. Hearts and Hibs would meet in the Championship the following season.

Hearts fans had their own relegation party that night. I think it's called Karma! The following football season in the Championship would be exciting. We would have Hibs coming down with us. Rangers were also on their ascent back to the Premier League and would be in the division as well. That made it a very exciting Championship League, but much more difficult for Hearts to get back up immediately. That was all factored in to the plan. The prudent financials that Kevin Windram was working to were prepared on the basis we would be out of the top division for two seasons. Kevin would soon join the Hearts Board.

It was only 48 hours after the documents were signed and there was a fans rally. It was more of a celebration than a rally. Graeme Kay had been at the centre of such events for a number of years. He and his colleagues generated tens of thousands of pounds for the Hearts cause. I was looking forward to the rally. Most of the first team would be in attendance along with Gary Locke and Billy Brown. There were very few people who didn't recognise what they had achieved in the most trying of times. I did a question and answer session that allowed me to thank the supporters for what they had done and to encourage them to keep going. Ann was in attendance as well. She was mobbed by adoring fans wanting a selfie and her autograph. It was a carnival atmosphere. I couldn't stay for the entertainment of comedian Sandy Strang or former referee Kenny Clark as I had a host of local constituency appointments. It raised a lot of very welcome resources.

The rebuilding of Hearts would commence in earnest. There was the regular preparation required for the new season and the longer term. It was not going to be an easy task for Ann and her new executive team. I wasn't primed for what was to happen the following day. The Monday was the first working day of the new regime. Ann had rightly taken full control as Chief Executive and Chairwoman. She brought in Eric Hogg as Operations Director and Ann Park as Head of Commercial. Robert Wilson would take on Deputy Chief Executive and Head of Strategic Planning. I was appointed to the Board as the FOH representative. What a privilege that was. Fiona Sinclair at Hearts had phoned me to ask that I go to Tynecastle as soon as I could to sign the forms for Companies House to become a Director. I had filled out these forms a number of times for both my own businesses and local organisations. This was very special though. We have all thought about scoring that winning goal for Hearts in a Cup Final, but that was as far as my ability took me. I was never very good at football so playing for Hearts was never a boyhood dream. However, it was unbelievable that I would have the honour of serving on the Hearts Board at such a crucial point in its history. I was so excited and determined to do it to the very best of my ability.

It were other additions to the Hearts Board that caused the press to term Monday 12 June 2014 as 'Budgement Day'. I know Ann had been taking advice from a large variety of experts and sources in advance of becoming the majority shareholder. That was wise planning. However, I wasn't made aware of the extent of changes on the footballing side of things. I guess Ann didn't want idle speculation filling newspapers at a time when all eyes had to be on saving the club. Ann knew from her earliest visits to Tynecastle and her initial meetings with senior staff that the club was 'broken'. Hearts had essentially been abandoned by the previous owners with no resources. Running the club became a day-to-day survival for David Southern and his staff. With no direction or money from the owners, there could be no overarching strategy either for how the club should be run or how football should be played. There had been no proper leadership from the previous regime for far too long. Ann had already met most of the staff during the long administration period and completed her own due diligence. She knew that first day on the job that it felt right for her to be there.

Administration had hollowed the club out and there was serious under-investment. Ann knew there would be no quick fix for these problems. That was why she set in place a three- to five-year plan to revamp the entire club and set it on a trajectory so that is would survive for another 140 years. It was about financial stability but, more than that, it was about refocusing on the football department to nurture the conveyor belt of young players.

The future for Hearts, and many other clubs, would be to put in place a pyramid youth academy system that allowed the very best youngsters to play in the first team and then be sold on for considerable transfer fees. This would then allow reinvestment in the playing squad and youth development. That was the only model Hearts could follow in the search for success. The days of spending big in the short-term to gamble on winning trophies was over. The strategy would have to start at under 8-year-olds all the way through to the senior football management. That would mean change on a fairly major scale.

I hadn't been involved in these discussions. My day job, FOH and trying to get the deal over the line consumed every waking hour so I was as shocked as anyone to be told by Ann on the Monday morning that Gary Locke and Billy Brown would be leaving Hearts. Ann wanted to make fundamental changes to the footballing department and that meant making a difficult decision not to offer Gary Locke and Billy Brown new contracts. There had been some speculation since the turn of the year that Gary and Billy were to be moved on. You never know how much stock there is in such speculation. Craig Levein would join the club with immediate effect as Director of Football with Robbie Neilson as Head Coach. Craig would assume total responsibility for everything to do with the football side. Ann was a big fan of Craig's. She knew he had a wealth of knowledge and a great deal to offer the club. He would be solely responsible for putting in place an end-to-end strategy for how Hearts was going to implement a youth-driven playing policy for the future. John Murray returned to his former role as a chief scout and temporarily running the academy.

I felt sorry for Gary and Billy, but I do remember what Bryan Jackson said on the first day he went into Tynecastle: 'Do all the bad things on day one as they have to be done.' I was fully supportive of Ann's strategy. My only regret was not knowing. I had sat between Gary and Billy at the fans rally the day before. We talked about the possibilities for the new season. They didn't have contracts as yet but they both gave the impression that they expected to be offered another season. It was an enormously difficult decision for Ann to make. She did say:

> Knowing the decisions we were about to implement on the football side made me quite uncomfortable. I was pretty uncomfortable in many ways but equally I was convinced our broad approach was right. I also hated the press and media side of things as it was so totally new to me.

Gary was immense both on and off the pitch in the last year. He had dealt with everything that had been thrown at him with dignity and love for Hearts. There would have been a large number of people in the club that were sorry to see them go. However, the club had to move on.

It was a big bang but honest approach on day one to start rebuilding our great club. Ann posted her positive vision in detail on the Hearts website. The fans were right behind Ann and her new team. At least we all could recognise that Ann would be making decisions in the best interest of the club. That would be a novelty given what had happened previously.

The other consequence of the deal being concluded was that all FOH Directors were to resign, and a new FOH Board appointed. I already had the resignation letters from the supporters group representatives. They submitted them at the very start of their tenure. Calum, Jane, Henry, Bill and Dougie had done their jobs. They came into this project to save the club that they loved and what a contribution they all made to make that happen. Their hours of sacrifice and tireless work should never be underestimated. They did it without personal gain. They are the real heroes of this process. Lawrence would also be calling it a day. He was immense. He transformed the public face of FOH and devised a marketing and PR campaign that should be winning national awards. His choreography of media messaging was superb.

The press release from the supporters' representatives caused a bit of a stir, but they deserved their proper public thanks. I'm convinced we wouldn't have been successful without them. These are very good people, very good Hearts people. Lifelong friendships were developed. They should be proud. Maybe the fan groups shouldn't have resigned when they did in hindsight, but they stuck to the agreements. Without them, our club would be dead. Whatever happens going forward they had done their bit, and then some. They brought our club home.

I had considered resigning at this time too. It had been a whirlwind 18 months and I felt I had done my bit. Despite being a professional politician, I didn't enjoy the often bruising and exhausting politics of FOH. I had a superb relationship with Ann, but I could go out on a high and let others take it forward. There was a General Election the following spring and I was defending the smallest majority in Scotland. I was also consumed by the Independence Referendum that September. It was Donald and Grigor that persuaded me to see it through a little bit longer. In my heart of hearts, that is what I wanted to do. It wasn't time to quit.

That left a much smaller FOH Board of myself, Garry Halliday, Brian Cormack, with a new formal additional of our marketing advisor, Alasdair Bruce. Jamie Bryant also stood down. His work commitments didn't allow him to be involved as much as others although the initial principle for FOH was his. He must have been pleased to see it come to fruition. We would also bring on Donald Cummings from D&W. This much smaller Board would be more manageable and be able to concentrate on maintaining and growing the number of members and income. That was really the only task now. The Hearts Board would be available for advice and the PR department at Tynecastle could be used for FOH purposes. We were essentially working hand-in-glove now so FOH had the resources of the club at our disposal. Given that Robert and Kevin would be busy advising Ann at the club, she introduced me to Marcia Campbell. Marcia wealth of experience had her dubbed 'Scotland's first lady of finance' by *The Scotsman*. She came onto the FOH Board with fresh eyes to advise us on the way forward. She had a number of non-executive positions including Sainsbury's Bank and Aviva. We were exceptionally lucky to have her advising us.

Ann made some other structural changes in her first week. She wanted to set a new family and community orientated culture. Wonga as a shirt sponsor did not fit with that so she made the very bold decision to break ties with them and give the away kit shirt sponsorship to FOH as a thank you to the supporters. What an incredible gesture. It would be a fitting recognition of what the supporters had done to save their club, especially in such a remembrance year. The home shirt would be sponsor-free given the gravity of what the tribute shirt was commemorating. The Argentinian-style away kit, with its blue and white panels, would be emblazoned with the FOH crest rather than a corporate sponsor, subject to SFA clearance.

The first Hearts Board meeting was a real pleasure. Ann, Eric, Robert, Craig and I couldn't quite believe we had got to this point. If someone had told me a year before that I would be plotting the path to a positive future for my football club, I would never have believed them. This was *Roy of the Rovers* stuff for me. I am sure it was for the others too. We got an update on the financials of the club from Eric. We had been surprised to receive an £85,000 contribution for the club academy scheme. An irritation was the Hearts annual accounts that had to be signed off. There were some matters to clear up in terms of share certificates for those who participated in the 2012 share offer. It was a minor and expensive issue but important for those fans to get what they were promised. SPFL and SFA regulations had to be complied with. I gave an update on FOH pledge levels that were just over 8,000. We had paid over the contracted £1 million and were well on track to exceed the £1.4 million working capital obligations. The most exciting part for me though were always the footballing reports from Craig Levein. He and Robbie had been working hard to identify new players for the coming season. It wasn't going to be easy with both Hibs and Rangers in the division, but they were confident of getting promoted.

To a layperson, the strategy was threefold: firstly, to bring through the best young talent in Scotland to the first team; secondly, to build on the team that was ever present from the previous season; thirdly, to identify players that would be unaffordable in normal circumstances but would maybe want to come to Hearts to resurrect their careers. The latter was obviously a risk but some would work out and others not. I think in hindsight many of the players that were risks came very good indeed – Öztürk, Bauben, Gomis, Zeefuik and, of course, Sow were prime examples of this approach. If only the club could sign players! The only proper decision we made at that first Board meeting was to action the payment of the Living Wage to all staff and contractors. This was a new beginning, with a new culture, and a new community. It was a superb decision and one that felt as if Hearts had turned the corner. Ann couldn't believe the positive reaction to this decision. It proved to her that it was both the right thing to do as an employer, but also to change the culture:

> I was completely surprised by the powerful reaction that followed the announcement of implementing the Living Wage. We didn't expect so much positivity. We did it because it was the right thing to do and it made good business sense.

Ann confirmed on 11 June that Heart of Midlothian Football Club had officially exited administration. This was the final hurdle. We were all ecstatic. It was a formal technical exercise but that lifted the transfer embargo. Ann announced that season tickets would go on sale with a 7 per cent price reduction and a plea for fans to pay with cash or cheque. This was one of the peculiarities of season ticket sales. If you purchased them on a credit card, you would have your purchase essentially insured. That meant though that the credit card company only paid out to the club a proportion of the cost after each home match had taken place. That was dreadful for Hearts cash flow when they required it most. Credit card transaction providers were also not very responsive to Hearts credit rating despite the new ownership and were imposing considerable charges. This was no impediment to the newly energised Hearts fans – they snapped up over 10,000 season tickets in a matter of weeks. There would be a host of friendly matches. The first and most glamorous would be against Manchester City at Tynecastle. Knowing Craig, he would have immediately got on the phone to agents to get players signed up. I have never known someone to work so hard. Both Robbie and Craig came to the next FOH Board to present their new footballing philosophy and what they would be doing to build an academy pyramid system that utilised satellite academies all over Scotland. That would help to identify the very best youngsters. They would sweat the academy at Riccarton to produce players ready for the first team. They also explained the exciting and open way they wished to play the game.

It was an exhilarating and frantic period. Messages from people wanting to help and congratulate the club and FOH were coming in from all over the world. The 1874FF was still raising money and made a donation of £12,500 to Hearts to help pay for stadium improvements. The press was also still very interested in what was happening at Hearts. I never ignored a call from the media as their role was hugely important. I'm glad I didn't miss a certain call from a BBC *Sports* reporter (who I promised never to reveal but he knows who he is). It was a normal day at Parliament for me. My mobile rang about 5.00pm. Terry Butcher had just been sacked as manager of Hibs and the reporter was phoning to ask if I was interested in taking the job. I was quite taken aback. It was lucky I was on the ball that evening. I explained that I already had a busy job and my football commitments were taking all of my spare time. Of course, the reporter thought he was talking to my namesake, Hibs legend and Dumbarton manager, Ian Murray. After a 10-minute conversation I revealed he had phoned the wrong Ian Murray. He saw the funny side, but politely – or reasonably politely – said if I ever mentioned who he was he would seek revenge. Maybe he will reveal himself when this book is published. I always wondered what would have happened if I had said I was taking the job and turned up at Easter Road as a result. It may not have pleased the Hibs faithful. They certainly wouldn't have been singing, 'There's only one Ian Murray.' In fact, there were two.

Another chapter was closed when David Southern announced he was leaving the club. David wanted to pursue new projects. He didn't really have a role with the new regime as Ann had brought in Scot Gardiner as Chief Operating Officer. He was remarkable for Hearts. A true maroon hero. He summed up his nine years:

> I feel very privileged to have worked at Heart of Midlothian Football Club. I have enjoyed some of the greatest days in the club's history and also been engaged in some of the most challenging. I have memories that will last a lifetime. Now that the club is safe, and the revival is well underway I feel my work here is complete. I am very proud of the job everyone associated with the club has done to create what we have here today.

My first game in the Directors Box was a Petrofac Training Cup victory over Annan Athletic. It was my first opportunity to see a game. There was a palpable feeling that this was a new era and the fans were going to enjoy every minute of it. And they did. The season started in earnest at Ibrox. Rangers were ploughing through the divisions and were desperate to get back to the top league. It was the worst possible fixture for Hearts to start the season. It just so happened to be my 38th birthday. I went to Ibrox to meet up with Ann, Eric and the rest of the Board. Over lunch, Eric ran through the etiquette for opposing Directors in the Directors Box. We could clap but celebrating goals or singing was not allowed. It would be inappropriate to do so. We all confirmed these instructions. It was our first official match as a Board and we wanted to show that Hearts was changing. What a Sunday afternoon match. After a tight first half, Hearts captain Danny Wilson scored with a header from a corner. It was a great first goal of the season. We, as instructed, clapped, looked gleefully at each other but knew, given we were at Ibrox, that anything could happen with 38 minutes remaining. And it did. As the clock ran down, Rangers equalised through Nicky Law. What a disaster but typical of Hearts in Glasgow. We just didn't carry the luck to win here. We were bitterly disappointed.

What a start to the season it would have been to take three points back along the M8 to Gorgie. Ah, but wait. As if by magic our new striker, Osman Sow latched on to Sam Nicholson's through ball to slip it past the Rangers goalkeeper into the corner of the net. I don't know what happened next but there was a sure-fire breach of etiquette in the Rangers Directors Box. I don't know if I was carrying Eric or he me, but we celebrated. It was a total release of emotion. It may have even been a culmination of the previous 18 months. There were lots of very dark days when it looked like there was no light at the end of the tunnel. Sow's goal not only gave us the light, but we were nearly out the tunnel. What a way to start the season and what a launch pad for Robbie Neilson and his team. We left Ibrox elated. and I went for the 'clockwork orange' back to Queen Street station. It was about an hour after the match so wasn't overly busy. One of the major disadvantages of having been so high profile with FOH was being recognisable. Supporters of all clubs knew who I was. Despite trying to be inconspicuous on the subway, I heard a call out from behind me, 'Hey you, ya fat bastard.' I froze as a Brutus of a man dressed head to toe in Rangers memorabilia ambled towards me. 'Here we go,' I thought. He had almost got to me when he said, 'Sorry mate, thought you were someone else.' Obviously, someone equally as fat I thought.

That opening match signalled the start of remarkable run of matches that saw only one defeat in 30. The sequence included a win and two draws against Hibs. A 10-0 home win against Cowdenbeath caught the eye. The only disappointments were heavy league and Scottish Cup defeats to Celtic. But what a season. Tynecastle was sold out every week. The fans were returning in their thousands. It was quite a sight.

Two games and a goal particularly stick in my own mind. As a Trustee of McCrae's Battalion, I was humbled to be the senior Director on duty for the home match against Raith Rovers before Armistice Sunday. Ann and Eric were on a short break. The game was taking place 100 years since the start of World War I. The afternoon would assume added poignancy for all involved. We were also hosting the Royal Navy from Rosyth. A 100-page commemorative programme was produced to mark the occasion and we had the band of the Royal Scots Association. There were formalities in the Directors Suite with the Royal Navy to name Hearts the 'official' football team of new aircraft carrier HMS *Queen Elizabeth*. This was to commemorate Hearts' long association with the armed forces dating back to 1914. I was privileged to perform the official exchange of pennants in the Boardroom before the match. Coincidentally, the officer from the Royal Navy was a friend of mine from university days. It all added up to a very appropriate day. The stadium was adorned with poppies. A lone piper played the lament 'Flowers of the Forest' before the players interlinked shoulder-to-shoulder throughout the pre-game minute's silence. It was a hugely emotional and poignant moment, a moment of reflection for the 1914 team of heroes. This is what Hearts was all about. At the annual Haymarket memorial service the following morning, I laid a wreath on behalf of all the FOH members.

The second match was Hearts' 4-0 victory over Dumbarton in March 2015. The title was all but wrapped up. The significance of this game was the tribute paid to Hearts legend, Dave McKay. He had passed away at the age of 80 earlier in the month. I was hosting the parents of a good friend, Andrew Frame, in the Directors Box that afternoon as their twin grandsons, Ewan and Duncan, were the mascots for the day. Andrew and his wife Suzanne were with the boys but didn't want their grandparents to miss out seeing them.

What a day it was for them and me. The Boardroom was wall-to-wall with Hearts legends who wanted to be at the game to pay their respects to Dave. He played 135 times for his boyhood heroes in maroon during the most successful period of Hearts history in the 1950s. He was Hearts through and through. Our club captain was transferred to Tottenham Hotspur for £32,000 in 1959. Well known as a true gentleman of the game, although he played combined 390 games for Spurs and Derby, his heart was always at Tynecastle. The legend's words adorn one of the walls in the home dressing room:

> For as long as I can remember, all I wanted in my life, nothing else, was to play for Hearts, which is my dream team. And to play for Scotland. I had no ambition for anything else. Always Hearts.

The best story from the Boardroom that day was from his former teammate, Alex Young. Alex was telling us that Dave was always slightly aggravated when he was asked if it was Tottenham or Derby for him. On one occasion, he was a studio guest for *Sky Sports* on a live match between the two sides. It was finely poised at half-time and Dave was asked by presenter Richard Keys where his loyalties lay in such a finely balanced match. Dave, without even having to think about it said, 'Neither, my heart lies at Tynecastle.' It certainly did. It was a pleasure to share the Boardroom with such footballing royalty and his family that afternoon to remember a man that epitomised the club.

And now to the goal I most remember. I am sure it sticks in everyone's mind from that season. We went to Easter Road in late October looking to extend our lead at the top of the table. I wasn't at the game that day as I was a guest for the live beam back to Tynecastle for their new initiative, *Gorgie Live*. The Gorgie Suite was packed in anticipation of another famous victory over our greatest rivals. I was sat at a table with former Hearts players José Quitongo, Scott Crabbe and Jimmy Sandison. The 'hammer of Hibs' John Robertson was also with us. He had been brought back to the club to assist

Ann Park in the commercial department. He could open many doors for Hearts, such was his reputation and popularity.

The game was heading for a Hibs win. The clock was about to tick on to 92 minutes when Alim Öztürk, our centre half, strode forward with the ball. As he pulled his right leg back to shoot from fully 40 yards Scot Crabbe shouted 'no, don't shoot'. The ball left his right foot, flew through the air at pace, clipped the bottom of the crossbar and bounced over the line into the Hibs net. The 3,600 Hearts fans behind the goal couldn't believe it. The Gorgie Suite erupted. Someone on our table tipped it up in the air. I was hugging, kissing and jumping around with the former Hearts players at the now upturned guests table. When it all died down a little, I found myself underneath what was left of the table with Scott Crabbe. The goal became emblematic of FOH as the picture of the day was Alim celebrating in front of the Hearts fans, arms stretched, showing the FOH badge adorned on his shirt. That reminded everyone what they had done by supporting FOH. These were the goals and events that became memories. It was those memories that we saved so the club could make more.

FOH was driving forward. Pretty much all our focus was on marketing and maintaining the numbers. We were just a small team of six, so we all got involved in everything. Alastair and Garry had developed the fan reward scheme website that would allow each FOH member to log in, see their 'maroon points' total (1.5 points per pound donated), read any FOH communications and manage their account. It would also tell them when they were nearing a milestone level.

FOH was at Tynecastle in the old reception building for every home match. It was useful to answer questions, sign up new members and give away pin badges and memorabilia for donations. These initiatives raised a lot of money. There were one-off initiatives like a '£1 top up' to the monthly pledge, sign up a friend and the #pledgeforlife campaign designed to show that the FOH was going to be sustained beyond the contracted period. From this came the #legendsinthestand enterprise to show that it was the club's supporters who were its heroes. We spent a lot of time on social media marketing. We didn't really have a public media role now. We did most of that jointly with the club. Hearts was the focus and we would support them in what they were doing. Month after month, I reported to the Hearts Board that member numbers and income were at record levels. It was truly amazing.

Brian Cormack ran the system to identify those members who had stopped pledging. There were a number every month and most were due to economic circumstances. There was not one that I can recall that was cancelled because of a decision of the FOH or Hearts Boards. That gave me confidence that, regardless of what was to happen, the supporters knew this was the mechanism to take ownership of the club. Most who did cancel, or default, would restart their pledges when they could afford to. In reality, although the FOH membership has always been around the 8,000 level (give or take a couple of hundred), the actual number of unique pledgers since the first drawdown in September 2013 is nearly 11,000 individuals. The 'drive to 10,000' campaign had already been achieved in practice. Donations were also flooding in.

The issue of governance still had to be dealt with. The BIDCO/FOH agreement stipulated that it should not change throughout the course of the agreement. That gave us some time to see what to do next. We took that spell to scrutinise a lot of governance models from other clubs. Would FOH members want shares or membership for a small fee or to keep pledging in the current way? There was no shortage of options. Barcelona has a fully democratic system where their 150,000 members elect both the President and the Board. They pay an annual fee of €180 and any of the members can be elected. Borussia Dortmund is always talked about as one of the best models. Their 140,000 members pay an annual fee of €60 and the fans own 51 per cent of the shares, giving them a collective majority vote. It is the German 50 per cent +1 model that is intended to stop a single individual controlling any club for their own gain.

There are advantages and disadvantages of all models and these would have to be explored. It is also the case that one size doesn't fit all. Hearts in the Scottish leagues was not Barcelona or Bayern Munich. I was keen for us to examine all options with the support of D&W. One of the proposals was for FOH to retain 51 per cent as a majority shareholding and give away the balance to fans pro rata, depending on how much they had contributed. When I left the FOH Board, the final model hadn't been agreed but there were proposals to ensure a fully democratic staged process for everyone to be involved and have their say. It is now settled and will remain mostly as it was when I stood down. The important aspect is that it can be altered at any point in the future by the fans themselves. The principle of #pledgeforlife seems to endure so the model will endure for as long as the FOH members want it to.

Garry, Dougie and Alasdair put a lot of thought into how you could reward the FOH members with something that was intangible but interesting.

The rewards scheme was great but was there something more visible. Dougie suggested some time before that the FOH should manufacture a tribute strip with the names of all 8,000 members on it. We thought he had gone mad. He hadn't. We saw examples of where it had happened before. Any member of FOH who had contributed £120 since we started (180 maroon points) would have their name on the strip. Everyone was on it, all 8,000.

The Puma kit looked great and from afar it was similar to the grey Hearts away kit of the mid-1980s. We managed to persuade Ann that we should have an official third kit for the 2015/16 and it should be this. The team would walk out onto the pitch in a 2-2 draw away to Motherwell in November 2015 wearing the strip bearing the names of all 8,000 who had helped save the club. It was a game dubbed by Well Society Secretary Tom Feely as 'a celebration of fan ownership' as Motherwell also headed towards fan ownership under their chair, Brian McCafferty. It was a great gesture. Fans could also purchase the strip. It became both a prized memento and money spinner for the club. It made international press headlines.

A lot of work went into the first FOH AGM in December 2014. We held it a week before the Hearts AGM. I was glad as I couldn't attend the Hearts AGM due to parliamentary business. The preparations were vast. Every time we concluded items, we would be presented with more and more. It was not easy to have 8,000 members. What if they all turned up? We also had to conduct our first democratic Director election of all members. Anyone who could obtain 20 signatures from other FOH Members would be nominated for the place on the FOH Board. It was new, so we weren't surprised when we only had one nomination in prize-winning accountant Barry McGonagle. He was elected to the Board unopposed.

I had been swamped with work in the run-up to the AGM so had put off my Chair's report and speech for weeks and weeks. I intended to write something on the sleeper on my way up from London for the meeting. I fell asleep. I think Ann and others were a little surprised that I cobbled together a speech and report in the Willie Bauld Suite in the 20 minutes prior to the AGM. I did have some great notes that Marcia had written to work from.

The AGM was a great success and Barry was a huge asset to the FOH Board. He took responsibility for developing a monthly FOH update newsletter that would go to all members. He also engrossed himself in all the data we were generating from members. It proved that the democratic process worked. At later AGMS, there would be contests for the Board. They were successful. Donald had devised a system that was robust and inclusive.

Marcia was working wonders in bashing us into proper corporate shape. We had reformed working groups on audit and governance, marketing and members and finance and the future.

Fans hadn't let up with fundraising efforts. Graeme Kay organised a marvellous 'Big Hearts – Big Reunion'. An array of former players attended – Fysass, Flögel, Aguiar, Karipidis, Adam and Rousset. Again, they raised a considerable sum. I couldn't believe I was in a nightclub later that evening dancing with Thomas Flögel and Stéphane Adam. We were truly through the looking glass!

Hearts went on to win the Championship by a record 21 points from second-placed Hibs, winning 29 out of 36 matches. Rangers finished a further three points back. Hearts was promoted back to the top of Scottish football where they belonged. It was an extraordinary achievement for Robbie's team. Disappointingly, I missed the trophy handover against Rangers on the last day of the season. I was on full election mode for the 2015 General Election, but I was on the pitch with Ann, Craig and Eric after a 2–0 home victory against Queen of the South just a few weeks previously to thank the fans after the title was mathematically secured. To stand on that hallowed turf in front of a full house at Tynecastle was something very special indeed. The Hearts Board wanted to personally thank each and every supporter who had backed FOH and also ploughed their hard-earned cash into the club. The Championship League title was for them. They deserved it. It was also Ann's favourite moment:

> Probably, the biggest 'high' for me was gaining promotion in the first year, especially given the style in which we did it. Everyone kept telling me 'Enjoy it! It won't always be like this.' They were right of course.

Ann's leadership was driven by the desire to turn Hearts into the best family club in Britain with an emphasis on a culture that supported that aim. A few days after celebrating what Hearts had achieved on the field, she announced a three-year shirt partnership with Save the Children. It was made possible by a large philanthropic donation that was to be used to support the club, the Big Hearts club charity and Save the Children. It was a step change in how the club wanted to be perceived and the values that would guide it. It was a really proud moment for Ann. This was what she was looking to achieve as owner of Hearts – honesty and integrity. There would be no more oligarch egos in charge, just genuine businesspeople who were also fans and desperate to do well for the club and the wider community. It was welcomed across the football fraternity. She recalls this period fondly:

Certain things were very clear when I took over: I had to tackle the 'business problems'. We had been planning this for so long, our vision and core objectives were clear. Being allowed to put Save the Children on our shirt was amazing and really made me believe we could succeed.

That community approach encouraged corporate sponsors and supporters to come back to the club. The perception was that it had changed. The actuality was that it had definitely changed. Donations were flooding in to the FOH. Cheques were being handed to FOH current and former Directors at matches. On one occasion, Henry Snedden was handed a rather sizable cheque from a Federation of Hearts Supporters club during a match at Motherwell. £1,000 was received from London Hearts. Supporters were still involved in fundraising activities. A Clifford Mullen raised £420 from a sponsored walk and handed it to a Hearts official whist he was in Belfast. Graham Stark & Son Plumbing and Heating got in contact with Jane Lewis and sent in over £1,000.

There were also donations made in the name of relatives who had passed away. An email came in from Ken Edwards who wanted to donate £1,000 in his father's memory. His father, Kenny Edwards, worked as Chief Steward in the Directors Box for over 25 years during the Wallace Mercer era. He was presented with an engraved crystal decanter and whisky glasses by Gary Locke upon retirement. He had died the previous year and 'would be turning in his grave at the plight of Hearts'. His son, Ken, wanted to help the cause.

Ken wasn't the only bequest. Out of the blue, I received an email from a solicitor at Turcan Connell. They were executors of an estate from a deceased Hearts fan in Edinburgh. His will stated that his estate was to be divided into four equal parts, with one part to be paid and made over to such body, constitution, company, supporters' group or charity which supports or promotes the aims, objectives or purposes of Heart of Midlothian Football Club. The executors were given an absolute discretion to determine which body or bodies qualify and in what proportion payment should be made. Turcan Connell decided to explore the possibility of making the payment to FOH. They wanted a proposal from FOH to show that we satisfied the criteria. We had to engage D&W to do this as it involved some legal work. I didn't want to engage their time unless it was going to be beneficial to FOH. If it was for a couple of hundred pounds, then it wouldn't have been economical to do so. I asked Turcan Connell what we were looking at in terms of value. I fell off my seat when they told me that FOH would receive

£108,725.78. I immediately phoned Donald Cummings and got it moving. We were successful and completely humbled.

It was important to work with the Ann and the club on how we would spend this bequest. It wouldn't have been right to merely have it used for the day-to-day running of the club. After much discussion, it was decided to use it to build the memorial garden. That would be a fitting tribute to the anonymous legacy. It would also allow others to have a place at Tynecastle where they could remember a loved one. It was a lovely tribute to a man who decided he would leave his estate to the club he loved. If you get a chance to visit the memorial garden at Tynecastle, give a thought to the 93-year-old Jambo who made it all possible.

Hearts was truly flying, being run by the best CEO and Chair in the country. Ann was transforming Hearts and shaking up Scottish football. That was no surprise to me or anyone who had worked with Ann. She had taken on a 'man's world' before:

> Being a woman in a man's world was not new to me, coming as I did from the IT sector. I had learned long before not to let misogynistic behaviour bother me. I ignored it and simply focused on doing my job well.

And doing the job well she was. Hearts were back in the Premier League, debt-free, sold out at every game, fans excited, the best CEO and Chair in the country, the most dynamic football department the club had ever seen and all backed by the funds of over 8,000 supporters who were striving to save and own their beloved Hearts. What a story. The club was off life support and in the recovery ward.

Job done. My time as FOH Chair and Hearts Board member was coming to an end...

CHAPTER 19

And Now, the End is Near...

IF A TWIST of fate had resulted in me becoming the Chair of the Foundation of Hearts, then more twists of fate would bring an end to my role with FOH and, by consequence, Hearts. The conclusion of the 2015 General Election left me as the sole Scottish Labour Party MP. The acting leader of the Labour Party, Harriet Harman, called me the day after the election to ask if I would serve in her Shadow Cabinet as the Shadow Secretary of State for Scotland. I couldn't refuse. I had a huge national responsibility now as well as to my constituents and party. Every slither of free time I had was consumed by FOH. Something had to give. My party needed me to help it recover. I suppose I had to do an FOH on the Scottish Labour Party. I had a big decision to make. My head was telling me that it would be impossible to stay in the role of FOH Chair. Even if I wanted to, there would not be enough hours in the day to satisfy all the demands on my time. I had also significantly neglected my own personal life over the previous two years. I had to try and put that right. My heart was telling me that I should stay and see if I could tough it out. Was that realistic? I did feel that the whole weight of the process over the last two years had rested on my shoulders as Chair and was only successful because Ann and I had a strong relationship with each other. That was supplemented by my friendly relationships with the supporter groups.

What helped my decision was the reaction from a small quantity of supporters. There was no doubt that my re-election as the sole Scottish Labour MP would vastly increase my public profile and, as a consequence, attract the ire of some. My postbag and emails were swelling with correspondence from 'fans' who said they would never go to Tynecastle again whilst I was involved. FOH was also receiving similar communications. It was only when Ann presented me with some that she had received that my decision to leave became much easier.

I did query if these were coming from Hearts supporters. The vast majority that we were able to cross reference with the FOH and Hearts databases showed they were. In fact, some had already cancelled their FOH membership. It was hurtful and upsetting but there was nothing I could do. I didn't want FOH or the club to be harmed in any way so it kind of helped to make my mind up to go. On reflection, it was the worst decision I have ever made. I walked away so I could concentrate on my political responsibilities at national level. I was never thanked or appreciated for that, so I should have stayed. It was not right to be forced out by political opponents. My constituency work never suffered one iota from my involvement in FOH or Hearts. That was all that mattered. Isn't hindsight a wonderful thing?

I sent my resignation to my fellow FOH Directors and Ann as the Chair of Hearts. It wasn't an easy letter to compose.

I write this letter with a very heavy heart.

It is with great regret and sadness that I write formally to tender my resignation as a Director of Heart of Midlothian Football Club. This is as a consequence of my resignation as Chair and Board Director of the Foundation of Hearts.

Since my re-election last week, I have taken on a number of senior responsibilities that will reduce the spare time I have available to dedicate to other interests. I have, after much soul searching, taken the decision that the FOH requires a new Chair and Director that can give maximum attention to the growing the membership beyond 10,000 and prepare the organisation for full supporter ownership.

I never envisaged that I would be involved in the saving of my beloved club. I always remember sitting on my father's knee when I was very young, and he would recall stories of Hearts greats and games. The main topic of conversation when the family got together at Christmas and for other social occasions was our favourite club. All those stories were not always favourable, but they were cherished memories nonetheless.

Hearts means so much to me and tens of thousands of others. We can all say why, but for me it is because my father died at the same age I am today. He left my older brother at 13 and me at 9. The glue that stuck our family together was the maroon glue from Tynecastle both before his death and certainly afterwards. The few memories I have of him are from the terraces watching Hearts. That is why we should never let any club die. It means too much to too many people.

Over 30 years later I, myself, can recall too many times watching Hearts that I have shed a tear of joy or disappointment, hugged and kissed a complete stranger, danced for joy on a concrete terracing, and sang myself hoarse. Those are what memories are made of.

When I answered my mobile a few years ago and was asked to help Hearts, I did it without hesitation despite the considerable political risks. It has not been an easy few years but just to see smiles on the faces of supporters that are proud of their club again has made it all worthwhile.

And to serve as Director of the club has been a dream come true. I was never good enough at football to even contemplate playing for Hearts so to have been able to serve the club and the supporters from the Boardroom has been a fantastic experience. It's been one of the greatest pleasures and privileges of my life.

I'm very proud that you, Ann, are transforming the club and Scottish Football. You are a marvellous Chair and CEO who has the respect of everyone from your Board colleagues and the players to the staff and supporters. It's been a great privilege to have been able to work alongside you and learn from the vast experience you have had at the top of business. Hearts is in good hands with you, Eric and the team. We are lucky to have such good, honest, kind and caring people involved.

When I look back on the last few years, it is a matter of huge pride when I think about each and every one of the supporters who dug deep time and time again to save our club. I'm very proud too of everyone, both past and present who have helped FOH both formally and informally.

I'm very proud that FOH and you at the club have made sure that fathers, uncles, mothers and aunties of the future can recall their stories of the past to their loved ones.

I'm very proud to have been part of the team who helped to own the history and create the future – but there is a time for everyone to move on.

Generations of future Jambos will look back on these times and say 'we did that' and I'm glad to have played a small part in that story.

I wish the new FOH Director at Hearts all the very best of luck in the future and offer my help and advice whenever it is required.

Long may our beloved club continue to play an integral part of Edinburgh, local communities and in the lives of everyone who loves her.

It's been one of the greatest pleasures and privileges of my life.

Best wishes and good luck.

Yours for Hearts,

Ian'.

I wrote it from the heart and sent it in. I received more positive communications on the back of that letter than I had in all my time as a politician or Chair of FOH. The most cherished came from my now supporters group friends. Ann and the Hearts Board were also very understanding and supportive. I would retake my seat back in the Wheatfield stand.

A few days later, my FOH colleague Brian Cormack became Chair and the Hearts Board representative. The FOH Board kindly treated me to a slap-up lunch and drinks as a thank you. He would be joined by Donald Cummings as the second FOH Director on the Hearts Board. Brian would stand down in 2016. The subsequent AGM elected Stuart Wallace and Louise Strutt from the FOH Membership. Stuart became the fourth Chair of FOH and a member of the Hearts Board. He wasn't the first Wallace to grace the boardroom at Tynecastle!

My formal role ended on 30 June 2015. Jacqui Duncan, the wonderful new Head of Finance and Technical Support emailed me, 'Just to confirm, I have lodged with Companies House, your resignation from the Board of Hearts with effect from 30 June 2015.' That was that.

I left a healthy and ongoing debate, on the back of FOH, if supporter ownership was a model for Scottish football. Many FOH Directors had presented our experiences at other clubs and sporting conferences. I was always of the view that not only did one size not fit all but every situation would be completely different. The situation at Hearts was unique. We were in a crisis, so it worked. Others have not had the same crisis where the very existence of their club has been called into question. The thrust behind FOH was borne out of crisis but became an example of how fan ownership can work. In Scotland, it seems to be working well at Dunfermline, Stirling Albion and Motherwell, with Hibs, Rangers and many others on the road to at least partial fan ownership. The financial ups and downs of Scottish football, and football in general, don't make it a model for everyone (Dundee only lasted two years) but fan ownership in some shape or form appears to be here to stay and will become much more prevalent in the future.

We were, and I still am, contacted by a large number of supporter organisations from clubs all over the UK: Leeds United, Coventry City, Portsmouth, Bolton, Milton Keynes Dons, York City, Oxford United and even Hibs, the latest to be Bury Town FC. They have all encountered crisis to one degree or another. If there was one bit of advice I would give them, it would be that there may be a lot of owners of football clubs that are looking for a full or partial exit strategy. The supporters are a possible route. Fans should organise themselves into a credible entity and talk to owners. If they are able to create a constructive partnership, then owners may be able to offer something to supporters that give them a stake in the club and feel they are part of it. It needn't be full ownership or even an exit strategy. It could just be investment in the club to create a voice.

I am glad that space has been found to bring Gary Locke back to the club as an ambassador. He is Mr Hearts. I have spent a lot of time at Tynecastle since I stood down from FOH. None of the occasions has been as pleasant as my own plot ceremony. Garry managed to get this idea in place for those members reaching a milestone of contributions and I hear directly that FOH members love it. They get on the pitch to claim their plot with an accompanying certificate. It is a special event for those invited. It just shows you what can be achieved when you doggedly keep pursuing an idea.

Hearts would go on to finish third in their first season back in the Premier League. That meant the supporters would get a chance to make some new memories when European football returned to Tynecastle. There were inevitably going to be ups and downs. One of my most challenging tasks at FOH was managing the expectations of the fans. There would be bad times, perhaps many more in the short term than the good times, but they all had to remember the position we were in just a few short months and years before. We football fans are impatient and fickle. Rightly so – we pay our money and want to win matches. However, when you are presented with an ultimatum that your club will die unless you step in and less than four years later you are looking forward to European football, you have to take a step back to reflect. That was why I was bitterly disappointed when Robbie Neilson left the club. He was a great Head Coach and an even better human being. I wouldn't go as far as to claim he was hounded out of Hearts but the increasing unease about him as our Head Coach must have been a deciding factor. Managing expectations will always be the challenge now.

The progress on the pitch and at the academy was there for all to see. The big issue was the old main stand and Ann would have to turn her attention to completing the modernisation of the stadium:

> When I realised just how bad the Old Stand was and how much this would limit our ability to grow and improve, it became a fairly easy decision to press ahead with plans for the new stand. I was blown away by the support I received from benefactors and from the FOH pledgers.

Her plans for a new 7,000-capacity main stand would be a lasting legacy and reduce the increasing maintenance required to keep the old stand functioning. There was no doubt that it had come to the end of its life some years ago. There were challenges that the Hearts Board would have to overcome to make the dream a reality, like the fact that a Romanov company in liquidation still owned the small administration block building by the stadium and the dilapidated former adult education building, owned by the Council, was an eyesore. There was also the small matter of the ethanol tanks at the distillery that had always hampered stadium redevelopment.

The catalyst for making the decision may have been partly down to the sustained success of FOH. The number of members was constant at around 8,000. The £3.8 million working capital requirements from the FOH/BIDCO contract had been fully satisfied in 2016. Ann approached FOH to see if they would consider altering the schedule of payments in the contract to delay the repayment of the £2.5 million BIDCO capital loan. FOH pledge income would be diverted into supporting the £12 million new main stand development. It seemed a no brainer for FOH. They were sustaining the pledge levels so could afford it and it would give a project for their funds over another two years. Ann would then be repaid in the following two years. It also had the added advantage of keeping Ann in post as the CEO and Chair. FOH would provide £3 million towards the cost of the stand. The club also received £4.5 million from benefactors to help finance it. The remainder would be made up of club profits and special appeals. It was barely believable. I was keeping my fingers crossed that all the song and dance we made about the danger of the ethanol tanks to reduce the cost of the stadium during the administration process didn't come back to bite the club. It didn't. The planning went through, the old Archibald Leitch structure was demolished and an impressive new stand appeared. Tyne-castle was well known as the most atmospheric stadium in Scotland. I think the new addition would challenge the atmosphere of any in Europe.

Hearts has now changed beyond all recognition since the day when we officially emerged from what was an uncertain, agonising and lengthy administration process. There were no fragments of the Romanov regime remaining. The Foundation of Hearts will become the majority shareholder and the fans will own the club. That would have been unimaginable just a few short years ago. The transformation of Hearts was incredible. One of the biggest tributes came from the father of football, Sir Alex Ferguson, who described Ann as 'a guardian angel' for galvanising the club. There will be ups and downs both on and off the park in the months and years to come. Personnel will change. Managers, players, staff and Boards will come and go, but the supporters with Ann Budge and all the others have put in place really solid foundations that will endure long into the future.

I can think of no better tribute to the team that sacrificed their lives for their country back in 1914, and all Hearts supporters before and since, than to have secured the future of Hearts. The magnitude of our 1914 team's com-mitment and ultimate sacrifice can never be overstated. They stepped forward when the risk was greatest and because of them – and thousands of other brave men and women including many Hearts supporters and shareholders – we have the luxury of watching Heart of Midlothian play football today.

Hearts may not have the sporting success of the Real Madrids, Barcelonas and Manchester Uniteds of this world, but we do have a history every bit as rich. Every one of us has enjoyed the highs of the Scottish Cup wins, Champions League qualification, regular European competition, the associated big nights at Tynecastle, and that unforgettable record- equalling league games winning run. That hugely successful chapter has closed, and we are now opening a new chapter in the club's history. The fans will rightly own the history and shape the future.

We asked the club's greatest asset, its supporters, to take the opportunity to establish certainty and stabilise the club for future generations. It was not the first time that they responded to this rallying call when our club needed them the most. Their sacrifice would be huge but it would be negligible when compared to the alternative of our beloved Hearts dying.

That was our moment. We didn't hesitate. Hearts is a club of the local community, it always has been. If anyone ever needed proof of that, it has been demonstrated time and time again particularly during Hearts darkest days, and not simply in financial terms. As Hearts supporters, we can rightly take pride in how we do things, not just what we do.

What summed up the experience for me was when I met a very elderly gentleman in Gorgie Road on my way to a game. He was wearing his flat cap and a heavy black winter coat. A real old timer. He stopped me and said, 'You're Ian Murray, aren't you?' My first reaction was, 'Here we go. Time for an earful.' He simply said, 'Thanks very much for giving us our club back.' I appreciated it. It was a lovely gesture. He was visibly emotional. I replied, 'Thanks, but it wasn't really me. You took it back. The fans.' I can't thank you – every single Hearts supporter – enough for saving Hearts. Coming together in such challenging times is as valuable as any sum of money that has been raised.

One thing is clear. We must always remember that we have come far too close to losing Heart of Midlothian Football Club. We must never allow this to happen again. Our club was saved because of you, the supporters. We grasped the opportunity to start afresh and it has been a whirlwind of progress. As one chapter in the history of the club ends, another begins. The next 145 years are secured. Future generations can enjoy what we have always enjoyed – supporting Heart of Midlothian Football Club.

That was my story, that was our song.

Some other books published by **LUATH PRESS**

Athens to Zagreb: A First Hand History of Hearts in Europe

Mike Buckle

ISBN: 9781908373410 HBK £14.99

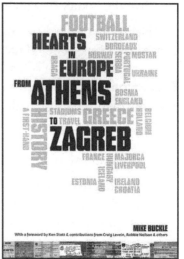

This book is the complete guide to all of the games played by Hearts in European competitions since the club become only the third Scottish team to enter the European Cup.

With contributions from several prominent Hearts players and celebrity fans, including Ken Stott and Scott Wilson, *From Athens to Zagreb* will evoke forgotten memories amongst fans of all ages.

A must-read for Hearts fans, Athens to Zagreb *is the definitive guide to all matches played by the team in European competitions since 1958.* SCOTTISH REVIEW OF BOOKS

Hands on Hearts: A Physio's Tale

Alan Rae

ISBN: 9781908373540 PBK £9.99

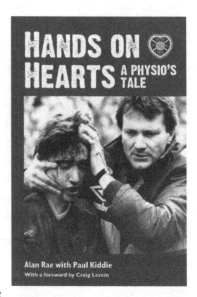

As Heart of Midlothian FC's physiotherapist, Alan Rae was a vital member of the Tynecastle backroom staff for more than two decades. He was one of the few constants during a tumultuous period in the club's rich history and his behind-the-scenes recollections will fascinate and entertain in equal measure. From international superstars to mischievous boot-room boys, Rae shares his unique insight into the life of a great Scottish football institution. *Hands on Hearts* is a must-read for football fans everywhere – Jambos or otherwise – and for anyone who has ever wondered about the healing properties of the physio's magic sponge!

From the brink of possible collapse to the arrival of Vladimir Romanov, most fans of football will find something of interest in this book. SCOTTISH FITBA

Details of these books can be found at www.luath.co.uk.

The Foundation of Hearts

The Foundation of Hearts (FOH) is the largest supporters' movement in Scottish footballing history. FOH currently have an active membership of around 8,000 individuals, all of whom contribute financially to the organisation. This financial contribution is used to provide working capital for the club we support, Heart of Midlothian Football Club, with a view to the club becoming fan owned.

FOH will acquire the majority shareholder in Hearts when it has fulfilled the legal provisions of an agreement with a company called BIDCO, owned by current Chief Executive and Chair of the Hearts, Ann Budge, to repay the capital loan used to get Hearts out of administration. At the final payment, the 79.9 per cent shareholding owned by BIDCO will transfer to FOH, thus delivering the central objective of fan ownership.

The vision of the Foundation of Hearts is:

- to have Hearts fans centrally involved in the ownership of this great club

- to establish a well-run club which operates with integrity and transparency and encourages entertaining football from a team built around the players produced by a thriving youth development programme

- to have the club remain at its 'spiritual home' of Tynecastle, unless dictated by other prevailing circumstances

- to ensure that the future of Heart of Midlothian Football Club remains secure for all time.

There have been over 11,000 individual contributors to FOH since its inception, contributing over £10 million to the saving and rebuilding of the club. You could be one of them by signing up to a contribution for as little as £10 per month and become an equal member of the Foundation of Hearts. This membership allows you to choose the direction of the organisation, vote for your FOH Board of Directors and stand for election yourself as a Director.

Find out all the information at www.foundationofhearts.org. Help us to own the history and use your voice as a member of FOH to shape the future.

Luath Press Limited

committed to publishing well written books worth reading

LUATH PRESS takes its name from Robert Burns, whose little collie Luath (*Gael.*, swift or nimble) tripped up Jean Armour at a wedding and gave him the chance to speak to the woman who was to be his wife and the abiding love of his life. Burns called one of the 'Twa Dogs' Luath after Cuchullin's hunting dog in Ossian's *Fingal*. Luath Press was established in 1981 in the heart of Burns country, and is now based a few steps up the road from Burns' first lodgings on Edinburgh's Royal Mile. Luath offers you distinctive writing with a hint of unexpected pleasures.

Most bookshops in the UK, the US, Canada, Australia, New Zealand and parts of Europe, either carry our books in stock or can order them for you. To order direct from us, please send a £sterling cheque, postal order, international money order or your credit card details (number, address of cardholder and expiry date) to us at the address below. Please add post and packing as follows: UK – £1.00 per delivery address; overseas surface mail – £2.50 per delivery address; overseas airmail – £3.50 for the first book to each delivery address, plus £1.00 for each additional book by airmail to the same address. If your order is a gift, we will happily enclose your card or message at no extra charge.

ILLUSTRATION: IAN KELLAS

Luath Press Limited
543/2 Castlehill
The Royal Mile
Edinburgh EH1 2ND
Scotland
Telephone: +44 (0)131 225 4326 (24 hours)
email: sales@luath. co.uk
Website: www. luath.co.uk